Praise for

Magnificent Mind at Any Age

"Learn the secrets of a balanced brain from a physician who has experience examining 50,000 scans of patients. Compare a failing mind to a brilliant brain and learn how to move in the direction you desire."

—Mehmet C. Oz, M.D., bestselling coauthor of *You: The Owner's Manual*

"A must-read . . . *Magnificent Mind at Any Age* blends scientific innovation with a clear and powerful writing style. Dr. Amen's SPECT scans are fascinating, his conclusions are life changing, and he provides practical health strategies you can utilize immediately."

—Michael Gurian, author of *What Could He Be Thinking?*
and *Leadership and the Sexes*

"I consider Daniel Amen to be the most innovative psychiatrist in America. His premise is simple: you can't have a healthy life without a healthy brain. His dietary and lifestyle strategies for maintaining brain health are based on the world's most comprehensive library of brain imaging technology. If you want a better and more fulfilled life, this book is a must-read."

—Barry Sears, Ph.D., bestselling author of *The Zone*

"Dr. Amen is without a doubt our nation's leader as a top clinician/researcher who has the gift of making the complexities of reaching brain health and potential understandable by everyone. . . . *Magnificent Mind at Any Age* is a gift for the baby boomer who is now facing how to live the rest of his or her life and for young parents who want to make sure they are providing the best they can for their children and teens. Everyone will find *Magnificent Mind at Any Age* a great resource."

—Earl R. Henslin, Psy.D., author of *This Is Your Brain on Joy*

"Providing brain basics from cradle to grave, Dr. Amen has written an indispensable handbook for handling emotions, cognition, relationships, and even our spiritual lives. It is comprehensive, inspiring, and user-friendly, explaining the most complex material in a way that's easy to understand and, better yet, to put into practice."

—Hyla Cass, M.D., coauthor of *Natural Highs*

"A user's manual to care for our precious brain. If you have a brain, buy this book!"

—Mark Hyman, M.D., bestselling author of *UltraMetabolism*

MAGNIFICENT
MIND
AT ANY AGE

Natural Ways to Unleash Your
Brain's Maximum Potential

DANIEL G. AMEN, M.D.

THREE RIVERS PRESS

NEW YORK

MEDICAL DISCLAIMER

The information presented in this book is the result of years of practice experience
and clinical research by the author. The information in this book, by necessity,
is of a general nature and not a substitute for an evaluation or treatment by a competent
medical specialist. If you believe you are in need of medical interventions please see
a medical practitioner as soon as possible. The stories in this book are true. The names and
circumstances of the stories have been changed to protect the anonymity of patients.

Copyright © 2008 by Daniel G. Amen, M.D.

Published in the United States by Three Rivers Press, an imprint of the Crown Publishing Group,
a division of Random House, Inc., New York.
www.crownpublishing.com

Three Rivers Press and the Tugboat design are registered trademarks of Random House, Inc.

Originally published in hardcover in the United States by Harmony Books,
an imprint of the Crown Publishing Group, a division of
Random House, Inc., New York, in 2008.

Library of Congress Cataloging-in-Publication Data

Amen, Daniel G.
Magnificent mind at any age : natural ways to unleash your brain's maximum potential /
Daniel G. Amen.—1st ed.
Includes bibliographical references.
1. Brain—Popular works.   2. Mental health—Popular works.   3. Brain—Tomography.
4. Single-photon emission computed tomography.   I. Title.
QP376.A4265 2009
612.8'2—dc22   2008030532

ISBN 978-0-307-33910-2

Printed in the United States of America

Design by Helene Berinsky

10 9 8 7 6 5 4 3 2 1

First Paperback Edition

For Dad

I love you.

CONTENTS

MAGNIFICENT
MIND
AT ANY AGE

PART ONE

A MAGNIFICENT
MIND
STARTS WITH
A HEALTHY BRAIN

|1|

Are You Wired for
Success or Failure?

THE SECRET BEHIND WHY SOME PEOPLE
ACHIEVE THEIR DREAMS AND OTHERS DON'T

At the Amen Clinics we have been balancing troubled brains for more than twenty years. We see small children and the elderly and everyone in between. People come to see us because we use sophisticated brain imaging technology to help us understand and treat our patients, plus we use natural treatments whenever possible. It is through the lens of our imaging work that I discovered that when I improve how your brain functions, not only do I help you overcome problems such as attention deficit disorder (ADD), anxiety, depression, addictions, and anger, I also help you be more thoughtful, creative, energetic, focused, and effective.

After looking at nearly fifty thousand scans, it is clear to me that a balanced brain is the foundation for a life that is happier, healthier, wealthier, and wiser. That is the promise of this book: if you really understand how to develop and take care of your brain, your life will be better no matter what your age.

One question people often ask me is whether the mind is separate from the brain. The answer is clearly no. The mind and the brain are completely dependent on each other. Just think with me about Alzheimer's disease, which is clearly a brain illness. Images 1.1 and 1.2 depict two brain single photon emission computed tomography (SPECT) scans. These are the scans we do in our clinics. SPECT is called a functional scan, because it shows how the brain works; it measures blood flow and activity patterns. Image 1.1 is of a healthy person. It shows full, even, symmetrical activity. Image 1.2 shows a

Image 1.1: Healthy Brain   Image 1.2: Alzheimer's Disease

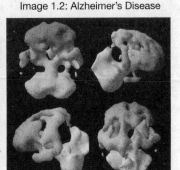

Full, even, symmetrical activity   Deterioration back half of brain

woman who has Alzheimer's disease. The holes indicate very low activity in several important areas of her brain.

Do people with Alzheimer's disease lose their minds? Yes, they do as the disease progresses. When you lose brain tissue you lose your memory and your ability to think clearly.

Now let's consider brain trauma. Image 1.3 depicts a soldier's brain that was damaged in an explosion in Iraq. He was discharged from the army within a year of the accident because he kept getting into fights with other soldiers, something that did not happen before the injury. Does brain damage

Image 1.3: Soldier's Brain Damage

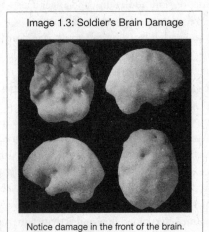

Notice damage in the front of the brain.

Image 1.4: ADD Before Treatment

Image 1.5: ADD After Treatment

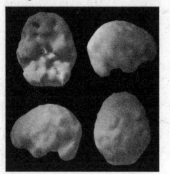
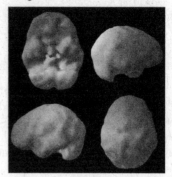

Decreased frontal lobe activity

Improved frontal lobe activity

affect a person's ability to get along with others? Of course it does! Damage the brain and you damage the mind and most everything else in your life.

But what if we improve the brain? Does that improve the mind? Here's an example. Jenny, age sixty-two, came to see us for dyslexia and ADD. She had suffered her whole life, underachieved at school and at work, and felt defective and stupid. She had been divorced twice and was estranged from her children. I had treated her son for ADD, and he subsequently reached out to her. With the proper diagnosis and treatment she was able to feel much better and was able to make peace with her children. (See Images 1.4 and 1.5.)

A balanced brain is the foundation for a magnificent mind. Here is a recent letter I received from the mother of one of my patients.

(with permission)

> Dear Dr. Amen,
>
> I am the mother of Dale B. who was treated at the Amen Clinic approximately 8 years ago. Dale was 17 and in trouble with the law. He was brought to the clinic in shackles. After evaluation and treatment, Dale was able to be gainfully employed for 1 year in retail sales. He then joined the Army where he excelled. Dale immediately became an Army Ranger. Dale was able to make a success of his life because of the treatment he received at the Amen Clinics. Dale was killed in action in Iraq on 3/18/06 just 3 days before his 24th birthday. We take great comfort in knowing Dale died a Hero. I thought you might be interested in the part

you played in this Hero's life. Dale was buried at Arlington Cemetery
with great honor.
Thank you,
Laura B.
Proud Mother of Sgt. Dale B.

Helping to unchain a young man from the shackles of failure to become a decorated war hero is a humbling experience. Even though Dale's death was very sad, he died on his own terms, doing something he loved. The details of Dale's story are unique, but the essence is not. I have received many, many letters thanking me for changing someone's brain and changing his or her life.

Most people have the *completely wrong idea* about accomplishment and about what holds people back from realizing their dreams. The majority of people, like me before I began this work, take a commonsense approach. This is the same approach espoused by most self-help gurus, business executives, and head coaches who write "how I won the championship" books. Try harder, they say, be your own person, visualize your success, work longer, take responsibility, stop complaining, change your attitude, and do not let anyone get in your way. With diligent devotion, you can be anything you want in life. If you are not successful, then you are lazy, willful, or need an attitude adjustment. Look at me. If I can do it, you can too.

The problem with this approach is that it simply doesn't work for many people who sincerely try to incorporate it into their lives. It often backfires. The harder many people try, the worse their brains, abilities, and behaviors get. No doubt the tough love, kick-in-the-butt approach works for some, but it leaves countless others feeling demoralized, disconnected, hopeless, and unworthy.

How effective do you think I would have been with seventeen-year-old Dale B. when he came to our clinic in shackles if I chewed him out and told him to try harder, just like all the other adults in his life had already done? Not very effective. What we did was completely different.

A magnificent mind starts with a healthy brain. For you to realize your dreams in any area of your life, requires your brain must work right. Your brain controls everything you do: how you think, how you feel, how you act, and how well you get along with other people. When the brain works right, you work right. When your brain is troubled, you have trouble in your life.

Before we did anything with Dale we understood the context of his life, listened to how he thought and took sophisticated images of how his brain worked. It was clear from the scans and his behavior that Dale suffered from a brain that was out of balance. As we optimized the three-pound supercomputer between his ears he was able to mature, gain self-control, and claim a more effective life. With understanding and a balanced brain, he was able to develop the abilities to live a hero's life, serving his country and making his parents proud beyond words. With an unbalanced brain, he likely would have remained ashamed of himself, a disappointment to his family and a drain on society.

The first key to a magnificent mind is a balanced brain. With a balanced brain we are able to learn from our own experiences and from other people to make our own lives the best they can be. **The first step in investigating failure is to understand the brain.** An unbalanced brain causes its owner immeasurable trouble, including difficulties learning, being distracted and impulsive, and making the same mistakes again and again.

The Secret Behind Why Some Achieve Their Dreams and Others Don't

With an unbalanced brain most self-help or societal strategies to improve behavior do not work. Consider prison. Clearly, it is an extreme and costly attempt to modify behavior. Yet the recidivism rate is 60–70 percent within five years. Few people ever consider looking at the brain in helping people whose behavior is so bad they end up in jail. In a 2007 study that my colleagues and I published in the *Journal of Neuropsychiatry,* we found that murderers had significantly lower overall activity in their brains compared with a healthy group, especially when they performed a concentration task. These findings were especially prominent in the prefrontal cortex, the area of the brain that acts as the supervisor, inhibiting impulses and difficult behavior. We will never improve bad behavior until we balance the underlying organ that drives it.

Or consider marital therapy. According to a 2005 *New York Times* article, two years after ending counseling, 25 percent of couples were worse off than when they started, and after four years up to 38 percent were divorced. Very few marital therapists ever consider looking at the brain in trying to help failing relationships, and that is a mistake. Consider the following example.

In 2006 I gave a lecture to one thousand people at Skyline Church in San Diego. The next year I was invited back. As often happens when I speak at a place for the second time, a number of people approach me as I walk into the lecture hall or sanctuary with their SPECT scans. My lecture motivated them to come to one of our clinics to have their own brain evaluated. On this oc-

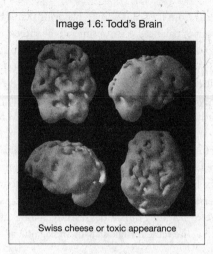

Image 1.6: Todd's Brain

Swiss cheese or toxic appearance

casion, a thirty-five-year-old man, Todd, came up to me to show me his scan (see Image 1.6). The scan shows a swiss cheese appearance, indicating seriously low overall activity, the same pattern we often see in our drug or alcohol abusers. As I looked at the scan, Todd said, "You think I am a drug addict, don't you?"

"The thought had crossed my mind," I replied.

"I have never used drugs," Todd said. "And I don't drink. Before I came to your clinic I used to paint cars in my garage, without much ventilation. I don't do that anymore."

"That is the sign of intelligent life," I replied. "New information causes you to change your behavior."

He went on to tell me that he and his wife had been in marital therapy for several years without any benefit. After his visit to the clinic in Newport Beach he started to live a brain-healthy life. He began taking a multiple vitamin and fish oil and the other brain-healthy supplements we recommended, and he improved his eating and exercise habits. The difference, he said, had been life changing. After his brain was better, he was able to be a better husband. I wonder how many marriages are suffering because one partner has a brain problem that no one is aware of. How do you do marital therapy with this brain? It will never work, until you help heal the brain first.

In every walk of life a magnificent mind is tied to brain function, but because we never directly look at the brain and rarely think about its impact on our own lives, we often miss this most important puzzle piece in trying to realize our dreams.

The Ideas of Change

Over the past three decades my primary work has been as a psychiatrist and brain imaging specialist. I became a psychiatrist to study human behavior to learn how and why people develop magnificent minds. I started imaging the brain eighteen years ago because I realized after nine years of being a psychiatrist that I was missing important information to help my patients. To really help people change, I discovered that I must understand and optimize the organ of change, the brain, in individual patients.

Shortly after beginning my brain imaging work with people hospitalized for psychiatric problems, a series of ideas started to percolate in my own brain. Over the next few years, the ideas crystallized and have become part of almost everything I have done since.

A magnificent mind starts with a balanced brain.

Failure is often the result of a brain gone wrong.

Not everyone has the same brain function.

Optimize the brain and you dramatically increase a person's abilities.

Use every option available to balance the brain, including natural supplements, diet, exercise, thinking strategies, and if needed, medication.

Teach people skills; do not just give them pills.

I ordered my first brain SPECT study on psychiatric patients in the spring of 1991. I was using the study to help understand the underlying brain problems of my patients to better target their treatment. At the time, I had a very busy psychiatric practice. I was treating people in my private clinic and those in the hospital where I was the director of the dual-diagnosis program for patients who had substance abuse and psychiatric problems. I was excited about SPECT because it helped me be a better doctor. It helped me be more effective in helping my patients. Even though SPECT scans are of tremendous value in understanding individual brains, you do not need a scan to benefit from this book. By studying tens of thousands of scans I have developed a checklist (see chapter 3) to help people predict what their scan might look like if they could get one. The checklist will help you understand your brain's specific needs and guide you on ways to help it.

Magnificent Mind at Any Age is ultimately about understanding how the brain is involved in the day-to-day operations of your life no matter what your age and giving you specific strategies to optimize it naturally. The book will help you unlock your abilities in work, school, and relationships, and bring you closer to your own potential for accomplishment, connection, and happiness.

|2|

A Magnificent Mind Starts
with a Healthy Brain

ESSENTIAL STRATEGIES

Brains run the world. They run the stock market and the local market. They run huge corporations and the mom-and-pop shop down the street. Brains run churches, banks, hotels, tennis clubs, dry cleaners, professional basketball teams, Internet dating services, and universities. Brains run marriages, choirs, homeowner associations, and terrorist groups. Your brain runs you and is significantly involved in running your family. Yet even though the brain is involved with everything we do at work and at home, we rarely think about or honor the brain. There is no formal education about the brain in MBA programs, no brain-training programs at church, no brain exercises in customer service or management programs, and no real practical education about the brain in school. The lack of brain education is a huge mistake, because success in all we do starts with a healthy brain.

The characteristics of a magnificent mind include personal responsibility, clear goals, good attention, consistent effort, effective social skills, impulse control, motivation, integrity, and creativity. Yet few people realize that all of these are brain functions. A healthy brain makes these characteristics easier to incorporate in your life, while a damaged or struggling brain makes these much harder. Taking great care of your brain is essential to a magnificent mind. Here is an example.

In one of the graduate psychology courses I taught I asked for volunteers for our healthy brain study. By the year 2000, we had amassed tens of thou-

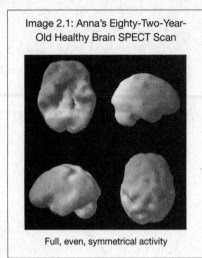

Image 2.1: Anna's Eighty-Two-Year-Old Healthy Brain SPECT Scan

Full, even, symmetrical activity

sands of SPECT scans for clinical reasons, such as attention deficit hyperactivity disorder (ADHD), anxiety, depression, autism, Alzheimer's disease, brain trauma, marital strife, and violence. To further our research efforts, we needed to build a large normal database to compare our clinical studies. I solicited normal people wherever I went. Surprisingly, they were not that easy to find. Christy, one of my favorite students, came up after class very excited. She said, "You have to scan my eighty-two-year-old grandmother, Anna. She is one of the most normal people I know. You will love her." On Christy's advice and with her grandmother's agreement, we screened Anna and indeed found her to be healthy (see Image 2.1). She met all of the criteria for the study: she had not suffered from psychiatric illness at any point in her life; there was no history of substance abuse, brain injuries, or first-degree relatives with psychiatric illness; and she was not on any medications. Anna had been married for fifty-eight years and was a loving wife, mother, and grandmother. She had a sharp, curious mind and was active in her church and community. She had solid relationships that spanned many years. Anna never drank alcohol, never smoked, and tried to eat healthy. She has one of the healthiest brains I had ever seen, out of nearly fifty thousand! Her brain fit her life.

The First Steps to a Healthier Brain

Most of us are never taught about how important the brain is, so we go through life thinking about everything (weight, skin care, finances, children,

Internet dating, vacations, careers, sports) but this critically important organ. I live in Newport Beach, California, the heart of Orange County. We have often been called the plastic society because we have more plastic walking around our streets and beaches than almost any other place in the world. I often say that we care more about our faces, our boobs, our bellies, and our butts than we do our brain. How stupid is that? When you really want to change, the place to start is with your brain. In the rest of this chapter I will tell you the first six things you should do to improve your brain health.

1. PROTECT YOUR AMAZING BUT FRAGILE BRAIN

The brain is the most complicated organ in the universe. It is estimated that the brain has one hundred billion nerve cells and more connections in it than there are stars in the universe. Even though the brain consists of only about 2 percent of your body's weight, it uses about 25 percent of the calories you consume. If you take a piece of brain tissue the size of a grain of sand, it contains a hundred thousand neurons and a billion connections all communicating with one another. If you are not thoughtful, the brain loses an average of eighty-five thousand brain cells a day, or one per second. Information in the brain travels at the speed of 268 miles per hour, unless of course you are drunk, which really slows things down. The brain is the organ of loving, learning, behaving, intelligence, personality, character, belief, and knowing.

The brain is also very soft and it is housed in a really hard skull. Most people think of the brain as firm, fixed, and rubbery. Yet that is not how it is inside your skull. That is how it is once it is fixed in formaldehyde on the pathologist's table. Inside your skull the brain is comprised of 80 percent water and is the consistency of soft butter or custard, somewhere between egg whites and Jell-O. In *Another Day in the Frontal Lobe*, neurosurgeon Katrina Firlik describes the brain "like tofu, the soft kind, which when caught in suction during surgery slurps into the tube."

Your soft tofulike brain is housed in a really hard skull that has many ridges. These ridges damage the brain during trauma, so why would you ever let a child hit a soccer ball with their heads, play tackle football (even with helmets), skateboard, or snowboard or ski without helmets? Unless you didn't like them, why would you buy your teenagers a motorcycle or take them four-wheeling in the desert? From a neuroscientist's point of view, these are dangerous activities that could grievously injure the brain. Sports like boxing, football, motocross, and cage fighting are simply not worth the risk. The brain loves physical activity and it is better to think about safer brain sports such as tennis, table tennis, track and field (although not pole vaulting), and basketball.

A 2007 study by John Adams and colleagues at the University of Cincinnati College of Medicine found that hitting a soccer ball with one's head may be linked to long-term brain injury and memory problems later in life. Researchers found evidence of reduced gray matter in the brains of male college soccer players, compared with young men who had never played.

The single most important thing I have learned from looking at tens of thousands of scans is that mild traumatic brain injuries change people's whole lives (by damaging their brain) and no one knows it. The brain-injured person often subsequent to the injury suffers from emotional, behavioral, or cognitive problems that may lead him to a psychiatrist or psychologist, who typically never looks at the brain. Problems that are physically based are often considered psychological. If you never look at the brain, you will likely miss what many researchers have called the silent epidemic. There are two million reported new brain injury cases every year, and millions of others that go unnoticed.

When I first started the imaging work, I saw a lot of brain injury patterns on scans. When I asked patients about a history of head injuries they denied them. When I pressed, a whole new world opened up. I found out that people often forgot significant injuries. I had to ask them three, four, even ten times. Many people forget or they did not realize that they have had a serious brain injury. You would be amazed by how many people after repeatedly saying no to this question suddenly get an "aha" look on their face and say, "Why yes, I fell out of a second-story window at age seven." Or they tell us they went through the windshield of a car headfirst, had concussions playing football or soccer, or fell down a flight of stairs. Not all brain injuries, even serious ones, will cause damage—there is an interaction between genetic vulnerability and trauma. Moreover, the brain is buffered by the cerebrospinal fluid that bathes it. Still, damage can occur more than most know.

So many of the troubled people we see at the Amen Clinics have had a brain injury (or two or three). Damaging your brain may limit or impair your ability to be successful in any area of your life. People who have experienced head injuries have a higher incidence of drug abuse, alcoholism, mood problems, divorce, domestic violence, arrests, financial problems, and every other type of trouble that leads to failure. Be smart. If you want to be your best, protect your soft brain.

2. DO A BETTER JOB OF TAKING CARE OF YOUNGER BRAINS

Most people think that we become adults when we turn eighteen years old. That is a societal definition, but it is not true from a brain science perspective. The prefrontal cortex, the part of our brain that makes us most human (forethought, judgment, impulse control, learning from our mistakes—the stuff of maturity), does not finish developing until we are about twenty-five years old. The insurance industry knew this long before neuroscientists, as twenty-five is the age when your car insurance rates go down because you become a more thoughtful driver.

As the brain matures, nerve cells become wrapped in a white, fatty substance called myelin (a process known as myelinization). Like wrapping copper wires with insulation, myelin protects and helps nerve cells work up to ten times more efficiently. Myelinization starts from the back part of the brain and works forward. The occipital lobes, involved with vision, myelinate within the first few months of life, so we can see more detail. It is not until we are much older that the prefrontal cortex becomes myelinated. Current research, including ours, suggests it is at about age twenty-five. From a study we did at the Amen Clinics, involving more than sixty-three hundred patient scans, we found that the activity in the prefrontal cortex does not become stable until we are in our midtwenties.

Why is this so important? Since the brain is not finished developing until we are in our midtwenties, we should be doing a much better job protecting our teenage and young adult brains. Too often parents give up on their teenagers and do not supervise what they eat, allow them to get little sleep, don't get terribly upset about early drinking or marijuana use, and permit them to drive in unsafe vehicles. We allow our kids to go away to college too soon, where they engage in brain-destroying behaviors, such as heavy drinking, nonstop violent video games, Internet gambling, and pornography, and we are ready to toss them out of the house when they are eighteen, if they irritate us. I know my three adult children (ages thirty-one, twenty-six, and twenty-one) have much better judgment now than they did at age eighteen. I can certainly say the same thing about my own behavior. Once this brain research was released, the Supreme Court banned executing murderers who committed their crimes when they were teenagers.

Take this concept a step further. Parents spend billions of dollars each year trying to help their children be successful. We spend money on private schools, summer camps, and lessons of all sorts, including martial arts, athletics, music, and dance. We spend time tutoring them or hiring tutors for them. With all the time and effort spent on helping them be their best, we should not forget the most important organ that actually tells the body how to hit the golf shot, remembers the karate kata, hears the prosody of music, and improvises in modern dance. Spending time and money on youth brain health is one of the smartest investments in your child's, teenager's, and young adult's future. Some simple things to do for children and teens is to teach them about the importance of their brain, how to take care of it, protect it, feed it properly, get enough sleep, avoid toxic substances such as drugs or alcohol, and share the major concepts with them from this book and another of my books, *Making a Good Brain Great*. Once properly educated, I find children and teens are much better at taking care of their own brains.

3. BOOST BLOOD FLOW

Blood is especially important to the brain. Even though the brain is composed of only 2 percent of the body's weight, it uses 20 percent of the body's blood flow and oxygen supply. Blood flow to the brain is rarely thought about as important by the general public, unless a disaster strikes, such as a stroke or an aneurysm. Yet good blood flow is absolutely essential to the brain's health. This is one reason I favor brain SPECT as our primary imaging study. It specifically looks at blood flow patterns in the brain.

Blood brings oxygen, sugar, vitamins, and other nutrients to the brain and takes away carbon dioxide and other toxic waste products. Anything that limits blood flow prematurely ages all of your body's organs. Consider the skin of smokers. Most people can tell if someone is a smoker by looking at his or her skin. A smoker's skin is more likely to be deeply wrinkled and even perhaps tinged with a yellow or gray color. Why? Nicotine in cigarettes is a powerful constrictor of blood flow to every organ in the body, including the skin and the brain. Deprived of vital nutrients, the smoker's body will look and the brain will think older than they are.

Unless you actively do something to change it, blood flow throughout your body decreases over time, especially to the brain. Blood vessels become droopy and blood pressure rises, limiting blood supply. To stay young of heart and mind, it is essential to understand the factors that limit blood flow and eliminate them. Improving blood flow is the fountain of youth.

Whatever is good for your heart is good for your brain. Since I wrote *Sex on the Brain*, I also realized that whatever is good for your heart is good for your brain is also good for your genitals. Blood flow to your genitals is essen-

MAGNIFICENT MIND AT ANY A

tial for both men and women to have healthy, passionate, satisfying s
Did you know that 40 percent of forty-year-olds have erectile (bloo
dysfunction? And 70 percent of seventy-year-olds have erectile dysfunction
too? No wonder commercials for Cialis, Levitra, and Viagra are everywhere.
The startling statistics for erectile dysfunction are an indication that heart
and brain problems are also much more common than most people think.

Here is a partial list of factors that limit or disrupt blood flow.

- Stress. The overflow of the stress chemical adrenaline constricts blood flow to many areas of the body.
- Caffeine. This substance directly constricts blood flow to the brain, disrupts sleep, and is involved in dehydration.
- Nicotine. This substance constricts blood flow everywhere.
- Dehydration. The brain is 80 percent water. Anything that dehydrates you makes it harder to think. I once did a scan of a famous bodybuilder. His brain resembled that of a drug addict's, but he vehemently denied it. Then I learned that he significantly dehydrates himself before photo shoots to look leaner for the camera, and he had one of these photo shoots the day after his first scan. When he was adequately hydrated the following week, his brain looked much better (see Images 2.2 and 2.3).
- Artery disease/heart disease. Both directly limit blood flow.
- Diabetes. A small blood vessel disease, diabetes limits blood flow, makes blood vessels brittle, and prevents the healing of damaged tissue.
- Environmental toxins. These toxins poison blood vessels.
- Lack of sleep. People who get less than six hours a sleep at night have lower overall blood flow to the brain.
- Lack of exercise. In addition to weakening the heart pump, too little exercise allows blood vessels to become droopy and less efficient.
- Drug or alcohol abuse. These substances are directly toxic to the vascular system. Drugs or alcohol cause a toxic swiss cheese appearance on scans from the overall decreased blood flow.

To increase healthy blood flow throughout your body and brain, you need to get enough sleep; drink plenty of water; avoid substances that dehydrate you, such as caffeine and alcohol; stop any medications or bad habits (like smoking) that may be constricting blood flow; and consider taking supplements such as fish oil, gingko, ginseng, and L-arginine that boost blood

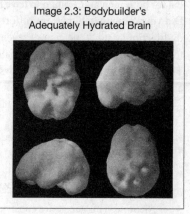

Image 2.2: Bodybuilder's
Dehydrated Brain

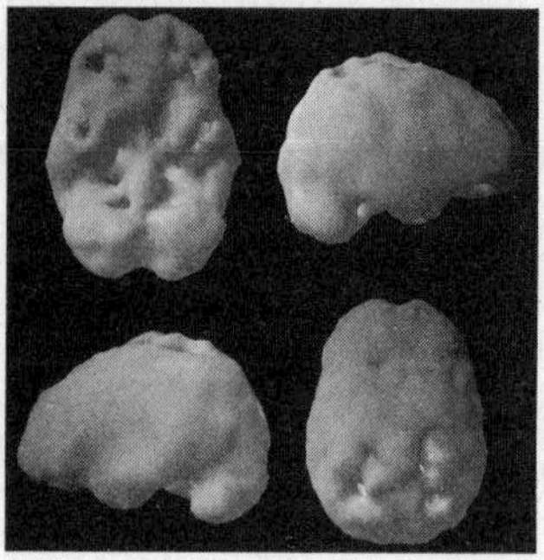

Image 2.3: Bodybuilder's
Adequately Hydrated Brain

flow. Probably the most important thing to do is to eliminate any toxins and to exercise.

4. INCREASE YOUR BRAIN'S RESERVE

Have you ever wondered why certain stresses or injuries affect some people and not others? I have. I have wondered why some people get depressed after losing a parent while others, although sad, keep going; why some people, after a minor head injury, seem to really be affected, while others don't; or why some people can work many hours straight, while others are completely spent after a short period of time. Several years ago, after looking at many thousands of brain scans, I started to think about the concept of brain reserve. Brain reserve is the cushion, margin, or extra neurons that we have, to deal with unexpected events or insults. The more reserve we have, the more stresses or injuries we can handle. The less reserve, the more vulnerable we are.

When we are conceived, we all start with the same reserve. Many things can erode it; many things can boost it. For example, if your mother smoked, drank much alcohol, or was under constant stress when she was pregnant with you, she decreased your brain's reserve. If she took fish oil, listened to classical music, and meditated every day, it is likely she increased your reserve. If you fell down a flight of stairs at age three, were exposed to chronic stress from an alcoholic mother or father during childhood, were sexually molested as a child or teenager, drank too much alcohol or used drugs, you decreased or limited your brain's reserve. On the other hand, if you were fed a healthy diet, took fish oil, were raised by loving, consistent parents, and were exposed to many different kinds of learning, your brain's reserve was likely increased.

Anything that harms brain function starts to erode your brain's reserve. Here are some factors known to decrease brain reserve.

- Prenatal or birth injuries
- Brain injuries
- Excessive alcohol
- Drug abuse
- Negative thinking
- Poor diet
- Environmental toxins
- Chronic stress
- Lack of sleep / sleep apnea
- Smoking
- Excessive caffeine
- Too much television or violent video games
- Lack of exercise

Likewise, maintaining a brain healthy life will increase your reserve or hardiness to deal with pending stresses or trouble. I always want to be increasing my brain reserve, so I can deal with the crises that inevitably will come my way. Here are a number of ways to do it.

- Make positive social connections.
- Engage in new learning.
- Maintain a healthy diet.
- Take a daily multiple vitamin.
- Take a fish oil supplement.
- Learn music.
- Exercise regularly.
- Dance (of course, without drinking).
- Engage in positive thinking.
- Express gratitude.
- Meditate.

If you wish to stay healthy during stressful times, you need adequate brain reserve. Start working today to add more neurons to your life.

5. MAINTAIN THE BRAIN'S HARDWARE

Your brain not only has to grow, develop, and mature, it has to repair itself on an ongoing basis. It is not like a car that can be taken into the mechanic when it needs a tune-up or a part replaced. Your brain has mechanisms to repair the damage as a result of the normal wear and tear of life. The hardware has to be maintained in order for the brain to consistently function at its best.

It is still commonly believed that we are born with all the brain cells we will ever have. Because of this notion, scientists considered brain damage irreversible and neurological disease unstoppable. In stunning research within the last decade, investigators demonstrated that adult human brains generate new cells after all. Since then, scientists have been furiously studying the implications that has accelerated research in this area.

Neurogenesis means birth, but the birth cycle is begun by death. Let's say you go to a New Year's Eve party and have a little too much champagne. You come home and sleep it off. By the time you awake, several hundred thousand neurons have died from alcohol toxicity. Somehow, the number of neurons in your brain has to be brought back up to normal. Neurogenesis is the process that develops and maintains the functional capacity of brain circuits by replacing neurons that are killed or damaged. The very act of the neurons' dying triggers certain growth factors in the brain to stimulate the formation of new neurons. But neurogenesis doesn't know when to stop; left on its own it will continue creating new neurons until the brain explodes. The brain has to regulate itself so that just the right numbers of neurons are maintained. When the number generated reaches a certain level, cell death is triggered, which miraculously brings the number back down. Yet once again, this death mechanism does not know when to stop killing, and thus new neuron formation is triggered again. This process allows the brain cell growth to stay within a certain range, so that the circuits can always function well—at least under normal conditions.

Think of this repair process as the brain's governor, whose main job is to *govern* the population. It must maintain the right balance or all hell will break loose. Aging occurs when more cells die than are made. Cancer occurs when cells overproliferate. Encouraging brain health encourages neurogenesis.

6. YOUR ABILITY TO CONTROL YOUR LIFE IS DIRECTLY TIED TO THE HEALTH OF YOUR BRAIN

Most people have a black or white conception of free will. That was my thought before I started my work with brain imaging. Growing up Roman

Catholic I had the idea that we could all equally decide to do good or bad. It was a simple decision that led to heaven or hell, and we all had the same ability to choose, unless of course someone was mentally retarded or had another brain illness, such as Alzheimer's disease or schizophrenia, that took away their self-control. After looking at tens of thousands of brains in my own patients I have come to realize the free will is really a very gray concept. I think most of us have about 85 percent free will, until you drink a six-pack of Bud Lite, which drops free will to about 50 percent. But what if someone, through disease or damage, starts with 50 percent free will? That same six-pack of Bud Lite could cause a disaster in their lives.

In the first several years of scanning the brain, criminal attorneys heard about my work and sent us people to scan who had done some really awful things. Most of the time, though not always, these people had really bad brain function. It became clear that the health of the brain was related to decision making.

In one very sad case from Healdsburg, a city about an hour north of San Francisco, a sixteen-year-old boy, Jose, senselessly attacked another teenager, Dillon, because of the color of the sweater he wore. Referred to as the Red Sweater Case, the city was outraged. Jose had been "hotboxing" before he lost his temper. A group of teenagers, including Jose, were inside a VW Beetle with the windows rolled up, smoking joints. Being in a closed space with multiple people smoking increases the concentration of marijuana in the body, thus the term *hotboxing*. Shortly afterward, Jose saw Dillon walking his dog across the street. Dillon was wearing a red sweater. Jose, a wannabe gang member whose color was red, confronted Dillon and asked him what color he claimed. Dillon said he didn't claim any color and started to walk off. Jose said, "Wrong answer," and senselessly beat him nearly to death. Dillon was in a coma for three weeks and ended up with serious brain damage.

As part of developing a defense, Jose's attorney sent him for neuropsychological testing, which revealed probable damage to his prefrontal cortex, the part of the brain involved in judgment, empathy, planning, and impulse control. The neuropsychologist suggested the attorney contact me to scan Jose's brain. The SPECT study was very abnormal. Jose had severe decreased activity in his prefrontal cortex and temporal lobes (implicated in learning disabilities and violence) and increased activity in the anterior cingulate gyrus, which is the brain's "gear shifter," causing him to be rigid and inflexible and to fixate on negative thoughts (see Image 2.4).

Clearly, Jose had an abnormal brain. He had suffered several brain injuries in the past, including being beaten unconscious by a heavy chain,

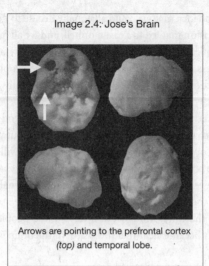

Image 2.4: Jose's Brain

Arrows are pointing to the prefrontal cortex
(top) and temporal lobe.

and he had experienced severe emotional trauma. His mother was murdered when he was eight years old and he had witnessed much violence. Even when he was not smoking marijuana, Jose suffered with a vulnerable brain. Put him in the wrong situation, under the influences of something that diminishes brain function further, even marijuana, and he is likely to explode.

I received a lot of criticism for testifying at Jose's trial, even threatening phone calls to my office. People said I was providing a high-tech excuse for bad behavior. But the truth was that Jose did not have full access to his own brain, the organ that controls behavior. It didn't mean that he didn't do the crime. He did. It didn't mean he was not responsible for it. He was. What it does mean is that the jury should take into consideration that he was literally not dealing with a complete set of brain cells and they should send him to a place where he could get appropriate treatment. Odds are, whatever the sentence, he will go home at some point. He will be less likely to reoffend, if his brain was helped. In fact, the jury did use imaging information for mitigation. Rather than receiving twenty-five years, which the prosecution wanted, the jury sentenced him to eleven years, recommending he go to a place that would provide Jose with treatment.

Why is it that some people explode in certain situations and others do not? I think we must consider the vulnerability of the brain. The better our brains work, the less likely we are to do bad or stupid things.

| 3 |

Brain Envy

ELIMINATE THE DAILY HABITS THAT HOLD YOU BACK

Bad habits are like chains that are too light to feel until they are too heavy to carry.

—WARREN BUFFETT

Lucy, a well-respected scientist and entrepreneur in her early fifties from Boston, came to see me after selling her company. Even though she was financially set for life, there was so much stress associated with the sale that she had trouble sleeping, was racked with anxiety, and had obsessive tendencies that she thought she had left behind in her twenties. As part of our evaluation we performed a set of brain SPECT scans. Her husband, Arnie, came along and also got scanned, in his mind, to support his wife. He was just curious. I looked at her brain and saw the trouble I had expected and recommended a course of treatment. When I looked at Arnie's fifty-six-year-old brain, it looked like he was eighty (see Image 3.1). I asked him what he was doing to hurt his brain.

"Nothing, Dr. Amen," he said with a look of disbelief.

"Really?" I said, feeling a little confused as to why his brain looked so bad. "How much do you drink?"

"Oh, not very much," he replied.

"What's not very much?" I asked. Through the years I have learned to always ask this follow-up, clarifying question.

"Oh, maybe I have three or four drinks a day."

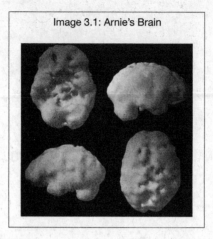

Image 3.1: Arnie's Brain

"Every day?" I said.

"Yeah, every day. But it's never a problem. I never get drunk. I have never gotten into trouble with it," Arnie said with anxiety.

"Why do you drink every day?" I asked.

"Since my daughter went off to college I have this empty nest thing going on. The time I used to spend with her, I now spend at a local pub, seeing my friends. It's a social time, kind of like the show *Cheers*."

"Well, you are poisoning yourself," I said. "You're fifty-six and your brain looks like it's eighty. If you keep this up, pretty soon your brain is going to look a lot worse, and with that comes trouble with everything in your life."

Arnie was shocked that his brain looked as bad as it did. As we talked, I could see he was beginning to develop "brain envy." After learning about his brain, it was clear he wanted his to function better. I gave him a very specific brain healthy plan that included abstinence from alcohol, regular exercise, mental exercise, vitamins, supplements, and fish oil. Four months later he wrote me saying that he mentally felt like he was twenty years old. His energy and memory were better, and he felt smarter and more articulate. His work as a business consultant had also improved, and he started writing a book about his work, something he had wanted to do five years earlier but could never find the time or motivation.

Personally Confronted with Bad Brain Habits

Over the years I have personally had ten brain SPECT studies, beginning at age thirty-seven when we first started to do scans. Looking back, my early scans showed a toxic, scalloped appearance that was definitely not consistent with great brain function (see Image 3.2). My last scan, at age fifty-two, looked healthier and much younger than my scan fifteen years earlier, even though scans usually become significantly less active with age (see Image 3.3). Why? In the intervening years, I developed "brain envy" and wanted a better brain. As I learned about brain health, I put into practice what I preached to my patients and readers.

All of my life I have been someone who rarely drank alcohol and never used an illegal drug. Then why did my brain not look great? Before I understood about brain health, I had many bad brain habits. I ate lots of fast food, lived on diet sodas filled with aspartame, often would get by on four to five hours of sleep at night, worked like a nut, didn't exercise with any regularity, and was living in a marriage filled with chronic conflict and stress.

Your daily habits and routines, as we will see, are either hurting or helping your brain. In this chapter we will look at one of the major obstacles to your success—your behavior each day. This chapter begins with a "Bad Brain Habit Quiz" to show you your strengths and weaknesses. Then we will explore fourteen bad brain habits that span all age groups and finish the chapter by considering bad brain habits across the life span as they relate specifically to childhood, adolescence, early adulthood, middle age, and the elderly.

As you read about these bad habits, I can hear some of you thinking, much like my patients or the teenagers who took our high school course "Making a Good Brain Great" have said, "How am I going to have any fun, if I have to watch everything I do every day?" My usual response is that you

Image 3.2: My Scan at Age Thirty-Seven	Image 3.3: My Scan at Age Fifty-Two

 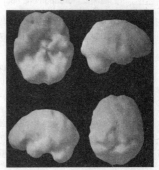

Notice there is less bumpiness or scalloping on the scan at age fifty-two.

have much more fun with a healthy brain than with one that is out of sync. A healthy brain is more thoughtful, playful, insightful, romantic, productive, and wealthier. Do you think you will have more fun if you can stay in a great relationship, keep a meaningful job, save your money to spend it on planned, fun activities, and be able to think well into your later years, as opposed to four-wheeling in the desert (rife for brain injuries), being drunk or high, or living with chronic anger?

BAD BRAIN HABIT QUIZ

Please rate each question on a scale of 0 to 4.

0	1	2	3	4	NA
Never	Rarely	Occasionally	Frequently	Very Frequently	Not Applicable

_____ 1. My diet is poor and tends to be haphazard.

_____ 2. I do not exercise.

_____ 3. I put myself at risk for brain injuries by doing such things as not wearing my seat belt, drinking and driving, engaging in high risk sports, and so on.

_____ 4. I live under daily or chronic stress, in my home or work life.

_____ 5. My thoughts tend to be negative, worried, or angry.

_____ 6. I have problems getting at least 6–7 hours of sleep a night.

_____ 7. I smoke or am exposed to secondhand smoke.

_____ 8. I drink or consume more than two normal-sized (8-ounce) cups of coffee, tea, or dark sodas a day.

_____ 9. I use aspartame and/or MSG.

_____ 10. I am around environmental toxins, such as paint fumes, hair or nail salon fumes, or pesticides.

_____ 11. I spend more than one hour a day watching TV.

_____ 12. I spend more than one hour a day playing computer or video games.

_____ 13. Outside of work time, I spend more than one hour a day on the computer.

_____ 14. I have more than three normal-sized drinks of alcohol (8 ounces of beer or wine or 1 ounce of hard liquor) a week.

0–6	Great brain habits
7–12	Really good; work to be better
13–20	Fair; you are prematurely aging your brain
>20	Poor; time to be very concerned

Fourteen Bad Brain Habits That May Affect All Age Groups

1. Lousy diet
2. Lack of exercise
3. Risking brain trauma
4. Chronic stress
5. Negative thinking, chronic worry, or anger
6. Poor sleep
7. Cigarette smoke
8. Excessive caffeine
9. Aspartame and MSG
10. Exposure to environmental toxins
11. Excessive TV
12. Excessive video games
13. Excessive computer or cell phone time
14. More than a little alcohol

1. LOUSY DIET

You literally are what you eat. Every cell in your body, including brain cells, make themselves new every five months. Some cells, like those that make up your skin, regenerate every thirty days. Eating a healthy, balanced diet provides the nutrients and fuel to drive optimal brain function. Your diet makes a big difference in how you feel. Yet so many of us are diet disasters. Obesity and diabetes are at epidemic proportions. Both of these problems are directly related to diet and are risk factors for Alzheimer's disease. What you eat on a daily basis helps or hurts your brain.

How are your eating habits? Do you skip breakfast? Do you grab two doughnuts in the morning on the way to work, with the large coffee filled with flavored cream and sugar? Or do you think you are being smart by saving the calories from the sugar and using aspartame? Do you grab a diet soda and think that all you are getting is sweet, bubbly water? Do you allow yourself to get so hungry that you gorge at lunch or dinner? Do you keep candy in your desk at work or easy to get at in the cabinets? Do you plan your meals or only think about them when you are hungry? Are you a sucker for supersizing meals? Do you gorge late at night?

The best brain diets include the following.

- Lots of pure water. The brain is 80 percent water.
- Few calories. Obesity is bad for your brain, as fat stores toxic materials and obesity doubles the risk for Alzheimer's disease.
- Lean protein. Fish, chicken, lean pork, and beef, for example, all help build neurons.
- Complex, low glycemic carbohydrates. These include whole grains, fruits, and vegetables.
- Healthy fats. Fish, avocados, and raw nuts all maintain nerve cell membranes and myelin.
- Lots of dietary antioxidants, such as blueberries. I often tell my patients to eat from the rainbow (food with many different colors, although this does *not* mean Skittles). See my book *Making a Good Brain Great* for more suggestions for a brain healthy diet.

2. LACK OF EXERCISE

No matter what your age, being a physical slug is bad for your brain, even if you are spending all of your time doing *New York Times* crossword puzzles. The brain needs physical exercise. Without it, the brain struggles. Exercise boosts blood flow to the brain, which helps supply oxygen, glucose, and nutrients and takes away toxic substances. Anything that limits blood flow results in poorer oxygenation, glucose delivery, and nutrient deficiencies. If the deep areas of the brain are starved of healthy blood flow you will have problems with coordination and processing complex thoughts. Exercise also increases brain-derived neurotrophic factor, a chemical that helps with neurogenesis. When we lose more cells than we make, aging occurs. In laboratory rats, research shows that exercise generates new brain cells in the prefrontal cortex (judgment and thoughtfulness) and temporal lobes (memory), which survive for about four weeks and then die off unless they are stimulated. If you stimulate these new neurons through mental or social interaction, they connect to other neurons and enhance learning. This is why people who *only* work out at the gym are not as smart as people who work out at the gym and then go to the library. At every age, exercise helps keep the brain healthy. Without it, we become fatter, less intelligent, and definitely not happier.

The best exercises combine aerobic elements, which means you get your heart rate up, with some form of coordination movement. Coordination movements activate the cerebellum, at the back bottom part of the brain, and enhances thinking, cognitive flexibility, and processing speed. Dancing is a perfect exercise, especially learning new steps, but if you drink when you dance that completely ruins the benefit. The other perfect brain exercise is table tennis. It is great for your cerebellum, because you have to get your eyes, your hands, and your feet all to work together at the same time, while you are thinking about the spins on the ball. I think of table tennis as aerobic chess. And it involves very few brain injuries. In 1999 I played in the U.S. National Table Tennis Tournament with hundreds of other people and there was not one brain injury. According to a new brain imaging study from Japan, table tennis helps balance your brain. Researchers studied a group of patients before and after playing table tennis and showed increased activity in the prefrontal cortex, the thoughtful part of your brain, and the cerebellum, just after playing for ten minutes. More table tennis, less football and boxing!

3. RISKING BRAIN TRAUMA

Even though I discussed this earlier, it bears repeating. Brain injuries can have a devastating impact on your life, no matter what your age. I have had patients who fell down a flight of stairs at age three, fell out of a second-story window at seven, and fell off the roof in middle age. I've had other patients suffer severe skateboarding accidents in their early teens, snowboarding accidents in their later teens, and four-wheeling accidents as young adults. I've had elderly patients who experienced bad falls. All of these injuries have the potential to damage the brain and compromise your abilities and happiness. Does your day-to-day behavior increase or decrease the risk of brain injuries?

- Do you speed in your car or text-message on your phone while driving?
- Do you head soccer balls? This has been shown to damage the front tips of your temporal lobes (potentially affecting memory, language, and emotional control).
- Do you play tackle football? In a study from Virginia Tech, high school football players get hit in the head an average of thirty to fifty times a game, sometimes with the force of a severe car accident.
- Do you ride bikes, skateboard, ski, sled, or snowboard without helmets that fit snugly? A helmet that fits is much more protective than one that doesn't. Bike riding is the number one cause of brain injuries in children and teens.

- Do you go four-wheeling, off-roading, with all-terrain vehicles, Jet Skiing, or boat racing?
- Do you drink alcohol? This increases your risk of a brain injury from a motor vehicle accident, falls, or making someone else mad enough at you to give you a brain injury.
- Are you taking medications or drugs that make you unsteady on your feet or decrease your reaction time, increasing your risk of injury?
- Do you drive without your seat belt buckled or while talking on a cell phone?
- Do you box or play extreme sports that place you at increased risk?

There are many more daily habits that increase your risk of injury. Remember that your brain is soft and your skull is hard. Respect and protect your brain.

4. CHRONIC STRESS

Chronic or severe stress, stemming from family conflict, financial hardships, health problems, or environmental challenges, can affect all age groups. When stress becomes unremitting, it hurts the brain. In a series of studies reported in the journal *Psychoneuroendocrinology,* researchers looked at the effects of long-term exposure to stress hormones, especially cortisol, on the brain function of older adults, young adults, and children. In the first study, researchers measured levels of cortisol in a group of older adults over a period of three to six years. They found that older adults with continuously high levels of cortisol performed worse on memory tests than older adults with moderate or low cortisol levels. In addition, older adults with long-term exposure to high cortisol levels also had, on average, a 14 percent smaller hippocampus, the area of the temporal lobes involved with memory. In tests with young adults, researchers found that short, temporary increases in cortisol negatively affected their thinking and memory skills. But these impairments were only temporary. Another study with young children and teenagers from different socioeconomic classes showed that children with lower socioeconomic status had higher average stress hormone levels than the other children. Taken together these studies show that chronic stress impairs the brain function for people of all ages.

High cortisol levels not only shrink the hippocampus, but they also make you fat by disrupting several hormones involved in appetite control. In addition, daily stress increases blood pressure, disrupts sleep patterns, and increases negative thinking patterns, all of which hurt brain function. Having techniques to counteract stress, such as daily relaxation, meditation, prayer, or exercise, can have a positive effect on how your mind works.

5. NEGATIVE THINKING, CHRONIC WORRY, OR ANGER

Thinking is a habit. Negative, worried, or angry thinking is a bad habit that results from a lack of "thoughtful" education. Most people think that thoughts just happen. We are not taught to question or correct the negative words or images that run wild in our heads. Yet these awful thoughts are often at the core of anxiety and depressive disorders, relationship and work problems, and they have a real, measurable, negative biological impact on brain function.

Our brain and body respond to every thought we have. At all ages, including young children, the quality of our thoughts is either helping us or hurting us. Positive, happy, hopeful thoughts release chemicals that help you feel good; negative, worried, or angry thoughts release a completely different set of chemicals that make you feel bad and erode the functioning of your brain. Depression, often the result of rampant, unquestioned negative thoughts, doubles the risk for Alzheimer's disease, increases your risk for substance abuse to self-medicate the bad feelings, and pushes other people away, increasing isolation and loneliness.

6. POOR SLEEP

Do you go to bed late and get up early? Do you toss and turn, look at the clock, wonder when morning will come, or become disgusted with yourself that you have no power to turn your mind off? Sleep is essential to healthy brain function. People who get fewer than six hours a night have decreased blood flow to the brain, and they have trouble thinking clearly during the day. Sleep problems are rampant in our society. According to the National Institutes of Health, 30 percent of the population has chronic sleep problems and 10 percent are affected by symptoms of sleep deprivation during the day. The prescriptions for sleep medications, such as Ambien and Lunesta, have skyrocketed in the past decade. We are in the midst of an insomnia epidemic. In 1900, Americans, on average, got nine hours of sleep a night. In 2008, we got only an average of six hours of sleep at night. Our brains were not designed to have a 33 percent decrease in sleep in such a short period of time. The advent of the lightbulb is the likely cause of the change.

Shift workers, those suffering from jet lag, teens who have their sleep schedules off-kilter, and those suffering from sleep apnea are all at risk for poorer brain function. Those who are sleep deprived score poorer on memory and math tests, have lower grades in school, and are at much greater risk for driving accidents. According to the National Highway Traffic Safety Administration, drowsiness and fatigue cause more than one hundred thousand traffic accidents each year and young drivers are at the wheel in more than half the crashes. Sleep deprivation is also associated with depression and attention deficit disorders. Recently, sleep apnea (snoring loudly, breath holding when sleeping, and tiredness during the day) has been linked to Alzheimer's disease.

Sleep is involved in rejuvenating the brain. Without it, people can become psychotic. When I was the chief of Community Mental Health at Fort Irwin in the Mojave Desert we saw a number of soldiers who started to hear voices and became paranoid after being sleep deprived for up to three days in a row. Fort Irwin is home to the National Training Center, which teaches soldiers desert warfare. Troops spent days at a time in war games without much sleep. Mental health casualties were always high during those periods of time.

Try to get seven to eight hours of sleep at night, more for children and teens. Practice good sleep habits, such as avoiding much caffeine or nicotine. Also, do not use alcohol as a sleep aid, as it will wear off and cause you to rebound and wake up in the middle of the night; avoid exercise before bed; and learn relaxation techniques to calm your mind.

7. CIGARETTE SMOKE

Nicotine prematurely ages the brain. Nicotine, found in cigarettes, cigars, chewing tobacco, and nicotine patches, tablets, and gums, causes blood vessels to constrict, lessening blood flow to vital organs. Smokers experience more problems with impotence because of low blood flow to sexual organs. Nicotine constricts blood flow to the skin, making smokers look older than they are. Nicotine also constricts blood flow to the brain, depriving the brain of the nutrients it needs, and eventually causing overall lowered activity. If this substance is so bad, then why do people use it? In the short run, nicotine, like alcohol and other drugs of abuse, makes many people feel better. It stimulates the release of several brain neurotransmitters, such as acetylcholine, which improves your reaction time and your ability to pay attention. It also stimulates dopamine, which acts on the pleasure centers of the brain, and glutamate, which is involved in learning and memory (although high glutamate levels cause programmed cell death and is associated with causing Alzheimer's disease). No wonder people use nicotine and have trouble quitting. But if you want a healthy brain, do what you can to stay away from it.

Secondhand smoke is harmful to everyone, especially developing minds. Mothers who smoke during pregnancy are more likely to have children who have behavioral and learning problems. Additionally, secondhand smoke increases asthma, infections, and cancer. Smoking is a very bad brain habit.

8. EXCESSIVE CAFFEINE

Found in coffee, tea, dark sodas, chocolate, and pep pills, caffeine constricts blood flow to the brain and many other organs. A little caffeine a day is not a problem, but more than a cup or two of coffee a day can be trouble. Caffeine does four bad things to the brain. First, it dehydrates it, and anything that dehydrates the brain causes us to have problems thinking. Second, it interferes with sleep. Caffeine blocks adenosine, a chemical that tells us to go to sleep. By blocking adenosine, we can get by with less sleep. But as we have seen, sleep is essential for healthy brain function. No wonder so many people need a cup of coffee in the morning to get going. They are treating their sleep-deprivation symptoms. Third, caffeine also constricts blood flow to the brain, causing premature aging. Lastly, caffeine is addictive. Many people have significant withdrawal symptoms, such as headaches and tiredness, when they try to stop. Less caffeine is better.

9. ASPARTAME AND MSG

Many people drink diet sodas by the gallons, thinking that they are drinking nothing more than sweet water. I have had my share of diet drinks in my life, but when I read about the negative effects of aspartame, I became concerned. From the age of thirty I started to have arthritis in my hands and knees. When I stopped the aspartame, my joints no longer hurt. I have also had many patients report feeling better after stopping the intake of artificial sweeteners. Their headaches went away, they could think more clearly, joint pain improved, memory improved, and surprisingly, some even lost weight. My sense is that it also depends on our own genetic makeup. Some people seem to have no problems with artificial sweeteners, while others have terrible reactions to them. Less is better.

Monosodium glutamate (MSG) is another problem for many. Personally, I get headaches when it is in something I eat. But it is nothing like the reaction of one of my patients. This man came to see us from the Midwest. He had attention deficit hyperactivity disorder (ADHD) and some anxiety and depressive symptoms. In his history, he told us he became violent when exposed to any MSG. As part of his evaluation we scanned him; at his request, we did an additional scan on MSG. The MSG scan showed a significant left temporal lobe deficit, which is often associated with violence or rage reactions. I told him he had a choice to stay away from MSG or take medication to protect his temporal lobes. To my surprise he decided to take the medication just in case. When asked why, he said that if he lost his temper one more time his wife would leave him and you never know what has MSG in it. When possible, hold the MSG.

10. EXPOSURE TO ENVIRONMENTAL TOXINS

Most people do not wish to think they are being poisoned or poisoning themselves on a daily basis, but the frightening fact is that they may be. Painting without appropriate ventilation, visiting nail or hair salons too often, breathing in gas fumes as you fill up your car, using pesticides, and even remodeling your home have been implicated in brain damage. Understanding the sources of brain toxins can help you avoid them.

Breathing paint fumes and other solvents, such as hair and nail products, are brain toxins to approach with care. As a group, indoor painters have some of the highest levels of brain damage I have seen. I once evaluated a famous movie director whose scan showed a toxic appearance. On questioning, it was clear he had been exposed to high levels of paint fumes on many of the sets he had worked on. Getting proper ventilation was one of the keys to helping him heal. In my conversation with him, he told me the painters were the nuttiest people he ever worked with. He said they often got into fights on the sets for little or no reason and were the most unreliable. "Even the women act crazy," he said. No wonder, if they are exposed to chemicals that hurt the viability of brain tissue. A recent study reported that hairdressers had a higher than normal risk for Alzheimer's disease. When you go into a hair or nail salon, they often reek with fumes. If you get your hair or nails done only go to shops that have great ventilation.

11. EXCESSIVE TV

No matter what your age, watching too much TV, playing too many video games, or spending too much time on the computer is bad for your brain.

Our brains were not developed or evolved for the rapid change in technology that is affecting us today.

Parents hoping to give their children an edge by using infant educational videos, such as Brainy Baby and Baby Einsteins, are actually holding them back, according to a report in the *Journal of Pediatrics*. For every hour a day that babies eight to sixteen months old were shown the videos they knew six to eight fewer words than other children. Parents are spending hundreds of millions of dollars on these videos. "Unfortunately, it's all money down the tubes," according to one of the study's authors, Dr. Dimitri Christakis, a professor of pediatrics at the University of Washington in Seattle. Christakis and his colleagues surveyed a thousand parents in Washington and Minnesota and determined their babies' vocabularies using a set of ninety common baby words, including *mommy, nose,* and *choo-choo.* The researchers found that 32 percent of the babies were shown the videos and 17 percent of those were shown them for more than an hour a day. The American Academy of Pediatrics recommends no television at all for children younger than twenty-four months.

Another study published in the *Journal of Pediatrics* reported that for every hour a day children watch TV there is a 10 percent increased chance of them being diagnosed with ADHD. This means that if the child watches five hours a day she has a 50 percent chance of being diagnosed with ADHD. According to the American Academy of Child and Adolescent Psychiatry, children spend an average of three to four hours a day watching TV.

In other studies, increased television watching in childhood put people at risk for brain problems as adults. Dr. R. J. Hancox and colleagues from the Department of Preventive and Social Medicine in Dunedin, New Zealand, assessed approximately one thousand children born in 1972–1973 at regular intervals up to age twenty-six. They found that there was a significant association between higher body-mass indices, lower physical fitness, increased cigarette smoking, and raised serum cholesterol (all affect the brain). These are all factors that are involved in brain illnesses, such as strokes or Alzheimer's disease. In yet another study adults who watched two or more hours a day of TV had a significantly higher risk of Alzheimer's disease. Watching TV is usually a "no brain" activity, and less is better.

12. EXCESSIVE VIDEO GAMES

As a father of four children and a child psychiatrist, I have thought a lot about video games over the past twenty years. At first, I found them great fun to play. But soon thereafter, I started to worry. Action video games have been studied using brain imaging techniques that look at blood flow and activity patterns. Video games have been found to work in an area of the brain called the basal ganglia, one of the pleasure centers in the brain. In fact, this is the same part of the brain that lights up when researchers inject a person with cocaine. My experience with patients and one of my own children is that they tend to get hooked on the games and play so much that their school work, job performance, and social time can deteriorate, a bit like the effect of a drug. Some children and adults actually do get hooked on them.

There is also scientific literature that reports video games may increase seizure frequency in people who are sensitive to them. You may remember the seizure scare on December 16, 1997, when the Japanese cartoon *Pocket Monster* (Pokémon) showed an explosion of red, white, and yellow lights that triggered 730 Japanese children to go to the hospital with new onset seizures. The condition is called photosensitive seizures (seizures triggered by light). I often think video games trigger subclinical seizures in vulnerable kids and adults, causing behavior or learning problems.

Two studies from the University of Missouri examined the effects of violent video games (a significant percentage of video games) on aggression. One study found that violent real-life simulation video game play was positively related to aggressive behavior and delinquency. The more people played, the more trouble they seemed to have. Academic performance deteriorated with increased time spent playing video games. In the second study, laboratory exposure to a graphically violent video game increased aggressive thoughts and behavior. The results from both studies suggest that exposure to violent video games will increase aggressive behavior in both the short term (e.g., laboratory aggression) and the long term (e.g., delinquency). In a comprehensive review of other studies it was found time and again that exposure to violent video games is significantly linked to increases in aggressive behavior, aggressive thoughts, aggressive feelings, and cardiovascular arousal and to decreases in helping behavior; none of this is good for overall brain health.

13. EXCESSIVE COMPUTER OR CELL PHONE TIME

Computers, e-mails, the Internet, instant messaging (IMing) and cell phones are taking over our lives, and not always to good effect. Some people, like me, get well over a hundred e-mails a day. Some teens are IMing up to fifteen people at a time. According to a recent study, the distractions of constant e-mails, text messages, and voice mail are a greater threat to IQ and concentration than is smoking marijuana.

Drowsiness, tiredness, and an increasing inability to focus reached "startling" levels in the trials of eleven hundred people, who also demonstrated that e-mails in particular have an addictive, druglike quality. Research subjects' minds were all over the place as they faced new questions and challenges every time an e-mail dropped into their in-box. Productivity at work was damaged and the effect on staff who could not resist trying to juggle new messages with existing work was the equivalent, over the course of a day, to the loss of a night's sleep.

"This is a very real and widespread phenomenon," said Glenn Wilson, a psychologist from King's College, London University, who carried out eighty clinical trials for the marketing research firm TNS, which were commissioned by the information technology company Hewlett-Packard. The average IQ loss was measured at 10 points, more than double the 4-point mean fall found in studies of cannabis users. The most damage was done, according to the survey, by the almost complete lack of discipline in handling e-mails. Dr. Wilson and his colleagues found a compulsion to reply to each new message, leading to constant changes of direction, which inevitably tired and slowed down the brain.

Constantly checking e-mails, IMs, voice mails, and the Internet is stressful, but it is also addictive as one is always waiting for the next good e-mail, IM, or voice message to hit, like waiting for the next blackjack in the card game 21. The anticipation of something good keeps us checking something routinely. It also distracts us from staying focused on the person or task at hand. Checking these messaging systems is an important way to communicate, but it is better to set aside specific times each day to work on them and leave them alone the rest of the time.

14. MORE THAN A LITTLE ALCOHOL

Contrary to popular belief, red wine, except in small quantities, is not a health food. In my experience as a brain imaging physician, alcohol is directly toxic to brain function. The SPECT scans of people who consume more than three alcoholic beverages a week look toxic. Alcohol lowers overall blood flow and activity in the brain, which is why alcohol calms anxiety and disinhibits people, but over time it negatively affects memory and judgment.

Alcohol affects the brain by reducing nerve cell firing; it blocks oxygen from getting into the cell's energy centers; and it reduces the effectiveness of many different types of neurotransmitters, especially those involved in learning and remembering. Alcohol is a double-edged sword, depending on the quantity of intake. Large amounts of it—four or more glasses of wine or the equivalent in hard liquor on a daily basis—increase the risk of dementia. However, it has been found that small amounts—a glass of wine once a week or once a month but not daily—may reduce the risk. The reduced risk seems to be related to the fact that alcohol and cholesterol compete with each other and sometimes it is good for alcohol to win. Small amounts of alcohol compete with high-density lipoprotein (HDL), the good cholesterol, which actually removes the harmful types of cholesterol. When a person drinks a little alcohol, HDL is not allowed to bind to the cell membrane, so it is forced back into the bloodstream where it lowers low-density lipoprotein and other harmful cholesterols. This reduces the person's risk of heart disease, atherosclerosis, and strokes, all of which are known causes for dementia. On the other hand, researchers from Johns Hopkins University found that even moderate alcohol consumption (about fourteen drinks a week) has been correlated with brain shrinkage. When it comes to the brain, size matters! My advice is that small amounts of alcohol after age twenty-five is okay, but don't push it. Why wait until you're twenty-five to drink? As discussed earlier, the brain, especially the prefrontal cortex, is not fully developed until age twenty-five. Why start poisoning it before it has had a chance to fully develop?

You might wonder why I put alcohol as a potential problem affecting all age groups. If a parent has a problem with alcohol, it definitely affects the whole family, including the children. Parents who drink regularly tend to be less available for their children and less able to see their needs.

Bad Brain Habits of Children

Bad brain habits seen in children include all of those mentioned above and more. Whenever you "give in to get along" by submitting to a child's demands for unhealthy foods, you perpetuate a brewing disaster. Poor brain healthy foods encourage difficult behavior, which only makes parents less able to provide healthy meals. As my friend the nutritionist Dr. J. J. Virgin says, "Exposure equals preference. What you feed children is what they will eat throughout their lives."

A study from the department of psychology at England's University of Southampton researchers confirmed what many people have suspected:

food dyes and additives are bad for children's brains. Over three one-week periods, three hundred three- to nine-year-old children were randomly assigned to consume one of three fruit drinks daily: one contained the amount of dye and sodium benzoate typically found in a British child's diet, a second drink had a lower concentration of the additives, and a third was additive-free. All the children spent a week drinking each of the three mixtures, which looked and tasted alike. During each weeklong period, teachers and parents rated such qualities as restlessness, lack of concentration, fidgeting, and talking or interrupting too much. Researchers found that within an hour children were significantly more hyperactive when drinking the stuff containing additives. Stay away from dyes and food additives. Read the food labels!

In general, I have found another disturbing trend over the past twenty-five years. Parents are giving in more and more to difficult behavior. If a child has a habit of whining or crying to get his or her way and the parents give in to such behavior, they have taught the child's brain to whine and cry, making him more vulnerable to mood and emotional problems later on. The two words I like best in effective parenting are *firm* and *kind*. Children need love, attention, and affection, but they also need rules and discipline for their brain to develop properly.

Another way to develop a bad brain habit with children is by allowing them to endlessly argue with parents. When you allow children to chronically oppose or argue with you, you actually encourage their brains to be less flexible. When the brain area called the anterior cingulate gyrus works too hard, owing to a deficit in the neurotransmitter serotonin, people get stuck on negative or oppositional thoughts and behaviors. Behavior therapy has been shown to help calm down this part of the brain. Stopping argumentative behavior actually helps the brain work better. One of the best ways to do this is to directly deal with the behavior. On the bulletin board in our five-year-old's room is a set of seven family rules. One of the rules is "No arguing with parents. As your parents, we want to hear your opinion. More than twice constitutes arguing." This way, no arguing is the expectation, and cooperation is encouraged. If Chloe argues, there is a consequence. When she cooperates, there are smiles and rewards.

Another concern for children is watching the same movie over and over. Once a child has seen a movie, there is little suspense or thought about what happens next. Repetitive watching turns out to be a no-brain activity.

Never reading to a child is a bad brain habit. Children need new learning to expand their brains and they learn best in an enriched environment. The more active parents and caregivers are in encouraging reading and education, the more children will see learning as a lifelong value. New learning throughout life is thought to be a major preventive factor for Alzheimer's disease.

Children often are filled with negative or frightening thoughts that they never learn how to challenge. Children need education in correcting the bad thoughts that go through their heads. I once taught a class for third-graders called "How to Think." I was shocked by the number of distorted negative, hurtful, scary thoughts that frightened and depressed the kids. By age eight they are able to understand and correct negative thought patterns. Negative thinking can be a very bad brain habit and needs to be corrected as early as possible. It is easy to do this by teaching them about ANTs (automatic negative thoughts) and ANTeaters, discussed in chapter 12.

Bad Brain Habits of Teenagers

Typical teenagers have many bad brain habits. Typically, they watch too much TV, play too many hours of video games, are on the computer into the wee hours of the morning, IM others to the distraction of all else, engage in high-risk sports, are often sleep deprived, get into motor vehicle accidents, and have terrible diets. No wonder suicide is the second-leading cause of death in this age group. We must do better at taking care of the teenage brain. I think many parents and school administrators prematurely abdicate the role of supervising this group, feeling helpless to have a real impact. Yet I have found through teaching our high school course, "Making a Good Brain Great," which is now used in over thirty-four states and seven countries, that these kids are amenable to education and informed influence. In my mind, lack of guidance for teens is a very bad brain habit.

Teens do best when their parents know where they are, who they are with, and what they are doing. Teens do best when they know their parents check on them. You need to be your teen's prefrontal cortex (the part of the brain that provides supervision, judgment, and impulse control), until they can properly monitor themselves. The prefrontal cortex does not fully develop until we are twenty-five years old, so even supervising young adults is appropriate.

Besides those bad habits listed above (diet, head injuries, lack of sleep, excessive caffeine, etc.), we now need to include drinking and drug use, which are especially problematic to developing brains. I am ever amazed at how much our teens drink and how many drugs they consume. Significant alcohol and drug use may arrest development. If people start drinking moderately or more during adolescence, when they stop, say, in their midtwenties, they are often still at the same emotional level as when they started.

Many teens also feel invincible. Risky behaviors, such as driving fast in the rain, jumping off rock cliffs into the ocean, or head banging in mosh pits, are nothing more than fun, until something terrible happens.

A bad habit that teenage girls often engage in is nonstop drama. It is great to have friends to talk about the ups and downs of teen life. Yet new research suggests that when girls talk on and on about the same problems, such as home or boyfriend troubles, it actually makes them feel worse.

Teens who have the habit of hanging out with other teens or young adults who do drugs, fight, or are involved in other dangerous activities are also at higher risk for brain damage that will diminish their chances for success. Who you spend time with matters, as we often become like the significant people in our lives.

Bad Brain Habits of Young Adults

As we leave our parents' home and supervision to go off to college or live on our own, the bad brain habits tend to flare. There is often increased drug or alcohol usage; less sleep; poorer diets; and the stress of doing things other people used to do for us, such as paying bills, grocery shopping, and planning vacations.

One of the unique stresses of this age group is that you are trying to be competent and successful on your own, which adds a burden of stress not seen before. Money worries are commonplace. Learning how to navigate intimate relationships can be challenging, as your brain is starting to interact with another brain on a deep level. Children may make their first appearance into your life, which, in my personal experience, dramatically increased my sense of responsibility and stress. No longer could I just be so focused on my own fun and happiness, I had another little life to look after.

Bad Brain Habits of Middle Adults (Age 30–65)

Middle age is a breeding ground for stress and bad brain habits. Being there myself, I can relate. We often work too hard, taking care of children and our own parents; have trouble sleeping; wake up feeling tired; start the day with two cups of coffee; finish the day with red wine (erroneously thinking it is health food); and worry about jobs, finances, teenagers, and myriad other issues. We are the world's caretakers and often get little respect for keeping everything going.

If we add getting your hair or nails done too often (the exposure to these toxic chemicals has been associated with increased Alzheimer's disease and bladder cancer), taking sleeping pills at night, not getting enough sex (sexual frequency has been associated with health and longevity) or being in a distant or stressful marriage, not getting adequate exercise, carrying around fifty extra pounds, focusing on our failures, you have the prescription for anxiety pills and forgetfulness. No wonder we start to look old.

Bad Brain Habits of Older Adults (> Age 65)

By this stage of life people have accumulated many or most of the bad habits described above. I once had an eighty-four-year-old patient whose daughter bought her a poker video game. She really enjoyed the game and played more than four hours a day. Her family noticed that she started to have trouble sleeping and was becoming more anxious and irritable. When she stopped playing, she went back to her normal, happy, sleeping, relaxed self.

A lack of exercise is now at its peak, as aches and pains start to creep in. Taking fish oil on a daily basis can significantly help joints feel more limber and less painful. Television watching is as high or higher than at any other stage, which is very troubling, as those who watch the most TV have the highest incidence of Alzheimer's disease.

Focusing on disappointments in the past is a common trait in the elderly, and it can be very harmful to mood and health. A lack of new learning causes the brain to become tired. To keep the brain young throughout life it must be challenged. Social isolation is also very common as friends and siblings die at ever increasing rates. Being involved with social activities is important to brain health.

I have treated many elderly patients who have taken up new hobbies. I love this for them, except when they take up painting and do not have good ventilation. The elderly brain is potentially very vulnerable to toxicity.

Dietary deficiencies are common, as many elderly live alone and are more reticent to cook for only one person. In addition, dehydration is common, as they may not be getting enough fluids, or they are taking diuretics to lower their blood pressure. In addition, many elderly are seeing multiple doctors and taking multiple medications every day, without having a personal physician who oversees everything a patient takes. I have seen truly awful brain function associated with myriad medications.

Once you learn to love your brain and eliminate the bad brain habits that destroy your best chances for success, you are ready to use your brain to its fullest potential to reach your dreams.

| 4 |

Hidden Short Circuits May
Be Ruining Your Life

LEARN HOW TO IDENTIFY AND CORRECT
YOUR VULNERABLE AREAS

When Edward came to the Amen Clinic he was driving a truck for a living. He had just split from his second wife, felt sad and extremely anxious, and was having suicidal thoughts. He frequently had the urge to drive his truck off a bridge or over a cliff. When I went to the waiting room to greet Edward for the first time I saw him drawing in an artist's sketchbook. When I asked, he hesitantly showed me his picture. It was amazing. I thought that he must have been a trained professional artist, yet it was not mentioned in the background information I had just read about him.

Edward's clinical evaluation and brain scans revealed he suffered from depression, anxiety, and ADHD. All of his adult life he had struggled to keep jobs and was a never-ending source of frustration to his romantic partners. He was sick of feeling bad and now motivated to get help. With treatment, which entailed a combination of dietary changes, exercise, nutritional supplements, medication, and targeted mind exercises, he began to heal.

Edward had always wanted to be an artist. His teachers told him that he was gifted from the time he was in grade school. Yet he was never able to follow through and finish the projects he started. As his treatment began to take hold, he started completing art pieces. He was able to sell several paintings in a local gallery. Over the next year the demand for his work increased and he was able to quit working for the trucking company to focus on his art full time. Three years after I first met Edward he sold a painting for more than a hundred thousand dollars. Many people think they cannot afford to get help. Yet living with an untreated or ineffectively treated psychiatric illness is much more expensive than spending money on the help you need.

The shocking statistic is that 49 percent of the U.S. population at some point in their lives will suffer from a psychiatric disorder. Anxiety disorders, depression, substance abuse, and ADHD are the most common. Twenty-nine percent of the population will have two distinct disorders, and 17 percent, like Edward, will have three. Having one or more of these illnesses can certainly interfere with your ability to be successful at work and in your relationships, and they rob many people of their ability to feel happy and content. They also rob many people of their lives, as suicide claims nearly one million people every year worldwide.

Our brain imaging work has taught me that these problems are frequently the result of short circuits in the brain that can be repaired or ameliorated. The sad truth is that most people never avail themselves of appropriate treatment either because of ignorance, fear, shame, or guilt. This chapter will explore how these short circuits interfere with success.

I love being a psychiatrist but hate the words *psychiatry, psychiatric, psychiatrist,* and *mental disorder.* To the general population these words conjure up notions of crazy, weird, unusual, weak will, character problems, and somehow not being authentic or real. When I first told my father that I wanted to be a psychiatrist, he was clearly disappointed and asked me why I didn't want to be a real doctor. Yet these problems are real, cause real suffering, have a real biological basis in brain dysfunction, and occur commonly in people most would consider normal.

We Are All Vulnerable, Even Me

Given how common these illnesses are, almost all of us are vulnerable to them at some point in our lives. I know some of you are thinking, not me, I will never go through depression or anxiety, I will never have a problem with drugs or alcohol. I used to be like that too. I treated people who had problems, but I was too strong, too together, to suffer like my patients. Wrong! Several years ago I lost someone important to me. For nearly nine months I suffered from extreme anxiety, had crushing chest pain, couldn't sleep, and had terrible thoughts running through my mind. The anxiety affected my work and relationships. It hurt, more than I could have imagined. Ultimately, that period in my life made me stronger and I am grateful for it. I learned more emotional management skills for myself and my patients and met some incredibly wonderful, helpful people, and it significantly increased the empathy I had for people who suffer.

Untreated or ineffectively treated brain problems or psychiatric problems, whatever we call them, limit a person's ability to be successful. Of course, this is not always true, as many people who suffer from these illnesses are highly successful. Think of people such as Ernest Hemingway (depression), Vincent van Gogh (psychosis), John Madden (fear of flying), Jane Fonda (bulimia), Brooke Shields (postpartum depression), and Howard Hughes (obsessive-compulsive disorder), to name a few. All of these people suffered. Still, even for these people, their illnesses disrupted their lives and limited their abilities. Getting the proper treatment decreases suffering and increases effectiveness.

A Completely New Way of Looking at Failure

Wesley was the leader of a research work group at a large university. He brought in millions of dollars of grant money each year. Yet his department was inefficient and had a high turnover rate. Most people who worked with him thought he was a narcissistic jerk, including his boss, with whom he was constantly at odds. His boss once asked him if he failed kindergarten, "because he never learned to share." Wesley had temper outbursts and very poor social skills. Eventually, he was fired for his difficult behavior after he publicly challenged his boss in front of the university chancellor.

J. D. was the CEO of a multimillion-dollar food service organization. Normally a reasonable guy, J. D. blew up during a staff meeting at Vince, his trusted vice president who had been close to him for several years. Vince was so embarrassed by the tirade that he walked out of the meeting. J. D. had to spend several hours convincing him not to quit his job. Their relationship was never quite the same again. J. D. had periodic temper outbursts for little to no reason, but this was the first one that happened at this job. He had tormented his family with these outbursts for several years.

Cherie was the office manager of a large law practice. Despite being hardworking and efficient, she was fired for being inflexible and rude to clients and the law partners. She had been counseled several times before her termination. She had significant trouble with change and believed that the way things had been in the past is the way they should always be. Her children all left home before they turned eighteen. They just needed some space where they could have their own minds and be themselves.

Bill was the general manager of a department store chain. After ten years of service he was fired for stealing from the business. His wife had left him three years earlier because of infidelity.

Danny was a manager of a local grocery store. He was fired after he was caught by the owner having sex with one of the cashiers in the manager's office.

Sima was a clerk in a large cell phone store. She was smart, warm, and caring. Her customers and co-workers liked her. Yet she would go through extended periods where she would be late to work, call in sick, and look sad and disheveled. Her unpredictable behavior led to her termination, which significantly upset the morale at the store and left them shorthanded.

Terry was a pharmacy manager for a local drugstore chain. He worked for a boss who was angry and inconsistent. He was afraid of his boss. Terry felt so anxious that he began to suffer from headaches and gastrointestinal problems and started to miss work. Terry never felt as though he could confront his manager or go above his head to the regional manager. After a year of inconsistent work production, Terry was fired.

Barbara, age sixty-two, was a high school English teacher. The students and faculty had loved her for many years. In the past four years, however, she was growing more and more forgetful, irritable, and unreliable. She seemed unmotivated, which was a marked change in her personality. After being counseled several times, which had no impact on her behavior, she was terminated. Her husband was beside himself. His wife had become a completely different person.

What do all of these people have in common? Brain troubles mislabeled as bad behavior, leading to failure. Wesley and J. D. had a problem in a part of the brain called the temporal lobe, causing temper outbursts and poor social skills. Cherie was seriously inflexible, caused by too much activity in a part of the brain called the anterior cingulate gyrus (known as the brain's gear shifter). Bill and Danny had problems with the prefrontal cortex (called the brain's executive center) and exhibited impulse control problems (stealing and having sex with employees). Sima suffered from periods of severe depression, likely caused by too much activity in her deep limbic system. Terry suffered with severe anxiety and situational stress, where his basal ganglia worked overtime. Barbara had Alzheimer's disease, causing her temporal lobes to deteriorate at a rapid pace. All of these people had skill and all had been previously promoted. Yet because of their brain problems, they exhibited intolerable behavior that cost them their jobs and stressed their families. Not once did their supervisors or family members give the brain one thought. Most of these people had treatable problems that could have saved their businesses and families large sums of money, heartache, and time.

To know when your brain is in trouble, it is important to have a basic understanding of how your brain works, including its strengths and weaknesses. In the rest of this chapter I will introduce you to six areas of the brain that are most intimately involved with success and failure. I will show you what these areas do and what happens when things go wrong. These brain areas will also be referred to a number of times throughout the book.

Before I describe these systems, take the following brain system quiz to see where you stand. I realize that not everyone is able to get a brain scan, so I have developed a checklist to help predict areas of strength and weakness. A word of caution is in order. Self-report checklists have advantages and limitations. On the one hand, they are quick, inexpensive, and easy to score. On the other hand, people filling them out may portray themselves in a way they want to be perceived, resulting in self-report bias. For example, some people exaggerate their experience and mark all of the symptoms as frequent, in essence saying, "I'm glad to have a real problem so that I can get help, be sick, or have an excuse for the troubles I have." Others are in total denial. They do not want to see any personal flaws and they do not check any symptoms as significantly problematic, in essence saying, "I'm okay. There's nothing wrong with me. Leave me alone." Not all self-report bias is intentional. People may genuinely have difficulty recognizing problems and expressing how they feel. Sometimes family members or friends are better at evaluating a loved one's level of functioning than a person evaluating himself. They may have noticed things that their loved one hasn't. Quizzes of any sort should never be used as the only assessment tool. They are simply catalysts to help you think, ask better questions, and get more evaluation if needed.

AMEN CLINIC BRIEF BRAIN SYSTEM QUESTIONNAIRE

Please rate yourself on each of the symptoms listed below using the following scale. If possible have another person who knows you well (such as a spouse, lover, or parent) rate you as well.

0	1	2	3	4
Never	Rarely	Occasionally	Frequently	Very Frequently

_____ 1. Has trouble sustaining attention

_____ 2. Lacks attention to detail

_____ 3. Is easily distracted

_____ 4. Tends to procrastinate

_____ 5. Lacks clear goals

_____ 6. Is restless

_____ 7. Has difficulty expressing empathy for others

_____ 8. Blurts out answers before questions have been completed, interrupts frequently

_____ 9. Is impulsive (saying or doing things without thinking first)

_____ 10. Needs caffeine or nicotine in order to focus

_____ 11. Gets stuck on negative thoughts

_____ 12. Worries

_____ 13. Has tendency toward compulsive or addictive behaviors

_____ 14. Holds grudges

_____ 15. Becomes upset when things do not go your way

_____ 16. Becomes upset when things are out of place

_____ 17. Has tendency to be oppositional or argumentative

_____ 18. Dislikes change

_____ 19. Needs to have things done a certain way or becomes very upset

_____ 20. Has trouble seeing options in situations

_____ 21. Feels sad

_____ 22. Is negative

_____ 23. Feels dissatisfied

_____ 24. Feels bored

_____ 25. Has low energy

_____ 26. Experiences decreased interest in things that are usually fun or pleasurable

_____ 27. Experiences feelings of hopelessness, helplessness, worthlessness, or guilt

_____ 28. Has crying spells

_____ 29. Has chronic low self-esteem

_____ 30. Experiences social isolation

_____ 31. Feels nervousness and anxiety

_____ 32. Experiences feelings of panic

_____ 33. Has symptoms of heightened muscle tension (headaches, sore muscles, hand tremor)

_____ 34. Tends to predict the worst

_____ 35. Avoids conflict

_____ 36. Has excessive fear of being judged or scrutinized by others

_____ 37. Has excessive motivation, trouble stopping working

_____ 38. Lacks confidence in their abilities

_____ 39. Always watches for something bad to happen

_____ 40. Is prone to quick startles

_____ 41. Has a short fuse

_____ 42. Experiences periods of heightened irritability

_____ 43. Misinterprets comments as negative when they are not

_____ 44. Experiences frequent periods of déjà vu (feelings of being somewhere you have never been)

_____ 45. Displays sensitivity or mild paranoia

_____ 46. Has a history of a head injury

_____ 47. Experiences dark thoughts, may involve suicidal or homicidal thoughts

_____ 48. Undergoes periods of forgetfulness or memory problems

_____ 49. Has trouble finding the right word to say

_____ 50. Experiences unstable moods

_____ 51. Has poor handwriting

_____ 52. Has trouble maintaining an organized work area

_____ 53. I tend to have multiple piles around the house.

_____ 54. I am more sensitive to noise than others.

_____ 55. I am particularly sensitive to touch or tags in clothing.

_____ 56. I tend to be clumsy or accident prone.

_____ 57. I have trouble learning new information or routines.

_____ 58. I have trouble keeping up in conversations.

_____ 59. I am light sensitive and easily bothered by glare, sunlight, headlights, or streetlights.

_____ 60. I seem to be more sensitive to the environment than others.

ANSWER KEY
Prefrontal cortex symptoms: 1–10
Anterior cingulate gyrus symptoms: 11–20
Deep limbic system symptoms: 21–30
Basal ganglia symptoms: 31–40
Temporal lobe symptoms: 41–50
Cerebellum symptoms: 51–60

In each system, if you or a significant other answered the following number of questions with the answer of 3 or 4, here is the probability that problems may be present.

Highly probable	5 questions
Probable	3 questions
May be possible	2 questions

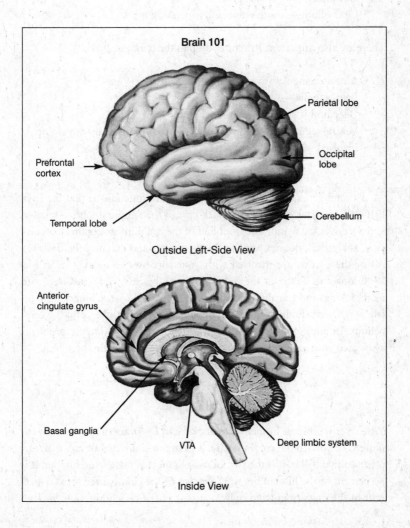

Brain 101

Outside Left-Side View

Inside View

Your Brain and Behavior

The brain is divided into five main lobes or regions.

- Frontal and prefrontal—forethought and judgment
- Temporal—memory and mood stability
- Parietal—sensory processing and direction sense
- Occipital lobes—visual processing
- Cerebellum—coordination and processing speed

There are also important structures deep in the brain, such as:

- Anterior cingulate gyrus—gear shifter
- Basal ganglia—anxiety center
- Deep limbic system—emotional center
- Ventral tegmental area—produces the neurotransmitter dopamine, involved with saliency (how important something is to do)

A useful generalization about how the brain functions is that the back half—the parietal, occipital, and back part of the temporal lobes—takes in and perceives the world. The front half of the brain integrates this information, analyzes it, decides what to do, then plans and executes the decision. All of these areas are involved with your successes and struggles in life. We'll look specifically at the functions of six brain systems involved with work, loving, and learning, including the prefrontal cortex, anterior cingulate gyrus, deep limbic system, basal ganglia, temporal lobes, and the cerebellum. In addition, there will be a brief discussion about the problems associated with each area along with some strategies to help them heal.

Prefrontal Cortex

Whenever we discuss humans, the first area of the brain that we have to explore is the prefrontal cortex (PFC). It is largest in human beings than any other animal by far. It is the part of your brain that makes you human. It is 30 percent of the human brain, 11 percent of the chimpanzee brain, 7 percent of the dog's brain, and only 3 percent of the cat's brain. Cats have no forethought and very little impulse control. My cat, Annabelle, lives totally in the moment. She doesn't think about the past or worry about the future. She also doesn't learn from mistakes and will drink out of the toilet, no matter how many times she has been told no.

The PFC is called the executive brain, because it acts in our head like the boss at work. When it is low in activity, it is as if the boss is gone, so there is little to no supervision and nothing gets done. When the PFC works too hard, it is as if the boss is micromanaging everyone, and people are left with anxiety and worry. The PFC helps us make decisions and keep us on track toward our goals. I also call it the Jiminy Cricket part of the brain. Jiminy Cricket was Pinocchio's conscience, that still, small voice in his head that helped him decide between right and wrong. Your PFC helps keep your behavior in check. Comedian Dudley Moore once said, "The best car safety device is a rearview mirror with a cop in it." The PFC acts like the cop in your head.

Problems with the PFC result in a "Jiminy Cricket deficiency syndrome" with a diminished conscience, poor judgment, impulsivity, short attention span, disorganization, trouble learning from experience, confusion, poor time management, and lack of empathy. Low activity in this part of the brain is often due to a deficiency in the neurotransmitter dopamine, and increasing it through supplements or medications is often helpful.

Images 4.1–4.3 depict three SPECT scans of Joan, a sixty-two-year-old woman who suffered from severe ADD and dyslexia her whole life. They

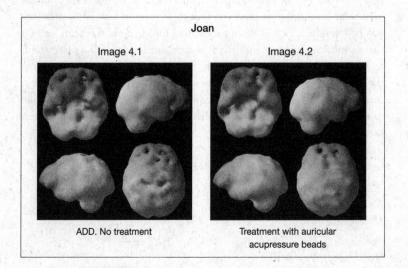

Joan

Image 4.1   Image 4.2

ADD. No treatment   Treatment with auricular
                           acupressure beads

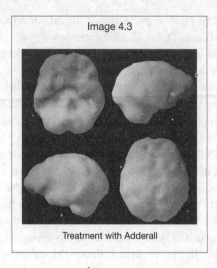

Image 4.3

Treatment with Adderall

were performed on three consecutive days. The first scan shows her untreated brain. In the second one, auricular acupressure beads were placed on both of her ears, resulting in some improvement. The third scan was done after Joan had been placed on Adderall, a stimulant medication, which dramatically improved her brain. These scans demonstrate that you can improve how your brain functions and change your life. With a better brain for Joan came a much better life, even though she was in her sixties when she was first scanned. One of the most exciting things about this scan series is that an innocuous treatment such as acupressure beads made a positive difference. Our imaging work has taught me to have more respect for alternative treatments, and even though they do not always work as robustly as medications, I have found these treatments can be used successfully in mild to moderate cases and used as additive treatments to help people use less medication.

Here is a quick summary of the PFC.

PREFRONTAL CORTEX (PFC) SUMMARY
(The Supervising Boss in Your Head)

PFC Functions	Low PFC Problems
Focus	Short attention span
Forethought	Lacks clear goals or forward thinking
Impulse control	Impulsivity
Organization	Disorganization
Planning, goal setting	Procrastination
Judgment	Poor judgment
Empathy	Lack of empathy
Emotional control	Failing to give close attention to detail
Insight	Lack of insight
Learning from mistakes	Trouble learning from mistakes
	Easily distracted

Diagnostic Problems Associated with Low PFC Activity

ADHD	Some types of depression
Brain trauma	Dementia, associated with bad judgment
Schizophrenia	Antisocial personality
Conduct disorders	

Ways to Balance Low PFC

Organizational help, coaching	Intense aerobic exercise (boosts blood flow)
Goal setting / planning exercises	Higher protein diet

Stimulating supplements: L-tyrosine, DL-phenylalanine, L-theanine, or S-adenosyl-methionine (SAMe) help boost dopamine or norepinephrine in the brain (see chapters 6, 7, and 8 for details on natural treatments; try only one at a time and discuss these supplements with your health care professionals too).

Stimulating medications (if appropriate): Adderall, Dexedrine, Ritalin, Concerta, Focalin, Wellbutrin, Strattera, or Provigil. We do not give stimulants to people with schizophrenia. Obviously, any medication recommendations need to be discussed with your doctor. These are just general suggestions.

Anterior Cingulate Gyrus

The anterior cingulate gyrus (ACG) helps you feel settled, relaxed, and flexible. It runs lengthwise through the deep parts of the frontal lobes and is the brain's major switching station. I think of it as the brain's gear shifter; it greases human behavior and allows us to be flexible, adaptable, and to change as change is needed. This part of the brain is involved in helping shift attention from idea to idea and seeing the options in your life. The term that best relates to the ACG is *cognitive flexibility.* When there is too much activity in the ACG, usually owing to lower serotonin levels, people become unable to shift their attention and become rigid, cognitively inflexible, overfocused, anxious, and oppositional. They may also hold grudges and get stuck on past hurts. Along with shifting attention, cooperation is also influenced by this part of the brain. When the ACG works in an effective manner it is easy to shift into cooperative modes of behavior. When it works too hard, people have difficulty shifting attention and get stuck in ineffective behavior patterns, where they may be uncooperative or difficult and stuck in their own mind-set.

ANTERIOR CINGULATE GYRUS (ACG) SUMMARY
(The Brain's Gear Shifter)

ACG Functions	Excessive ACG Activity Problems
Cognitive flexibility	Preoccupation with negative thoughts or behaviors
Cooperation	Worries
Moving from idea to idea	Grudge holding
Seeing options	Obsessions/compulsions
Going with the flow	Inflexiblity, may appear selfish
Seeing errors	Tendency to be oppositional/argumentative
	Tendency to become upset when things do not go your way
	Tendency to become upset when things are out of place
	Intense dislike for change
	Tendency to say no without thinking
	Seeing too many errors

Diagnostic Problems Associated with Excessive ACG Activity

Obsessive-compulsive disorder	Eating disorders
Premenstrual tension syndrome, some types	Chronic pain (stuck on pain)
Post-traumatic stress disorder	Oppositional defiant disorder
Difficult temperaments (need to have one's own way)	Tourette's syndrome

Ways to Calm Excessive ACG Activity

Intense aerobic exercise	Distraction
Relationship counseling, anger management	Lower protein / complex carbs diet

ACG supplements: 5-hydroxytryptophan (5-HTP), St. John's wort, or inositol help boost serotonin to the brain (see chapters 6, 7, and 8 for details on natural treatments; try only one at a time and discuss these with your health care professionals too)

ACG medications (if appropriate): selective serotonin reuptake inhibitors (SSRIs) (Paxil, Zoloft, Celexa, Prozac, Luvox), Effexor, atypical antipsychotics in refractory cases (Risperdal, Zyprexa, or Geodon)

Deep Limbic System

The deep limbic system (DLS) lies near the center of the brain. About the size of a walnut, this part of the brain is involved in setting a person's emotional tone. When the DLS is less active, there is generally a positive, more hopeful state of mind. When it is heated up, or overactive, negativity can take over. Because of this emotional shading, the DLS provides the filter through which you interpret the events of the day; it tags or colors events, depending on the emotional state of mind. The DLS also affects motivation and drive. It helps get you going in the morning and encourages you to move throughout the day. Overactivity in this area is associated with lowered motivation and drive, which is often seen in depression. The DLS is intimately involved with bonding and social connectedness. This capacity to bond plays a significant role in the tone and quality of our moods. The DLS also directly processes the sense of smell. Because your sense of smell goes directly to the deep limbic system, it is easy to see why smells can have such a powerful impact on our feeling states.

The problems in the DLS are associated with depression and negativity along with low motivation, libido, and energy. Because sufferers feel hopeless about the outcome, they have little willpower to follow through with tasks. High activity in the DLS may be due to deficiencies in the neurotransmitters norepinephrine, dopamine, or serotonin, and increasing these chemicals through supplements or medications may be helpful. Here is a quick summary of the DLS.

DEEP LIMBIC SYSTEM (DLS) SUMMARY
(The Mood and Bonding Center)

DLS Functions	Excessive DLS Activity Problems
Mood control	Depression, sadness
Charged memories	Focused on the negative, irritability
Modulates motivation	Low motivation and energy
Sets emotional tone	Negativity, blame, guilt
Bonding	Social disconnections/isolation
Sense of smell	Low self-esteem
Libido	Low libido
	Decreased interest in things that are usually fun
	Feelings of worthlessness or helplessness
	Feeling dissatisfied or bored

Diagnostic Problems Associated with Excessive DLS Activity

Depression	Cyclic mood disorders
Pain syndromes	

Ways to Balance High DLS Activity

Intense aerobic exercise
Cognitive-behavioral strategies to deal with automatic negative thoughts
Balanced diet, such as the one described by Barry Sears in *The Zone Diet*

DLS supplements: DL-phenylalanine, SAMe, or L-tyrosine (see chapters 6, 7, and 8 for details on natural treatments; try only one at a time and discuss these with your health care professionals too)

DLS medications (if appropriate): antidepressants (Wellbutrin, Effexor, or Cymbalta), SSRIs (if high ACG also present), anticonvulsants or lithium for cyclic mood changes

Basal Ganglia

The basal ganglia (BG) are the large structures toward the center of the brain that surround the deep limbic system. The BG are involved with integrating feelings, thoughts, and movement, which is why you jump when you get excited or freeze when you are scared. The BG help to shift and smooth motor behavior. When activity in this area is low, as in Parkinson's disease, people can develop tremors and problems with movement (writing, walking, jumping, etc.). In our clinic we have noticed that the BG are involved with setting the body's idle or anxiety level. When the BG work too hard, people tend to struggle with anxiety and physical stress symptoms, such as headaches, intestinal problems, and muscle tension. High BG activity is also associated with conflict avoidant behavior. Anything that reminds them of a worry (such as confronting an employee who is not doing a good job) produces anxiety, and high BG people tend to avoid it, because it makes them feel uncomfortable. People with high BG activity also have trouble relaxing and tend to overwork. When the BG are low in activity, people tend to have problems with motivation, attention, and moving their lives forward. In addition, the BG are involved with feelings of pleasure and ecstasy. Cocaine works in this part of the brain. High activity in this part of the brain is often due to a deficiency in the neurotransmitter gamma-aminobutyric, or GABA, and increasing it through supplements or medications is often helpful. Here is a quick summary of the BG.

BASAL GANGLIA (BG) SUMMARY
(The Anxiety Center)

BG Functions	Excessive BG Activity Problems
Integration of feelings, thoughts, and movement	High anxiety levels
Regulator of the body's idle	Panic
Smooth movement	Hypervigilance
Motivation modulator	Muscle tension
Pleasure mediator	Conflict avoidance
	Predicting the worst
	Excessive fear of being judged by others
	Tendency to freeze in anxiety situations
	Shy or timid appearance
	Bites fingernails or picks skin
	Excessive motivation, inability to stop working

Diagnostic Problems Associated with Excessive BG Activity

Anxiety disorders   Workaholism
Physical stress symptoms   Insecurity
(headaches, stomachaches)

Ways to Calm High BG Activity

Cognitive therapy to quell   Hypnosis, meditation
the bad thoughts
Relaxation training   Relaxing music
Assertiveness training   Limiting caffeine and alcohol intake

BG supplements: GABA, kava kava, or valerian root (see chapters 6, 7, and 8 for details on natural treatments; try only one at a time and discuss these with your health care professionals too)

BG medications (if appropriate): antianxiety medications such as benzodiazepines (low dose, short time), Buspar, anticonvulsants, blood pressure medications such as propranolol

Temporal Lobes

The temporal lobes (TLs), underneath your temples and behind your eyes, are involved with language (hearing and reading), reading social cues, short-term memory, getting memories into long-term storage, processing music and tone of voice, and mood stability. They also help with recognizing objects by sight and naming them. It is called the "what pathway" in the brain, as it is involved with recognition and naming objects and faces. In addition, the TLs, especially on the right side, have been implicated in spiritual experience and insight. Experiments that stimulate the right temporal lobe have demonstrated increased religious or spiritual experiences, such as feeling God's presence.

Trouble in the TLs leads to both short- and long-term memory problems, reading difficulties, trouble finding the right words in conversation, trouble reading social cues, mood instability, and sometimes religious or moral preoccupation or perhaps a lack of spiritual sensitivity. The TLs, especially on the left side, have been associated with temper problems. Abnormal (high or low) activity in this part of the brain is often due to a deficiency in the neurotransmitter GABA, and balancing it through supplements or medications is often helpful.

TEMPORAL LOBES (TLS) SUMMARY
(Memory and Mood Stability)

TL Functions	TL Problems
Understanding and use of language	Language problems, dyslexia
Memory	Memory problems
Retrieval of words	Trouble finding the right word
Reading	Mood instability
Recognize words and objects	Anxiety for little or no reason
Emotional stability	Headaches or abdominal pain, hard to diagnose
Reading faces and social cues	Trouble reading facial expressions or social cues
Rhythm	Dark, evil, awful, or hopeless thoughts
Temper control	Aggression, toward self or others
Spiritual experience	Learning problems
	Illusions (shadows, visual or auditory distortions)
	An overfocusing on religious ideas

Diagnostic Problems Associated with Abnormal TL Activity

Head injury	Dissociation
Anxiety	Temporal epilepsy
Amnesia	Serious depression with dark or suicidal thoughts
Religiosity	Dyslexia

Ways to Balanced the TLs

Anger management	Increased protein diet

TL supplements: GABA or valerian to calm TLs if needed; for memory, consider gingko biloba, huperzine, or phosphatidylserine (see chapters 6, 7, and 8 for details on natural treatments; try only one at a time and discuss these with your health care professionals too).

TL medications (if appropriate): antiseizure medications for mood instability and temper problems (Depakote, Neurontin, Tegretol, or Lamictal), memory-enhancing medications for more serious memory problems (Namenda, Aricept, Exelon, or Reminyl)

Cerebellum

The cerebellum, at the back bottom part of the brain, is called the little brain. Even though it represents only 10 percent of the brain's volume, it houses 50 percent of the brain's neurons. It has long been known that the cerebellum is involved with motor coordination, posture, and how we walk. Only recently has it become clear that the cerebellum is also involved with processing speed, like clock speed on a computer, which may be the reason it has so many neurons. It is also involved in thought coordination or how quickly you can make cognitive and emotional adjustments. The cerebellum helps you quickly make physical adjustments, such as while you are playing a sport, as well as helping you make emotional adjustments in stressful or novel situations. When there are problems in the cerebellum, people tend to struggle not only with physical coordination, but they also tend to get easily confused. Our research has found that low cerebellar activity is also associated with poor handwriting (coordination); problems maintaining an organized work area; being sensitive to light, noise, touch, or clothing (such as tags); and being clumsy or accident prone. The cerebellum has been found low in activity in autism, ADD, and learning disabilities.

Given that the cerebellum is the major coordination center in the brain, coordination exercises, such as sports and music, are some of the major strategies to keep the brain tuned to work at its best. At this point there is un-

CEREBELLUM (CB) SUMMARY
(Coordination and Processing Speed)

CB Functions	Low CB Activity Problems
Motor control	Coordination problems
Posture, gait	Slowed thinking
Executive function, connects to PFC	Slowed speech
Speed of cognitive integration	Poor handwriting
	Trouble learning routines
	Disorganization
	Sensitivity to noise or touch
	Tendency to be clumsy or accident prone
	Light sensitivity

Diagnostic Problems Associated with Poor CB Activity

Trauma	Alcohol abuse
Autism, Asperger's syndrome	Some forms of ADHD
Coordination problems	Sensory integration problems

Ways to Balance Low CB Activity

Prevention of brain injury	Cessation of alcohol use and avoidance of other toxic exposure
Juggling	Coordination exercises, such as dancing or table tennis

CB supplements and medications: unknown at this time

certainty about the neurotransmitter deficiency in this part of the brain, so we do not know what supplements or medications may be helpful.

Knowing the part of your brain that needs help is a shortcut to optimizing the brain in the fastest, most efficient way possible. You will notice under each brain section that there are a number of interventions to help people heal. There are myriad ways to optimize the brain, including dietary interventions, physical and mental exercises, targeted behavioral exercises, supplements, and medications. One treatment doesn't fit everyone. My hope in providing these options is for you to start a conversation with your health care professionals so that you can better tailor or target the treatment to the brain systems that need help.

| 5 |

If You Were My Family,
How Would I Treat You?

────

THE FOUR CIRCLES OF HEALTH AND HEALING AND
WHY YOU SHOULD CONSIDER NATURAL TREATMENTS

One question I always ask myself when treating patients is, what would I prescribe if this were my mother, my wife, or my children? How would I treat them? More and more I find myself recommending natural or alternative treatments for my patients because this is exactly what I would do for myself or the people I love. I am not opposed to medication, but I want people to use all of the tools that are available to them, especially the ones that are less expensive and have fewer side effects. Although I am not opposed to medication when needed, unlike so many of my colleagues, I see them as options of later resort, not first resort. My bent since medical school has been to use natural treatments and to teach patients skills, not just give them pills.

When I first started brain imaging work in 1991, I thought my tendency toward natural solutions might change in favor of medications, as most of the problems we treated were clearly considered biological; we could see the brain abnormalities on scans. What I didn't know at the time, but have been excited to learn since, is that many natural treatments, even certain types of psychotherapy, meditation, and nutritional supplements, can improve brain function.

In this chapter I will update you on the latest thinking on treating common mental health issues using natural treatments. I will also tell you when I would use them and when medications may be necessary. I will explain the approach we use at the Amen Clinics in diagnosing and treating the common problems that come to our clinics, including ADD, anxiety, depression, bipolar disorder, memory problems, insomnia, and brain injuries. In addition I will give a summary box for each natural treatment, stating the current scientific evidence for its use.

Before I turn to natural treatments, I want to share an important way to think about diagnosis and treatment of brain-related problems. At the Amen Clinics we use a biological-psychological-social-spiritual model in evaluating and treating the brain. I call these the four circles of optimal health (see Figure 5.1).

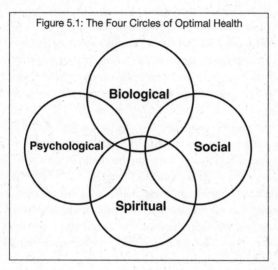

Figure 5.1: The Four Circles of Optimal Health

Biological

Psychological

Social

Spiritual

The Biological Circle

The first circle of health, illness, and healing is the biological or physical aspects of the brain, how it functions moment by moment. For the brain to operate at peak efficiency, its machinery (cells, connections, chemicals, energy, and blood flow) needs to physically work right. As mentioned earlier, the brain is like a supercomputer, having both hardware and software. Think of the term *biology* akin to the hardware of a computer. Contained within the biological circle are such factors as genetics, overall physical health, nutrition, exercise, and environmental issues (e.g., physical stress, toxins, and sleep). When the brain is healthy, all of these factors work together in a positive way to maximize our success. Illness strikes the brain when potentially any of these factors become disrupted or out of sync. When we do not get enough sleep, there is overall lower blood flow to the brain, which disrupts thinking, memory, and concentration. When there is an injury it hurts the machinery of the brain and we may struggle with depression, memory, and temper problems. When we eat a high-sugar meal, our blood sugar often rebounds low and we feel stupid and sluggish.

As an example, here are some of the biological factors associated with depression. It's first important to look at the family history. We know there is often a genetic link to depression and it tends to run in families, especially where there is alcohol abuse. It's also important to evaluate patients from a medical point of view, as there are a number of illnesses that can cause depression. These include thyroid disease, infectious illnesses, cancer, and certain forms of anemia. A heart attack or stroke also leave a person vulnerable to depression. Periods of dramatic hormonal shifts (postpartum or menopausal) often precipitate problems with depression. Additionally, certain medications can cause depression. Most notable among these are birth control pills, certain blood pressure or cardiac medications, steroids, and chronic pain control medicines. In evaluating depression, it's essential to take a good alcohol and drug abuse history. Chronic alcohol or marijuana use often causes depression, while amphetamine or cocaine withdrawal is often accompanied by serious suicidal thoughts.

Healing occurs by bringing these biological factors back into balance, by getting good sleep, protecting ourselves from brain injuries, treating any medical illnesses, avoiding toxins such as drugs, eating a healthy, balanced diet, getting plenty of exercise, taking a fish oil tablet and a multiple vitamin, and taking targeted supplements or even medication if needed.

The Psychological Circle

Psychological factors fall into the second circle of health, illness, and recovery. This circle includes how we think and how we talk to ourselves, the running dialogue that goes on in our minds, plus our self-concept, overall upbringing, and significant developmental events. Being raised in a reasonably happy home, getting positive messages growing up and liking ourselves, our bodies, height, and abilities all contribute to psychological health. When any of these areas struggle we are more likely to have mental problems. If, in our minds, we perceive ourselves as short, ugly, or less able than our peers, then trouble starts to brew. If our thinking patterns are excessively negative, harsh, or critical, they will have a negative impact on our moods and anxiety levels.

Going back to our example of depression, psychological factors that contribute to it include major losses, such as the death of a loved one, breakup of a romantic relationship and loss of a job, self-esteem, status, health, or purpose; multiple childhood traumas, such as physical or sexual abuse; negative thinking that erodes self-esteem and drives down the mood; and learned helplessness, the belief that no matter what you do things won't change. This comes from being exposed to environments where you are continually frustrated from reaching your needs or goals.

Healing our thoughts and hurts from the past are essential to wellness and optimal mental health.

The Social Circle

The social circle of health, illness, and recovery emphasizes the current events in our lives. When we are in good relationships, experience good health, have a job we love and enough money, our brain tends to do much better than when any of these areas are stressed. Stress negatively impacts brain function and dealing with difficult events makes us more vulnerable to illness. Depression is often triggered by current stressful life events, such as marital problems, family dysfunction, financial difficulties, health problems, or work-related struggles. Optimizing your present life, including relationships, work, financial situation, and health, improves brain health. Decreasing the daily stresses in your life also improves brain function, so having daily stress management techniques are important to overall brain health.

The Spiritual Circle

Many people have a spiritual side, where life takes on deeper meaning than just the everyday tasks of living. Having a deep sense of purpose, a connection to a higher power, and a connection to past generations and the future of our planet allow us to reach beyond ourselves to say our lives mattered. Many people go through spiritual crises, not knowing why their life has meaning, which sets them up for depression or substance abuse. Morality, connection, values, and a spiritual connection to others and the universe is critical for many people to feel a sense of wholeness and connection.

BIOLOGICAL-PSYCHOLOGICAL-SOCIAL-SPIRITUAL SUMMARY

Biological—Genetic tendencies, nutrition, exercise, neurotransmitter health, blood flow and oxygenation, sleep, overall physical health

Psychological—Thinking patterns, self-concept, upbringing, and development

Social—Current life opportunities and stresses, which includes relationships, finances, and work

Spiritual—Deeper life meaning, which includes a sense of purpose and connection with a higher power and the past and future

CAUSES OF MENTAL ILLNESSES

Biological—Genetic vulnerabilities, dietary deficiencies, poor exercise, neurotransmitter deficiencies, trauma, infection, toxicity, oxygen deprivation, lack of sleep, allergies, dehydration, physical illnesses (e.g., thyroid disease, diabetes, or heart disease)

Psychological—Negative thinking patterns, poor self-concept, stressful upbringing and development

Social—Current life stresses, which includes relationships, finances, work, and legal issues

Spiritual—Lack of personal meaning or purpose, a feeling of hopelessness, helplessness, or worthlessness

TREATING MENTAL ILLNESSES AND OPTIMIZING OUR LIVES

Biological—Healthy diet, adequate exercise and sleep, avoiding toxic substances, replenishing neurotransmitters, healthy supplements, medications when appropriate, novel treatments (e.g., acupuncture, hyperbaric oxygen treatment), protecting the brain from injury

Psychological—Optimizing a person's psychology through correcting negative thinking patterns, healing past traumatic wounds, and improving self-concept

Social—Strengthening a person's ability to deal with stress (stress management techniques) and enhancing social relationships

Spiritual—Discovering a deeper sense of purpose and connection

Why Consider Natural Treatments?

What are the pros and cons of using natural treatments to maintain health and prevent and treat illness? There are significant advantages of natural treatments, as well as a few downsides or controversies you need to know about. The most significant benefit to using natural treatments is that these strategies are geared toward preventing illness rather than just treating it. Preventing problems is dramatically more cost effective than treating problems that have occurred. Engaging in natural strategies helps build an attitude of prevention and hopefully leads to a healthier lifestyle overall. Waiting until you have an illness, such as a stroke or Alzheimer's disease, is *always* more expensive than spending time, effort, and money to prevent it. In addition to using natural methods for prevention, they are often very effective for mild to moderate problems and have fewer side effects than most pharmaceuticals. Compliance tends to be higher for these products, which means that people are more likely to take them over the long run. Generally, natural strategies are less expensive than pharmaceutical alternatives. In addition, you never have to tell an insurance company that you have taken them. As awful as it is, taking prescription medication for brain problems, or even to enhance brain health, can affect a person's insurability. This is true for medications that treat anxiety, depression, bipolar disorder, ADD, and many other problems. I know many patients, colleagues, and friends who have been denied medical or life insurance because of the medications they were taking. If there are natural alternatives, it is worth considering.

The natural supplement picture is not all rosy, and some of the disadvantages have to be considered. Even though natural supplements are generally less expensive than medications, you may pay more out of pocket because they are not covered by insurance. In addition, many people are unaware that natural supplements can have side effects. Just because it is natural does not mean it is innocuous. For example, St. John's wort, one of my favorite natural antidepressants, which works like a mild form of Prozac in the brain, can cause sun sensitivity and can deactivate the effectiveness of other medications such as birth control pills or antiviral drugs.

One of the major issues of concern regarding natural products is the lack of standardization and quality control. Rigid quality control is not required for these products and there are many variables in the manufacturing process. Variables associated with plant-based supplements, for example, include age, ripeness when harvested, growing environment, and storage conditions. The therapeutic and toxic components of the supplement may vary considerably. There also may be issues with contamination. Different components of each herb can exhibit different pharmacologic effects. It is critical to get brands you trust that have been tested and shown to be reliable. Another disadvantage is that people get a lot of their advice about supplements from the clerk at the grocery store, who may not have accurate information. I often send patients to www.consumerlab.com, which is an independent laboratory that posts tests of quality control on the Web.

Even when looking at the cons of natural supplements, in my mind, they are worth serious consideration. We can be targeted and thoughtful in our recommendations, and we can find dedicated companies that produce high-quality products. It amazes me how many physicians have a knee-jerk negative reaction to natural supplements despite the large amounts of research on them. I teach the course on supplements to the psychiatric residents at the University of California–Irvine. I have noticed that many of the residents start with a negative attitude about them. Invariably one of the residents will say there is not enough research on them and that they do not really contain the ingredients on the labels. At the end of the course, when they learn about the extensive research and good-quality companies, many of the young psychiatrists are excited about the possibility of using supplements to help their patients and many even start to take the ones I discuss below. I have enough personal experience prescribing pharmaceuticals with side effects that I believe patients deserve to know about natural alternatives. Let me give you an example of how effective natural treatments can be.

The president of a local college came to see me with her teenage daughter, Jennifer, who was depressed, angry, and did poorly in school. Her pediatrician had tried her on Prozac but she experienced bad side effects. The mother heard that I used natural treatments. After scanning Jennifer and seeing that the front part of her brain worked too hard, I put her on St. John's wort, an herbal antidepressant that settles down brain function, along with fish oil and a specially formulated multiple vitamin. Within three weeks Jennifer's behavior dramatically improved, as did her schoolwork. When I did a follow-up scan, the hyperactivity in the front part of her brain had also calmed down.

Natural treatments can change the brain. But whether we are using natural treatments or medication to help balance the brain, it is critical for us to know the individual pattern of each person. As we will see, not everyone with a mood disorder or ADD will have the same brain. I have described seven different types of anxiety and depression and six different types of ADD. There are also different types of autism and memory problems. One size does not fit everyone. Each person is different and needs an individualized plan based on their own unique brain. I will discuss this in length in the coming chapters.

NATURAL TREATMENTS: ADVANTAGES	NATURAL TREATMENTS: DISADVANTAGES
1. Often effective for mild to moderate problems. 2. Less expensive than most medications. 3. Usually significantly fewer side effects (although not no side effects) 4. Geared to both prevent and treat illness 5. Never have to tell an insurance company you are taking them; psychiatric medications can decrease insurability 6. Compliance generally higher as they usually have fewer side effects 7. Many backed by solid research suggesting their effectiveness	1. Possible side effects (as with all medications) 2. Not covered by insurance, may entail high out-of-pocket expenses 3. Usually fewer studies because drug companies cannot obtain patents on natural treatments so they are less lucrative 4. Less standardization and quality control than is performed on pharmaceuticals 5. Consultant may be the seventeen-year-old clerk at the grocery store

Natural Strategies That Apply to Us All

To keep your brain balanced, there are certain natural treatments that apply to us all. These include a healthy diet, exercising, killing the negative thoughts that steal our happiness, goal setting, stress management techniques (e.g., meditating), and taking a multiple vitamin and fish oil supplement daily. I address most of these issues in other chapters of the book, except for multiple vitamins and fish oil.

Multiple Vitamins

Because of our poor diets, I recommend that all of my patients take a high-quality 100 percent multiple vitamin every day. Over the last twenty years, our understanding of the benefits of vitamins has rapidly advanced, and it now appears that people who get enough vitamins may be able to help prevent such common chronic illnesses as cancer, heart disease, dementia, and osteoporosis, according to Drs. Robert Fletcher and Kathleen Fairfield of

Harvard University, who wrote the guidelines for vitamins published in the *Journal of the American Medical Association* (*JAMA*) in 2002. The last time *JAMA* made a comprehensive review of vitamins, about twenty years before, it concluded that people of normal health shouldn't take multivitamins because they were a waste of time and money. People can get all the nutrients they need from their diet, *JAMA* advised, adding that only pregnant women and chronically sick people may need certain vitamins. That was at a time when knowledge about vitamins was just beginning to expand. The role that low levels of folate, or folic acid, play in neural tube defects, for instance, was not known, nor was its role as a major risk factor for heart disease. Ninety-one percent of Americans do not eat at least five helpings of fruits and vegetables a day, the recommended minimum amount believed to provide sufficient essential nutrients. Humans do not make their own vitamins, except for some vitamin D, so they must get them from an outside source to prevent problems.

Omega-3 Fatty Acid Supplements

Fish oils, also known as marine oils, are fats found in fish, particularly cold-water fish, and other marine life, including phytoplankton and krill. These oils are rich sources of long-chain polyunsaturated fatty acids, also called omega-3 fatty acids. The two most studied fish oils are eicosapentaenoic acid (EPA) and docosahexaenoic acid (DHA). DHA is a vital component of cell membranes, especially those in the brain and retina. Supplemental fish oils have been shown to have many positive effects on the body. They lower triglyceride levels and have anti-inflammatory, antiarrhythmic, immune-enhancing, and nerve-cell-stabilizing properties. In addition, they also help maintain normal blood flow as they lower the body's ability to form clots. DHA is vital for normal brain development for the fetus and infant and for the maintenance of normal brain function throughout life. DHA appears to be a major factor in how fluid or flexible brain cell membranes are. This could play a major role in the maintenance of how we think and feel. Fish oils appear to have mood-stabilizing properties when used in the treatment of bipolar disorder. On SPECT scans, bipolar disorder shows overall increased activity in the brain, and EPA and DHA tend to calm or dampen these overactive brain signals.

A four-month double-blind, placebo-controlled study of thirty subjects with bipolar disorder compared the effects of fish oil supplements with placebo. Fourteen subjects received 9.6 grams daily of fish oil consisting of

6.2 grams of EPA and 3.4 grams of DHA, and sixteen subjects received olive oil as a placebo. This study showed improvement in the short-term course of the disorder with fish oil supplementation. Among those taking fish oils, longer periods of remission were observed in nearly every outcome category, and the results were statistically significant. Mild gastrointestinal side effects were reported in the fish oil group.

In a landmark study published in the journal *Lancet*, researchers examined the effect of dietary fish oil and vitamin E supplementation on death and disease in over eleven thousand subjects who had suffered a heart attack within three months of entering the trial. The trial lasted for forty-two months. The most significant result of this trial was the reduction in risk for overall and sudden cardiac death, which it is believed was due to the antiarrhythmic effect of the fish oil. The study suggests that up to twenty lives per one thousand post–heart attack patients could be saved by consuming daily doses of less than 1 gram of EPA and DHA.

An analysis of seventeen studies with fish oil indicates that supplementation with 3 or more grams of fish oil daily can lead to clinically relevant blood pressure reductions in individuals with untreated hypertension, although it did not lower blood pressure in those who were normal. An analysis of another group of studies on the effect of fish oils following coronary angioplasty indicates that subjects who had undergone successful angioplasty had a significantly lower rate (13.9 percent) of recurrent problems when given 4–5 grams daily of mixtures of EPA and DHA for three months to one year following the angioplasty. What's good for your heart is also good for your brain.

There are many other physical benefits of fish oil supplements. Daily use of fish oil of at least 3 grams of EPA and DHA mixtures for a period of twelve weeks or longer has been found to reduce the number of tender joints and amount of morning stiffness in people with rheumatoid arthritis, to the extent that they were reported to have lowered or discontinued use of nonsteroidal anti-inflammatory drugs or other antirheumatic drugs. The supplements appeared to be well tolerated in these individuals, and no serious side effects were reported.

Because of the possible anticlotting effect of fish oil supplements, hemophiliacs and those taking warfarin (Coumadin) should exercise caution in their use. Fish oil supplements should be stopped before any surgical procedure. Diabetics who take fish oil supplements should be monitored by their physicians. There have been no reports of serious adverse events in those taking fish oil supplements, even up to 15 grams daily for prolonged periods of time. The side effects that have been reported include mild gastrointestinal upsets such as nausea and diarrhea; halitosis; burping; and fishy-smelling breath, skin, and even urine. The blood-thinning effects can cause occasional nosebleeds and easy bruising.

The typical dosage of fish oil is 1–3 grams a day for prevention and 4–6 grams a day to treat illness. High-quality fish oil can be taken by pregnant women and has been shown to help the moods of those women prone to bipolar disorder.

|6|

Natural Ways to Heal

ATTENTION DEFICIT DISORDER

ADD and ADHD are essentially the same thing. Because at least half the people who have this disorder are not hyperactive, I prefer the term *ADD*.

I often tell people that I know more about ADD than I want to know. My son, Antony, was diagnosed with ADD when he was twelve years old. His room used to follow the second law of physics, meaning that things went from order to disorder. I used to ask him if he planned to have his room that messy. Moreover, his handwriting was a mess, and a half an hour of home-work used to take him three hours to do with his mother's yelling at him to sit down and get it done.

On the surface, Breanne, my oldest daughter, was the perfect child. She was always easy, always sweet, her room was always clean, and her homework always done. If I only had Breanne, I would have been a terrible child psychiatrist. I would have thought Breanne was so wonderful because I was such a good dad. If I saw your child acting up in the grocery store, I would have thought to myself, "Give me your child for a week and I will straighten him out and then teach you how to be a good parent." Well, God knew I was like that, so God gave me Kaitlyn.

Hyperactive from before birth. We thought Kaitlyn was going to be a boy, because the lore is that the more active babies are inside their mother's womb, the more likely they are to be boys. Well, she wasn't. Trying to hold Kaitlyn when she was a year old was like trying to hold a *live* salmon.

I had a spiritual crisis because of this child. Many Catholic churches allow young children to sit with their parents at mass. It was no fun with Kaitlyn, because she was the worst behaved child at church, which was not only embarrassing, but it was bad for business. I treated half the children in the congregation and if my child was the worst one, people would lose confidence in me. So after a while I stopped going to church.

Have you ever seen children on little yellow leashes in the mall? After having Kaitlyn, I became a firm believer in little yellow leashes because she was always trying to get away. But my problem was that I wrote a column in the local newspaper where I lived, and whenever I went to the mall people recognized me and said things like "Hey, you are Dr. Amen, I loved your column." I just could not deal with "Hey, you're Dr. Amen, why is your child on a leash?" So what I used to do with Kaitlyn was put her in her stroller and tie her shoelaces together so she couldn't get out. Now, I am not proud of that, but when you have a hyperactive child you do things just to survive.

When Katie was three years old, I went back to church but left her at home. I went to pray for a healing. I believe in healings. At the time I knew that 30 percent of three-year-olds *look* hyperactive, but only 5–10 percent of four-year-olds *are* hyperactive. So the first time you can really diagnose ADD with confidence is when the patient is four years old. I lit candles at church and even put an extra fifty dollars in the offering, trying to bribe God. I wrote to the pope and asked him to send a blessed picture that I could put by her bed. But he must have had an ADD secretary because no one wrote me back. At the age of four, I brought Kaitlyn to a colleague who diagnosed her with ADD.

The hallmark symptoms of ADD are short attention span, distractibility, disorganization, procrastination, and poor internal supervision. Some people are hyperactive like Kaitlyn, but many are not.

Short attention span is the key symptom of ADD, but it is not short attention span for everything. People with ADD have trouble with regular, routine everyday attention—the kind of attention that makes life work, such as getting your homework done, paying bills on time, doing your expense report at work, or listening to your spouse. For activities and events that are new, novel, highly stimulating, interesting, or frightening, people with ADD can pay attention just fine. It is as though they need stimulation in order to pay attention, which is why they ride motorcycles, go to scary movies, engage in high-risk activities, and tend to be conflict seeking in their relationships. Many people with ADD play this game I call "let's have a problem." If they are upset, they can focus and may even overfocus on the problem. This trait often fools people, even doctors, because if you can pay attention to things you love, but not most things, then people do not think you have ADD; they just think you are lazy.

Distractibility is another common symptom. Most of us can block out things we do not need to think about, but this is not the case for people with ADD. If someone drops a pencil three rows over, their attention immediately goes to the pencil. People with ADD also tend to feel everything. They hate tags and their clothes have to be just right or they get upset. They are often sensitive to touch and may need white noise at night to sleep; otherwise they hear everything in the house. Distractibility often affects a woman's ability to have an orgasm. What does an orgasm require? Attention! You have to pay attention to the feeling long enough to make it happen. After properly treating ADD, many people's sex lives get much better.

Many people with ADD are disorganized. Their rooms, desks, and bookbags are often a mess and they tend to be late. You can tell the ADD people at work because they are always ten minutes late and usually show up with a big cup of coffee in their hands. Many people with ADD self-medicate with stimulants, such as caffeine and nicotine.

Many people with ADD also have what I call poor internal supervision. They don't think before they say things and they don't think before they do things, which gets them into lots of hot water. Many people with ADD have trouble with long-term goals. The moment is what matters to them, not five moments from now or ten moments from now, but now. They wait till the last minute to get things done and have trouble saving for retirement. They also take what I call a crisis management approach to life. It seems as though their life goes from one crisis to the next.

For many people with ADD, the harder they try the worse it gets. On brain SPECT studies we see that the brain is usually normal at rest, but when the patient tries to concentrate there is decreased activity in the front part of the brain (see Images 6.1 and 6.2). Stimulant medications seem to help because they prevent this shutdown from occurring so people can concentrate. This is like putting your foot on the gas pedal and the car goes slower.

There are many myths and misconceptions about ADD. Here are just a few.

The first myth is that ADD is a fad or something new. Yet it has been described in the medical literature for well over a hundred years. It is true not as many people were diagnosed with ADD fifty years ago, but they existed and they were punished more in school or just labeled as bad or lazy kids.

The second myth is that everyone outgrows ADD by the time they hit pu-

ADD Scans

Image 6.1	Image 6.2

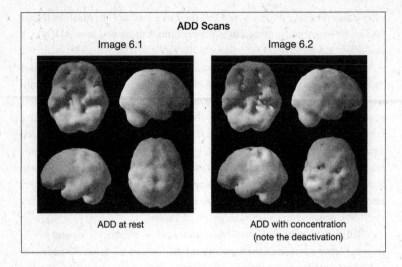

ADD at rest

ADD with concentration
(note the deactivation)

berty. About half the people who have it as children will have symptoms as adults, even older adults. I have treated many three- or four-generation families with ADD. In one of my favorite families I treated the six-year-old son, the mother, the grandfather, and the ninety-four-year-old great-grandmother. When the great-grandmother came in my office, I asked her why she was there. She said, "I want to finish the newspaper. I have never been able to finish the paper." On treatment a month later she came back into my office with a big smile and told me she had read her first book.

The third myth is that ADD is only a minor problem. Yet 35 percent of these children left untreated never finish high school. According to one study 52 percent of untreated ADD teens and adults will abuse drugs or alcohol. And according to another study 43 percent of untreated aggressive hyperactive boys will be arrested for a felony by the time they are sixteen. Seventy-five percent of people with untreated ADD have interpersonal problems. Why? In my lectures I often ask the audience, "How many of you are married?" Most of the audience raise their hands. I continue, "Is it helpful for you to say everything you think in your marriage?" The audience laughs. "Of course not," I continue. "Relationships require tact. They require forethought. But when you have low activity in the front part of your brain, as most people with ADD do, you often say the first thing that comes into your mind, which hurts other people's feelings."

I often say the brain is a sneaky organ. We all have weird, crazy, stupid thoughts that no one should ever hear. It is the front part of our brain that protects us from saying those stupid thoughts out loud. It acts as the brain's brake. I was once at a conference with one of my friends who has ADD and a brain injury. Two obese women were sitting in front of us talking about their weight problems. One woman said to the other, "I don't know why I am so fat. I eat like a bird." My friend looked at me and said loud enough for everyone around us to hear, "Yeah, like a condor." I looked at my friend in total embarrassment. Horrified, my friend put her hand over her mouth and said, "Oh my God, did that thought get out?" I nodded yes as the women moved away from us in disgust.

The last myth is that ADD is a disorder mostly of males. Some studies indicate that girls have ADD nearly as much as boys, but they are not diagnosed because, unlike Kaitlyn, most of them are not hyperactive. They frequently suffer with ADD symptoms and never get anywhere near their potential. They are passed off as lazy or not that smart.

Even though Breanne, my oldest daughter, was the perfect child, the truth is I never thought she was very smart. It embarrasses me to say that, but that was how I felt. I had to teach her simple things over and over and she did not learn her times tables until she was in fifth grade. I had her tested by a colleague in the third grade who basically told me the same thing, that she wasn't that smart. She didn't say it that way, but I could read between the lines. But the psychologist said Breanne would be okay because she worked so hard. In fact, in eighth grade Breanne won a presidential scholar award, not for academics but for effort. In tenth grade, however, things started to fall apart. She was in a college prep school and stayed up every night until one or two o'clock in the morning to get her homework done. Then one night, while studying biology, she came to me in tears and said she thought she could never be as smart as her friends. It broke my heart. The next day I pulled up her original scan, taken when she was eight years old. When I first started to do scans in 1991, I scanned everyone I knew. I had scanned my three kids, my mother, even myself. At the time I only had the experience of someone who had seen fifty scans. Now, seven years later, I had seen thousands of scans. With experienced eyes I was horrified with what I saw. Breanne had low overall activity, especially in the front part of her brain.

I came home that night and told Breanne what I saw and told her I wanted to get a new scan. Because of the injection with the procedure, she protested, "I don't want a scan, Dad. All you think about are scans." But I am a child psychiatrist. I know how to get my way with kids. I felt this was very important and so I asked her what it would take to get a scan. She told me she wanted a telephone line in her room. I started to think that maybe she was smarter than I thought. Her new SPECT study was virtually identical to the one seven years earlier. I cried when I saw it.

The next night on a low dose of medication I rescanned her, and her brain normalized. Breanne's learning struggles had nothing to do with her intelligence. The low activity in her brain was limiting the access she had to her own brain. I put her on a low dose of medicine along with some supplements. A few days later she said that learning was much easier for her. She started bringing home A's on her tests, which had never happened before. When she went to biology, she said she understood concepts for the first time. Usually a shy child in class, she started raising her hand and even participated in debates. At dinner one night she winked at me and said, "I kicked butt in a debate today." This was not the same child I knew. Four months after her scan, she got straight A's for the first time in her life. She repeated the feat all the way through high school and most of college. She has a completely different perception of herself—one that fits her reality of being smart, competent, and able to look forward to a bright future.

When you effectively treat someone with ADD you can change their whole lives. Then why are medications like Ritalin so controversial? Because although they work for some people with ADD, they can make other people much worse. Until I started doing scans I did not know why. What I found out from imaging was that ADD was not one thing, it was at least six different things, and giving everyone the same treatment helped some people but created disasters in others.

Here is a brief description of the six types and treatments.

Type 1: Classic ADD

Primary ADD symptoms plus hyperactivity, restlessness, and impulsivity. On SPECT scans we see decreased activity in the prefrontal cortex, especially with concentration. Usually diagnosed early and effectively treated with stimulant medications (e.g., Adderall, Concerta, Ritalin, Dexedrine, Strattera, or Provigil), fish oil, exercise, and a higher protein, lower simple carbohydrate diet. Supplement alternatives to medication include L-tyrosine, DL-phenylalanine, L-theanine, acetyl-L-carnitine, and grape seed extract (see pages 85–90).

Type 2: Inattentive ADD

Primary ADD symptoms plus low energy and motivation, spaciness, and internal preoccupation. On SPECT scans we see decreased activity in the prefrontal cortex and cerebellum, especially with concentration. Type 2 is diagnosed later in life, if at all. It is more common in girls. These are quiet kids and adults, often labeled lazy, unmotivated, and not that smart. It is also effectively treated with stimulant medications (e.g., Adderall, Concerta, Ritalin, Dexedrine, Strattera, or Provigil), fish oil, exercise, and a higher protein, lower simple carbohydrate diet. Supplement alternatives to medication include L-tyrosine, DL-phenylalanine, L-theanine, acetyl-L-carnitine, and grape seed extract (see pages 85–90).

Type 3: Overfocused ADD

Primary ADD symptoms plus cognitive inflexibility, trouble shifting attention, preoccupation with negative thoughts or behaviors, worrying, grudge holding, argumentative and oppositional behaviors, and a need for sameness. Often seen in families with alcoholism, addiction problems, or obsessive-compulsive tendencies. On SPECT scans we see decreased activity in the prefrontal cortex with concentration plus increased anterior cingulate activity. Stimulants, by themselves, usually make this type worse; people become more focused on the things that bother them. Effectively treated with the antidepressant Effexor, or a combination of a selective serotonin reuptake inhibitor (SSRI; e.g., Prozac) and a stimulant, fish oil, exercise, and a higher carbohydrate diet. Supplement alternatives to medication include a combination of a stimulating supplement, such as L-tyrosine with a serotonin-boosting supplement such as 5-hydroxytryptophan (5-HTP) and St. John's wort (see pages 90–92).

Type 4: Temporal Lobe ADD

Primary ADD symptoms plus a short fuse, tendency to misinterpret comments, periods of anxiety, headaches or abdominal pain, history of head injury, family history of rages, dark thoughts, memory problems, and a struggle with reading. Often seen in families with learning or temper problems. On SPECT scans we see decreased activity in the prefrontal cortex with concentration and decreased temporal lobe activity. Stimulants, by themselves, usually make people with this type more irritable. Effectively treated with a combination of antiseizure medications (such as Neurontin) and stimulants, fish oil, exercise, and a higher protein diet. Supplement alternatives to medication include a combination of a stimulating supplement, such as L-tyrosine with gamma-aminobutyric acid (GABA) to help stabilize moods or gingko, phosphatidylserine, or huperzine to help with learning and memory (see pages 92–93).

Type 5: Limbic ADD

Primary ADD symptoms plus chronic mild sadness, negativity, low energy, low self-esteem, irritability, social isolation, poor appetite, and sleep patterns. On SPECT scans we see decreased activity in the prefrontal cortex at rest and with concentration and increased deep limbic activity. Stimulants, by themselves, usually cause problems with rebound or cause depressive symptoms. Effectively treated with the antidepressant Wellbutrin or the supplement S-adenosyl-methionine (SAMe) plus fish oil, exercise, and a balanced diet. Supplement alternatives to medication include SAMe, L-tyrosine, or DL-phenylalanine.

Type 6: Ring of Fire ADD

Primary ADD symptoms plus extreme moodiness, anger outbursts, oppositional, inflexibility, fast thoughts, excessive talking, and extreme sensitivity to sounds and lights. I named it Ring of Fire after the intense ring of overactivity that I saw in the brains of affected people. This type is usually made much worse with stimulants if used alone. I usually start with a supplement combination called Neurolink, which contains GABA, 5-HTP, and L-tyrosine. Sometimes a stimulant may also be needed. Medication alternatives include anticonvulsants (e.g., Neurontin) and an SSRI medication, the use of the novel antipsychotic medications (e.g., Risperdal or Zyprexa) plus fish oil, exercise, and a balanced diet.

Knowing your type is essential to getting the right help for yourself. If these descriptions are not clear enough, consider picking up my book *Healing ADD* or taking our ADD Type Test at www.amenclinics.com.

Common Treatments for All Types

There are many treatments common to all people with ADD. Here are the most important ones to start with today.

1. Take a 100 percent multiple vitamin every day. Studies have reported that they help people with learning and help prevent chronic illness. No matter what type of ADD you or your child has, take a 100 percent vitamin and mineral supplement a day. When I was in medical school the professor who taught our course in nutrition said that if people eat a balanced diet they do not need vitamin or mineral supplements. I have seen that balanced diets are a thing of the past for many of our

"fast-food families." In my experience, ADD families in particular have problems with planning and tend to eat out much more frequently than non-ADD families. Protect yourself and your child by taking a 100 percent vitamin and mineral supplement. In a 1988 study published in the British journal *Lancet*, ninety children between the ages of twelve and thirteen were divided into three groups. One group took no tablet, one group took a typical multiple vitamin and mineral tablet, and the last group took a tablet that looked and tasted just like the vitamin and mineral tablet yet contained no vitamins or minerals. The results of this well-controlled study was that the group who took the vitamin and mineral tablet had a significant increase in nonverbal intelligence, while the other two groups showed no difference at all. The subclinical vitamin and mineral deficiency may have been contributing to these students performing below their abilities.

2. Omega-3 fatty acids have been found to be helpful in children with ADD. There are three double-blind studies suggesting their value, plus people with ADD have been found to have low levels of omega-3 fatty acids in their blood. Omega-3 fatty acids have two major components: epicosapentaenoic acid (EPA) and docosahexaenoic acid (DHA). EPA tends to be stimulating while DHA tends to be sedating (personal communication with Joe Hibbeln at the National Institutes of Health in 2007). For Types 1 and 2 I recommend the EPA component of fish oil (NeuroEPA from Amen Clinics) and for the other types a combination of EPA and DHA (NeurOmega). For adults I recommend taking 2,000–4,000 milligrams a day and 1,000–2,000 milligrams for children. An easy form for children to take is Coromega.

3. Eliminate caffeine and nicotine. They both interfere with sleep and decrease the effectiveness of other treatments.

4. Intense aerobic exercise daily for thirty to forty-five minutes. Kids should engage in a safe exercise like long, fast walks (no brain injuries, please).

5. Turn off the television and video games, or limit them to no more than thirty minutes a day. This may be hard for kids and teens, but it can make a huge difference.

6. Food is a drug. Most people with ADD do best with a higher protein, lower simple carbohydrate diet. In a 2008 study from Holland, researchers found that putting children on a restricted elimination diet

reduced ADD symptoms by more than 50 percent in 73 percent of children, which is basically the same effectiveness of stimulant medication without any of the side effects. Elimination diets are not easy to do. Basically, during the study the children could only eat rice, turkey, lamb, vegetables, fruits, margarine, vegetable oil, tea, pear juice, and water. But the results were stunning. Elimination diets may be a place to start; by gradually adding back other foods you will be able to see what items may be causing the abnormal behaviors. Working with a nutritionist may make a big difference. In this study the researchers also found that the children's moods and oppositional behaviors were also improved. People with Type 3 do better with more carbohydrates in their diet. Types 5 and 6 seem to do better with more balanced diets, like the Zone Diet described by Barry Sears.

7. In dealing with kids, employees, and even spouses with ADD, *no yelling*! Many people with ADD seek conflict or excitement as a means of stimulation. They can be masters at making other people mad or angry. Do not lose your temper with them. If they get you to explode, their unconscious, low energy prefrontal cortex lights up and likes it. Never let your anger be their medication. They can get addicted to it.

Natural Supplement Strategies for Each Type

In this section I will reexamine each ADD type and provide more details about the supplements that I have seen to have clinical benefit. I'll give you the rationale and dosage protocols that I suggest to my patients. If you decide to use these supplements instead of medication, as many people do, make sure you keep tabs on their effectiveness. I only want my patients to take something that is clearly beneficial to them. I also want them to take medication if the supplements are not effective. Many parents say that they want to try the natural supplements before they try medication. I'm not opposed to that, but I worry that if the supplements are not fully effective that they will not pursue more effective treatments, as people with ADD are masterful at procrastination. Follow through to find what works for yourself or your child. Be open to new ideas and persist until you get the best brain and life functioning. Of the different options, try them in the order I list and initially try them one at a time unless I note differently. Please be sure to discuss these options with your health care professionals.

TYPE 1: CLASSIC ADD AND TYPE 2: INATTENTIVE ADD

Supplement alternatives for Type 1 and 2 include L-tyrosine, DL-phenyl-alanine, acetyl-L-carnitine, L-theanine, or grape seed extract. These types seem to be due to deficiencies of the neurotransmitter dopamine.

L-TYROSINE

A search of the medical literature on L-tyrosine found eighteen studies that apply to mental health and learning involving approximately 503 patients. Of the eighteen studies, eleven are positive and seven are negative. In my experience, L-tyrosine can have a mild positive effect on Types 1 and 2 ADD.

I frequently prescribe the amino acid L-tyrosine in doses of 500 milligrams to 1,500 milligrams two to three times a day for adults and 100 milligrams to 500 milligrams two to three times a day for children under age ten. L-tyrosine is the amino acid building block for dopamine, the neurotransmitter implicated in ADD. It is reported to increase the level of phenylethylamine, a mild stimulant that is found in high concentrations in chocolate. Many of my patients have reported that it is helpful for them. It is softer in its effect, but nonetheless they notice a positive effect. Because of absorption patterns, I recommend that they take it on an empty stomach (a half hour before meals or an hour after meals). I have not seen any side effects with L-tyrosine, except for mild weight loss. If it is given by itself to Type 3 ADD patients, it tends to increase the intensity of overfocused symptoms. Patients with a history of mania should exercise caution with the use of L-tyrosine because the energizing properties of this compound may trigger a manic episode.

L-tyrosine is also the amino acid building block for epinephrine and norepinephrine. L-tyrosine has been reported to help boost energy levels, mood, focus, and metabolism. L-tyrosine may increase motivation and improve concentration. Research suggests that L-tyrosine acts to help the body adapt and cope with stress. Taken ahead of time, L-tyrosine allows some people to avoid typical bodily reactions and feelings from stressful situations like surgery, emotional upset, and sleep deprivation. L-tyrosine appears to be a successful addition to conventional treatment for cocaine and nicotine withdrawal. L-tyrosine levels are also low in some depressed patients. A number of studies conducted in the 1970s showed encouraging results regarding the use of L-tyrosine to ease symptoms of depression, especially when used together with the supplement 5-HTP.

Phil, age sixteen, had been treated for Type 1 ADD for several years. He was taking Ritalin, which would work for a while and then seem to wear off. The up-and-down effectiveness of the medication frustrated him. He tried Adderall, but it seemed to have the same effect. I stopped the stimulant medications, put him on 1,000 milligrams of L-tyrosine three times a day, was firm about dietary guidelines, and encouraged Phil to walk fast for an hour five times a week. Within a week, he said he felt better. He has maintained the regimen for four years now.

DL-PHENYLALANINE

A search of the medical literature on DL-phenylalanine found four studies that apply to mental health and learning involving approximately ninety-three patients. Of the four studies, all are positive. In my experience, DL-phenylalanine can have a mild positive effect.

DL-phenylalanine is an essential amino acid, which means that it is essential to human health but is not manufactured in the body, so it must be obtained from food or supplements. The body converts DL-phenylalanine into L-tyrosine, another amino acid essential for making proteins, certain brain chemicals, and thyroid hormones. Symptoms of DL-phenylalanine deficiency include confusion, lack of energy and decreased alertness, memory, and appetite. A number of studies show norepinephrine and epinephrine (adrenaline) to be low in patients with depression. The antidepressants imipramine and desipramine work in part by increasing norepinephrine in the brain. Theoretically, when more precursor is available, more neurotransmitters will be made. Therefore it makes sense that by boosting DL-phenylalanine we can increase norepinephrine and have a positive impact on concentration and mood. In fact, in a number of studies DL-phenylalanine has been found to be helpful for depression, energy, and pain control. I have used it for twenty years as an antidepressant in children, teens, and adults. It is milder in its effect than prescribed antidepressants, but it also causes significantly less side effects. People who have phenylketonuria, commonly known as PKU, should not take DL-phenylalanine, because they do not have the enzyme that metabolizes it. The recommended dose is 400 milligrams three times a day on an empty stomach for adults and 200 milligrams three times daily for children.

ACETYL-L-CARNITINE

A search of the medical literature on acetyl-L-carnitine (ALC) found twenty-six studies that apply to mental health and learning involving approximately twenty-one hundred patients. Of the twenty-six studies, twenty-three are positive and three are negative. In my experience, ALC can have a mild positive effect.

ALC is a nutrient that has been reported to improve mental focus, enhance energy, and slow aging. Research has shown that ALC increases levels of neurotransmitters needed for memory, focus and learning, and repairs the damage done to brain cells caused by stress and poor nutrition. About 95 percent of energy production in your cells occurs in the mitochondria. Many diseases of aging are increasingly being referred to as "mitochondrial disorders." ALC has been shown to help increase energy production in the mitochondria.

From Italy comes a fascinating study about the use of ALC for ADHD and Fragile X syndrome. It is a treatment we should consider for ADHD children and adults. Fragile X syndrome is the most common hereditary form of mental retardation. Many children with Fragile X syndrome also suffer from ADHD, which complicates social relationships at home and at school. Although stimulant medication such as Ritalin is often effective, it also causes side effects such as increased irritability, decreased verbalization, and social withdrawal. A previous study showed that ALC significantly reduced hyperactive behavior in Fragile X syndrome boys with ADHD who were treated with it for one year without causing adverse side effects. The same authors have now conducted a randomized, double-blind, placebo-controlled multicenter study to determine the effectiveness of ALC in a larger group. Led by M. Giulia Torrioli and Giovanni Neri of the Università Cattolica in Rome, the study involved fifty-one boys between six and twelve years old with Fragile X syndrome and ADHD who were treated in one of eight centers in Italy, France, and Spain. Each patient followed the treatment for twelve months, which involved 500 milligrams of ALC or a placebo given twice daily. Patients were evaluated by a team of child neuropsychiatrists and psychologists at the start of the study, after one month, six months, and twelve months. The effects of the drug and placebo were evaluated using a set of neuropsychological tests to assess behavior. Those treated with ALC demonstrated reduced hyperactive behavior and increased attention. No side effects were exhibited, confirming that ALC is a safe alternative to stimulants. The patients treated with the placebo also showed reduced hyperactive behavior, although not nearly to the extent as the ALC-treated patients. The patients treated with ALC also had significantly improved social ability compared with the placebo-treated group. The authors proposed that ALC be recommended as a treatment of ADHD in Fragile X syndrome children, since it effectively reduces hyperactive behavior and improves social abilities without adverse side effects. They also suggest that these results may be applicable to children with autism, who also do not easily tolerate stimulants.

Some people report feeling an increase in mental energy and focus within twenty minutes, which is why you should not take it too late in the day, as it may give you insomnia. Even though ALC is not a stimulant, it seems to naturally increase energy in the brain. Over thirty studies show that ALC slows or prevents age-related decline in mental function. In one study, 1.5 grams a day of ALC given to 236 older adults for forty-five days significantly increased the effectiveness of performance on all the measures of cognitive functioning, memory performance, and constructional thinking. Twenty adults given 1.5 grams of ALC experienced reversal of many of the signs of brain aging. Alcoholics with cognitive impairment have also benefited from ALC. ALC is potentially valuable in helping depression. One hundred sixty patients who had suffered from a stroke a year or more ago were given 1.5 grams of ALC a day for eight weeks. This led to increased speed of recovery, as well as improved mood and attention span. A total of over 600 patients with Alzheimer's disease have been studied in over twenty years of research, demonstrating that ALC benefits patients with dementia.

Because of lack of long-term safety studies, ALC is not advised for pregnant women or nursing mothers. Mild gastrointestinal symptoms may occur in those taking ALC, including nausea, vomiting, abdominal cramps, and diarrhea. Increased agitation has been reported in some with Alzheimer's disease when taking oral ALC. In those with seizure disorders, an increase in seizure frequency has been reported in some taking ALC.

You should consider ALC if you suffer with tiredness, mental fatigue, memory loss, or attentional problems. The typical dose is 500–1,500 milligrams a day.

L-THEANINE

A search of the medical literature on L-theanine found six studies that apply to mental health and learning involving approximately eighty-five patients. Of the six studies, all showed some positive effect. In my experience, L-theanine can have a mild positive effect.

L-theanine is an amino acid mainly found naturally in the green tea plant. L-theanine is the predominant amino acid in green tea and makes up 50 percent of the total free amino acids in the plant. L-theanine is considered the main component responsible for the taste of green tea. It is marketed in Japan as a nutritional supplement for mood modulation. L-theanine may also have activity in modulating the metabolism of cancer chemotherapeutic agents and ameliorating their side effects.

L-theanine has been shown to penetrate the brain and produce significant increases in the neurotransmitters serotonin and/or dopamine concentrations. These findings led to recent studies investigating the possibility that L-theanine might enhance learning ability, induce relaxation, and relieve emotional stress. Memory and learning ability were said to be improved in young male Wistar rats given 180 milligrams of L-theanine daily for four months. Human performance was assessed using a test for learning ability and passive and active avoidance tests for memory. The mental effects of L-theanine were tested in a small group of volunteers divided into "high-anxiety" and "low-anxiety" groups. The volunteers were females ages 18–22. Their level of anxiety was assessed by a manifest anxiety scale. Subjects received water, 50 milligrams of L-theanine, or 200 milligrams of L-theanine solution once a week. Brain waves were measured 60 minutes after administration. The 200-milligram dose (dissolved in 100 milliliters of water) resulted in significantly greater production of alpha waves than was observed in subjects receiving water. The effect was dose-dependent. The researchers regarded the significantly increased production of alpha-brain wave activity as an index of increased relaxation.

Pregnant women and nursing mothers should avoid L-theanine supplements. Use of L-theanine supplements concomitantly with cancer chemotherapeutic agents must be done under medical supervision. There are no known adverse reactions.

L-theanine supplements are available for the promotion of relaxation and modulation of mood. Doses used are between 50 and 200 milligrams, as necessary. L-theanine is available in some green tea preparations. The amino acid constitutes between 1 percent and 2 percent of the dry weight of green tea leaves.

GRAPE SEED / PINE BARK EXTRACT (PYCNOGENOL)

A search of the medical literature on Pycnogenol found five studies that apply to ADD involving more than a hundred patients. Of the five studies, four showed some positive effect. In my experience Pycnogenol can have a mild positive effect.

Grape seed or pine bark extract has also shown some mild benefit for Type 1 and Type 2 ADD. Grape seed or pine bark extract are proanthocyanidin compounds. These compounds have been found to increase blood flow and they act as superantioxidants, twenty to fifty times as powerful as vitamin E. There are several published studies with grape seed or pine bark extract in ADD and a number of published case reports.

Here is an example from Slovakia. Sixty-one children were supplemented with 1 milligram per kilogram per day of Pycnogenol or placebo over a period of four weeks in a randomized, placebo-controlled, double-blind study. Patients were examined at start of trial, one month after treatment, and 1 month after end of treatment period by standard questionnaires. Results show that one-month Pycnogenol administration caused a significant reduction of hyperactivity, improved attention and visual-motoric coordination and concentration of children with ADD. In the placebo group no positive effects were found. One month after termination of Pycnogenol administration a relapse of symptoms was noted. The authors concluded that "the results point to an option to use Pycnogenol as a natural supplement to relieve ADHD symptoms of children."

There is a body of medical literature that reports these compounds are very helpful for people with varicose veins. If you have ADD and varicose veins, then grape seed or pine bark extract may be for you.

Crystal, age forty-eight, came to the clinic for symptoms of ADD. Her whole life she had been restless, inattentive, easily distracted, terribly disorganized, and impulsive. After her third child she also developed terrible varicose veins, which I had noticed in the initial interview. When we talked about treatment options for her classic Type 1 ADD she said that she wanted to try the grape seed extract. Then she would see about other options. After three weeks she noticed that she felt better, had more energy, and her legs looked and felt better. Eventually we added L-tyrosine to give her more help with focus, but the regimen has worked well for her over the past several years.

TYPE 3: OVERFOCUSED ADD

This type of ADD seems likely due to a relative deficiency of both serotonin and dopamine. In this type I use something to enhance serotonin such as St. John's Wort or 5-HTP plus something to enhance dopamine such as L-Tyrosine.

St. John's Wort

A search of the medical literature on St. John's wort found thirty-two studies that apply to mental health and learning involving approximately one thousand patients. Of the thirty-two studies, thirty were positive and two were negative. In my experience, St. John's wort can have a significantly positive effect on mild to moderate depression and overfocused ADD when combined with L-tyrosine.

A high number of studies support the usage of St. John's wort as an effective treatment for minor to moderate cases of major depression. St. John's wort has also been shown to be better tolerated by individuals than prescription medication, with less side effects. In addition, randomized, double-blind studies have shown St. John's wort to be equally as effective as antidepressant prescription medications (e.g., citalopram, paroxetine, fluoxetine, sertraline, and imipramine).

I have seen that a combination of St. John's wort and L-tyrosine is often very helpful. St. John's wort comes from the flowers of the Saint-John's-wort plant (*wort* is Old English for "plant"). It got its name from the fact that it blooms around June 24, the feast day of St. John the Baptist, and the red ring around the flowers when crushed looks like blood, the blood of the beheaded John the Baptist. St. John's wort seems to increase serotonin availability in the brain. The starting dosage of St. John's wort is 300 milligrams a day for children, 300 milligrams twice a day for teens, and 600 milligrams in the morning and 300 milligrams at night for adults. Sometimes I'll go as high as 1,800 milligrams in adults. The bottle should say that it contains 0.3 percent hypericin, which is believed to be the active ingredient of St. John's wort. I have done a number of before-and-after SPECT studies with St. John's wort. It clearly decreases cingulate gyrus hyperactivity for many patients. It also helps with moodiness and trouble shifting attention. Unfortunately, I have also seen it decrease prefrontal cortex activity. One of the women in the study said, "I'm happier, but I'm dingier." When cingulate symptoms are present with ADD symptoms, it's important to use St. John's wort with a stimulating substance like L-tyrosine or a stimulant such as Adderall.

It has been reported that St. John's wort increases sun sensitivity (you could get sunburned more easily) and may decrease the effectiveness of birth control pills and antiviral medications. Also, don't use it if temporal lobe symptoms are present, without first stabilizing the temporal lobes.

Elaine, age sixteen, had always been a worrier. She also had problems with anger at home. If things did not go her way she would explode at her parents or at her younger sister. As a student she was a perfectionist, which caused her to spend excessive time on assignments. Her mother, a school principal, brought her to my clinic after she heard me lecture. She told me that she was sure Elaine had Type 3 ADD, causing her to overfocus. Her SPECT study showed marked increased activity in her anterior cingulate gyrus. She also had mild decreased activity in her prefrontal cortex. I placed her on St. John's wort, 600 milligrams in the morning and 300 milligrams at night. I also had her take 500 milligrams of L-tyrosine two to three times a day. Within a month Elaine was much better. She was more relaxed, less reactive, and did much better in her classes. She said that studying was easy because she no longer felt the need to have everything just so. She still wanted to excel, but didn't have to copy pages over three and four times until things were perfect.

5-HTP

A search of the medical literature on 5-HTP found twenty-five studies that apply to mental health and learning involving approximately one thousand patients. Of the twenty-five studies, twenty-one were positive and four were negative. In my experience, 5-HTP can have a significantly positive effect on anxiety, worry and sleep, and overfocused ADD when combined with L-tyrosine.

5-HTP is a step closer in the serotonin production pathway. It is also more widely available than L-tryptophan and it is more easily taken up in the brain. Seventy percent is taken up into the brain, as opposed to only 3 percent of L-tryptophan. 5-HTP is about five to ten times more powerful than L-tryptophan. A number of double-blind studies have shown that 5-HTP is as effective as antidepressant medication. It boosts serotonin levels in the brain and helps to calm cingulate gyrus hyperactivity (greasing the cingulate, if you will, to help with shifting of attention). The dose of 5-HTP for adults is 50–300 milligrams a day. Children should start at half dose. Take 5-HTP and L-tryptophan on an empty stomach. The most common side effect of 5-HTP is an upset stomach. It is usually very mild. Start slowly and work your way up slowly.

TYPE 4: TEMPORAL LOBE ADD

Temporal lobe ADD is a combination of temporal lobe dysfunction and poor prefrontal cortex activity. Strategies geared toward temporal lobe stabilization and enhancement have proven valuable for this ADD type. From a medication standpoint, I have seen antiseizure (also called anticonvulsant) medications be the most helpful. One of the mechanisms by these medications works by enhancing the amino acid GABA.

GABA

A search of the medical literature on GABA found only one study that applies to mental health and learning. GABA is a major neurotransmitter widely distributed throughout the brain. Because too much excitation in the brain can lead to irritability, restlessness, insomnia, seizures, and movement disorders, it must be balanced with inhibition. GABA—the most important inhibitory neurotransmitter in the brain—provides this inhibition, acting like a brake during times of runaway activity. Medications for anxiety, such as Valium and anticonvulsants, stimulate GABA receptors and induce relaxation. Either low GABA levels or decreased GABA function in the brain is associated with several psychiatric and neurological disorders, including anxiety, depression, insomnia, and epilepsy. Studies indicate GABA can improve relaxation and enhance sleep. GABA is available as dietary supplements in the United States.

The mechanisms of most antiseizure drugs involve direct or indirect GABA enhancement. The drugs act in a variety of ways by increasing GABA availability. The ketogenic diet, employed in particular for treatment of childhood epilepsy, is theorized to work via a GABA mechanism. Ketosis increases brain metabolism of acetate, which is converted to glutamine by glial cells. Glutamine is then taken up by GABA neurons and converted to GABA. Electroencephalogram tracings in healthy human subjects on a ketogenic diet yielded patterns consistent with increased GABA activity. Research indicates oral GABA supplementation may be beneficial for epilepsy. Several animal and clinical studies have examined the effect of a combination of GABA and phosphatidylserine (PS) in the treatment of various types of seizure disorders. A pilot study of forty-two subjects with drug-resistant epilepsy (ten with absence seizures [periods of spaciness]) found a combination of increasing doses of GABA (1,500–2,500 milligrams daily) and PS (300–500 milligrams daily)—in separate capsules—resulted in a significant, dose-dependent decrease in absence seizures, but not in simple or complex partial seizures.

I have seen GABA have a calming effect on people who struggle with temper, irritability, and anxiety (all of which may be temporal lobe symptoms). The doses of GABA range from 250 milligrams–750 milligrams twice a day for adults, half that for children.

Many people with temporal lobe ADD suffer from memory problems. I have found a number of natural substances helpful to enhance memory, including gingko biloba, PS, and huperzine A. These are discussed in chapter 8.

TYPE 5: LIMBIC ADD

Limbic ADD has many symptoms of mild depression, including negativity, sadness, feelings of hopelessness, and an overabundance of automatic negative thoughts. Frequently I have seen stimulants make people who have this type of ADD more negative and moody. The supplements that seem to help this type of ADD best are SAMe, DL-phenylalanine, or L-tyrosine. DL-phenylalanine and L-tyrosine were described earlier.

SAMe

A search of the medical literature on SAMe found forty-nine studies that apply to mental health, learning, and pain involving more than a thousand patients. Of the forty-nine studies, thirty-eight were positive and eleven were negative. In my experience, SAMe can have a significantly positive effect on mood, pain, energy, and focus.

SAMe is involved with the production of many important brain compounds, including neurotransmitters. It donates "methyl" groups to these compounds so that they can function properly. Normally, the brain manufactures all the SAMe it needs from the amino acid methionine. In depression, however, this synthesis has been found to be impaired. Supplementing the diet with SAMe has been found to increase the neurotransmitters involved with depression and improve cell membrane fluidity. SAMe is one of the best natural antidepressants; a number of recent studies have shown that it is as effective as antidepressant medication. SAMe has also been found helpful for people who suffer from fibromyalgia, a chronic muscle pain disorder. Fibromyalgia and ADD run commonly together. I think the chronic stress associated with ADD is in part responsible for the muscle pain. *People who have bipolar disorder or manic-depressive illness or Type 6 (Ring of Fire) ADD should not take SAMe.* There have been a number of reported cases of SAMe causing manic or hypomanic episodes (excessively up or happy moods, extreme impulsivity in sexuality or spending money, pressured speech, or decreased need for sleep). I think these reports highlight that SAMe is an effective antidepressant, as all of the prescription antidepressants have that capability as well.

In one study from UCLA, Walid Shekim and colleagues used oral SAMe in a sample of well-diagnosed adults with ADHD, in a four-week open trial to establish SAMe effectiveness and safety and in a nine-week, double-blind, placebo-controlled crossover trial. Preliminary data from the open trial reveal that 75 percent (six out of eight male) patients improve on it. The two who did not improve had not improved on the methylphenidate trial. Improvement ranged from moderate to marked, with minimal and transient side effects that did not interfere with functioning.

The dosage of SAMe is between 200 milligrams and 400 milligrams two to four times a day, half that for children. Nature's Made is a good brand and is sold at Costco, lowering the cost significantly.

TYPE 6: RING OF FIRE ADD

Type 6 ADD is often associated with intense ADD symptoms, such as intense hyperactivity and distractibility, severe impulsiveness, hypersensitivity to the environment, pressured speech, and cyclic mood changes. I think that this type of ADD may be related to bipolar disorder. Stimulants, by themselves, tend to make it worse. At the Amen Clinics we use the supplement Neurolink and high-quality fish oil. Neurolink is a combination of GABA, 5-HTP, inositol, and L-tyrosine. GABA is an inhibitory neurotransmitter and may help to calm overactive areas, 5-HTP and inositol act to increase serotonin availability and may help increase mood and flexibility, while L-tyrosine is the amino acid building block for dopamine and may help with focus and motivation. I usually start with two capsules twice a day for three weeks, then increase to three capsules twice a day for three weeks, then if needed go to four capsules twice a day. Patience is needed as it often takes several weeks for it to be effective. In addition to Neurolink, we also use high-quality fish oil, which has been found to be helpful in mood disorders and to calm hyperactive brain function. We recommend 2,000–4,000 milligrams a day of Neur-Omega from the Amen Clinics or Coromega. For more severe clinical presentations, I recommend fish oil plus an anticonvulsant medication or atypical antipsychotic to start and often an antidepressant after mood stabilization is obtained.

Cody came to see me from Georgia. He had all of the symptoms of ADD, but when he was placed on Ritalin he became more obsessive, couldn't sleep, and bit his fingernails until they bled. His scan did not show the typical ADD pattern but showed that he had too much activity in his brain. He needed something to calm his brain down, not stimulate it. On Neurolink, a natural supplement we produce that contains GABA, 5-HTP, and L-tyrosine, he did much better.

Through the years I have treated many pilots with ADD who cannot take medicine and keep their Federal Aviation Administration licenses, which seems a bit backward to me. I want my pilot to be able to concentrate and really don't want him to be distracted or conflict seeking when he is flying the plane. But because of the regulations pilots need natural treatments in order to keep their jobs. Many people, although not everyone, can find success with natural treatments for ADD.

| 7 |

Natural Ways to Heal

ANXIETY AND DEPRESSION

In this chapter I am going to continue our discussion about the common brain problems that can interfere with having a magnificent mind. I will discuss anxiety, depression, and bipolar disorder. According to the National Institutes of Health nearly seventy-five million Americans, or one in four of us, will suffer from one of these disorders at some point in our lives.

Many famous people throughout history have struggled with anxiety and depression, including Mark Twain, Ernest Hemingway, J. K. Rowling, and Princess Diana. It is no secret that Abraham Lincoln suffered from periods of severe depression, including suicidal thoughts. In 1836 he told a friend that there were times he was "so overcome with depression that he never dare carry a knife in his pocket." It's possible that Lincoln inherited the tendency for depression from his mother, whom he described as melancholy with "eyes as pools of sadness." Or it may have been the result of a severe brain injury he had when he was twelve years old. Brain injuries often predispose people to mood disorders. Without effective medication or natural supplements to rely on, Lincoln used laughter as a form of self-medication. If his friends could get him to laugh with a funny story or have him tell one of his humorous anecdotes, Lincoln's mood would begin to brighten. On the election night of 1864 Lincoln was very nervous and tense, anticipating a bad outcome. He read a book of humor to calm his nerves. When a member of his cabinet saw what Lincoln was reading, he left the White House in disgust, thinking that the president did not understand the seriousness of the evening. Apparently, Lincoln understood what modern-day doctors are now just discovering—laughter is healing.

Even now, many people think that anxiety and depression are the result of a bad attitude or a weak will. If only you tried harder, the bad feelings would go away. Yet these disorders are often the result of a brain that is out of balance, just like diabetes is a disorder of insulin. Seeing these as medical problems rather than moral problems enables people to get the help they need.

One common misconception is that anxiety and depression are separate problems. They actually run together nearly 70 percent of the time. Through our brain imaging work I have described seven different types of anxiety and depression, and knowing which type you have is critical to getting the right help. Shortly, I will tell you about all of the types, but first I want to share with you the treatments I recommend for all types.

Treatments for All Types of Anxiety and Depression

I recommend a general five-step approach for treating anxiety and depression. First, it is important to rule out a medical cause of anxiety or depression. Thyroid abnormalities, anemia, sleep apnea, brain injuries, and certain medications can all cause these problems. Getting a physical exam is one of the first, most important steps in dealing with these issues. One of my best friends from college came to see me because she was feeling overwhelmed and depressed. When I scanned her, she had severe overall low activity in her brain. Her brain looked like she was a drug addict. But I had known her for many years and knew that was not the case. Her blood work indicated a severe vitamin B_{12} deficiency, causing her to be very anemic. Treating her medical problem helped her mood and her brain.

Second, exercise helps all of the types. Exercise boosts blood flow and helps bring nutrients to the brain. In one head-to-head study comparing exercise with Zoloft, one of our effective antidepressants, they were equally effective after twelve weeks and exercise was actually more effective after ten months.

Third, I recommend that all of my patients take a multiple vitamin and fish oil supplement every day. Why? People who are depressed often do not eat balanced diets and vitamins can provide essential nutrients, such as vitamin D, that have been found to be low in many depressed patients. Vitamin D is made in our skin from sun exposure, but because we are exercising less outdoors and using sunscreen when we do, many people even in sunny climates have vitamin D deficiencies. Taking a supplement or walking in the sun every day for twenty minutes without sunscreen may be good for you.

Fish oil contains omega-3 fatty acids, which have been found to be low in people suffering from depression, ADD, Alzheimer's disease, and in those who have suicidal thoughts. A search of the medical literature on omega-3 fatty acids found twelve studies that apply to mood enhancement. Of the twelve studies, ten were positive and two were negative. I think omega-3 fatty acids are an essential component to the treatment of depression. As I mentioned in the last chapter, omega-3 fatty acids have two major components: eicosapentaenoic acid (EPA) and docosahexaenoic acid (DHA). EPA tends to be stimulating while DHA tends to be sedating. For unfocused anxiety and depression, I recommend the EPA component of fish oil (NeuroEPA from Amen Clinics) and for the other types a combination of EPA and DHA (NeurOmega). For adults I recommend taking 2,000–4,000 milligrams a day and 1,000–2,000 milligrams for children. An easy form for children to take is Coromega.

Fourth, people with anxiety and depression are often filled with automatic negative thoughts, or ANTs. These are the thoughts that automatically come into your mind and ruin your day. For many people, learning how to correct these negative thought patterns have been found to be as effective as antidepressant medication, without any side effects. There will be more on this technique later.

Fifth, natural supplements or medication can be very helpful. My bias usually is to start with natural supplements, while others prefer to start with medication. Either way, it is critical to know the type of anxiety or depression you have so you can get the right help. If these descriptions are not clear enough, consider picking up my book *Healing Anxiety and Depression* or taking the Brain Systems test at www.amenclinics.com.

7 Types of Anxiety and Depression

Type 1: Pure Anxiety
Anxiety is the main issue. People with this type suffer from feeling anxious, tense, and nervous. They live with a sense that something bad is about to happen and often have physical feelings of anxiety, such as headaches, stomachaches, and heart palpitations. People with "pure anxiety" tend to avoid anything that makes them nervous, such as new places, and they are not good with conflict and tend to avoid it like the plague. I often say people

with this type have way too many "fortune-telling" ANTs. They are masterful at predicting the worst and look to the future with fear.

Here's an example: Gary had gone to his doctor for back pain. When the doctor examined him he found a tender spot over his kidneys. He told Gary he wanted to order a kidney x-ray. That is when Gary's thoughts ran wild.

"The doctor is going to find out I have cancer," he thought. Notice the little leap in logic! But his thoughts didn't stop there. "I'm going to have to have chemotherapy. I'm going to vomit my guts out, lose all my hair, be in a tremendous amount of pain, and then I'm going to die!" All in about thirty seconds. Then in a panic Gary said to the doctor, "I can't have that x-ray."

"Why?" the doctor asked. "I need this x-ray, so I can figure out—"

Gary said, "No, you don't understand! I can't have the x-ray!"

That is when the doctor found my number and referred Gary to me.

As Gary told me this story, I knew that he suffered with a panic disorder. Gary was a master at predicting the worst, which was driving his panic symptoms. In treating Gary, I used deep relaxation and taught him to correct the ANTs that were feeding his anxiety. After two sessions I went with Gary to have the kidney x-ray. I hypnotized him to be calm during the procedure, and he did well until the technician came back into the room with a worried look on his face and asked Gary what side his pain was on. Gary grabbed his chest and looked at me as if to say, "I knew you were lying to me! I am going to die." I patted him on the leg and said, "Look Gary, before you die, let me take a look at the x-ray." Gary had a big kidney stone, which can be terribly painful, but kidney stones usually don't kill anyone! Gary's anxiety was ruining his life.

In treating pure anxiety, I teach my patients deep relaxation techniques and how to correct the negative thoughts that cause their suffering. In addition, certain supplements such as gamma-aminobutyric acid (GABA), vitamin B_6, L-glutamine, valerian, or kava kava may be helpful. I don't much like the typical antianxiety medications, like Xanax, because on scans the effects look very similar to those of alcohol, plus they can be addictive and affect memory.

Type 2: Pure Depression

Sadness is the main symptom. People with this type also struggle with low energy, sleep and appetite problems, and they may have little interest and get little pleasure in things that are usually fun. Their ANTs are different from the fortune-telling ANTs of Type 1 patients and tend to be more focused on feeling hopeless, helpless, worthless, and guilty. For this type I like the natural supplement S-adenosyl-methionine (SAMe), which has been found to be helpful for depression and pain, or I prescribe the antidepressant Wellbutrin.

Type 3: Mixed Anxiety and Depression

A combination of both anxiety symptoms and depressive symptoms, which is much more common than the pure types alone, calls for a combination of Types 1 and 2 treatments.

Type 4: Overfocused Anxiety and Depression

People with this type have anxiety or depression, and they get stuck on negative thoughts or behaviors. When this type is combined with anxiety, people get stuck on fearful thoughts. When it is combined with sadness, people get stuck on depressing thoughts. Obsessive-compulsive disorder occurs when people get stuck on obsessions or compulsive behaviors. With phobias, people get stuck on a fear, such as snakes. With post-traumatic stress disorder, people get stuck on something bad that happened in the past. Overfocused anxiety and depression is also associated with people who tend to worry, hold grudges, are rigid, and tend to be oppositional or argumentative. I have noticed that this type occurs more frequently in children or grandchildren of alcoholics.

In treating Type 4, it is important to boost serotonin, an important mood chemical in the brain. Supplements that do this include 5-hydroxytryptophan (5-HTP), L-tryptophan, and inositol, and there are currently six medications that do it as well: Prozac, Zoloft, Celexa, Paxil, Luvox, and Lexapro.

Type 5: Temporal Lobe Anxiety and Depression

The temporal lobes are underneath your temples and behind your eyes. They are very important to learning, memory, and emotional control. When there are problems in this part of the brain, people struggle with temper outbursts; memory problems; mood instability; and sometimes dark, evil, or frightening thoughts. People with this type tend to misinterpret comments as negative when they are not and they have trouble reading social cues. This type is common after a brain injury.

The supplements used to treat this type include GABA and fish oil. An antiseizure medication can also be helpful for this type. When there are memory issues present, I may use the supplements gingko, phosphatidylserine, or huperzine, or if they are severe I may use the medications Aricept or Namenda.

Type 6: Cyclic Anxiety and Depression

Mood cycles, sometimes mild, sometimes severe, is the typical symptom. The classic cyclic mood disorder is called bipolar disorder; people's moods swing between two poles, from depression to mania. It affects nearly 3 percent of Americans in any given year and seems to have been increasing over the last few decades. Mania is the opposite of depression. During a manic episode, people need less sleep, often have racing thoughts, and feel pressure to keep talking. They also may be irritable and very impulsive. People with bipolar disorder can become hypersexual, hyperreligious, or spend large amounts of money they do not have. One of my first patients with this disorder spent thirty thousand dollars the family did not have and she had no idea how she would tell her husband.

Sometimes bipolar disorder is mistaken for ADD. The distinction between the two is critical, however, because if you give people with bipolar disorder stimulant medications you can make them much worse. Like ADD and other forms of anxiety and depression, there are degrees and types of bipolar disorder. Some people suffer with mild mood swings while others have trouble staying out of hospitals or jails. For severe bipolar disorder medication is usually important. I have not found natural supplements to be as effective to fully treat this illness. Having said that, I give all of my bipolar patients fish oil in addition to medication, as researchers from Harvard found it helpful to decrease mood swings and relapse.

Type 7: Unfocused Anxiety and Depression

People suffering from this type exhibit very low energy, trouble thinking, and feeling as though they are in a fog. Rather than worry, they tend to have trouble holding on to thoughts and often have memory problems. In treating Type 7, it is important to find out why the brain is so underactive, treat any problems that might be present, and then find ways to stimulate the brain. The best supplement for this type is SAMe, and Wellbutrin is the best antidepressant.

Matilda was brought to our clinic by her family after she nearly burned down her house by forgetting something on the stove. Her family was at their wits' end. At age sixty-nine Matilda had been diagnosed with Alzheimer's disease and had been getting worse. She had also lost her driver's license because she had been in four minor accidents. Five of her six children thought she should be in a facility for her own safety. One of her daughters, however, had heard about me and brought her for more testing. "One more try," she told me. "You are our last hope." When I first met Matilda I thought she had Alzheimer's disease too, but the results of her scan suggested otherwise. She had good activity in the areas usually affected by Alzheimer's. Her scan was more consistent with depression. Sometimes in the elderly it can be hard to distinguish Alzheimer's disease from depression. Based on her scan I put Matilda on the antidepressant Wellbutrin. Within three weeks Matilda came out of the fog she had been in. Her memory was better and she became more talkative. After a month she asked if I would write the DMV to help her get her driver's license back. I told her, "Matilda, I drive on the same highways you drive. I need you to take your medicine and do the other things we discussed. If in six months you are still better and your scan is better, then I will write the DMV."

Six months later she remained better, her scan had improved, and I wrote the DMV!

Natural Supplement Strategies for Each Type

In this section I will reexamine each type of anxiety and depression and provide more details about the supplements that I have seen to have clinical benefit. I'll give you the rationale and dosage protocols that I suggest to my patients. Some of these I have discussed in the last chapter and will refer you there if the information is repeated. As I mentioned in chapter 6, if you decide to use these supplements instead of medication, as many people do, make sure you keep tabs on their effectiveness and inform your health care professional about what you are taking. I only want my patients to take something that is clearly beneficial to them. I also want them to take medication if the supplements are not effective. Many patients say that they want to try the natural supplements before they try medication. That's okay, but if the supplements are not fully effective, they should pursue more effective treatments, including medication. Anxiety, depression, and bipolar disorder can be potentially very harmful when left untreated or inappropriately treated. Follow through to find out what works best for yourself or your child.

TYPE 1: PURE ANXIETY

For this type of anxiety, GABA, B_6, L-glutamine, kava kava, or valerian may be helpful. I discussed GABA in the last chapter but include more information here as well.

GABA

A search of the medical literature on GABA supplementation found only two studies for anxiety and depression. Of the two studies, both were positive. In my experience, GABA can have a calming effect on anxiety and irritability, and can help with sleep.

GABA is an amino acid that also functions as a neurotransmitter in the brain. GABA is reported in the herbal literature to work in much the same way as the antianxiety drugs and the anticonvulsants. It helps stabilize nerve cells by decreasing their tendency to fire erratically or excessively. This means it may have a calming effect for people who struggle with temper, irritability, and anxiety, whether these symptoms relate to anxiety or to temporal lobe disturbance. Natural therapies that produce relaxation also act, at least in part, by enhancing GABA levels. A controlled pilot study found brain GABA levels were significantly increased after a single sixty-minute yoga session compared with a sixty-minute reading session.

The effect of orally administrated GABA on relaxation and immunity during stress has been studied in humans. One study evaluated the effect of GABA intake on the brain wave patterns of thirteen subjects. Electroencephalograms were obtained after three tests on each volunteer as follows: water as only intake, GABA, or L-theanine. After sixty minutes, GABA significantly increased alpha waves (calming brain waves) and decreased beta waves compared with water or L-theanine. These findings suggest that GABA not only induces relaxation but also reduces anxiety. In another study evaluating the effect of GABA on anxiety and immunity, eight people who were afraid of heights were divided into two groups (placebo and GABA). All acrophobics were crossing a suspended bridge as a way to induce stress. Immune response was measured by sampling immunoglobulin A (IgA) levels in their saliva while crossing the bridge. The placebo group showed marked decreases of their IgA levels, while the GABA group showed significantly higher levels. The authors of this study concluded that GABA could work effectively as a natural relaxant and its effects could be seen within one hour of its administration to induce relaxation and diminish anxiety. Moreover, GABA administration could enhance immunity under stress conditions.

GABA can be taken as a supplement in doses ranging from 250 milligrams–1,500 milligrams daily for adults and from 125 milligrams–750 milligrams daily for children. For best effect, GABA should be taken in two to three divided doses.

Vitamin B₆ and L-glutamine

Vitamin B_6 supports the action of the enzymes that convert the amino acid L-glutamine to GABA in the brain. Anxious people may not have enough L-glutamine or they may have vitamin B_6 deficiencies, which render them deficient in the building blocks necessary for GABA production. GABA is one of the amino-acid-based neurotransmitters with inhibitory properties and decreases the rate of nerve cell firing. The recommended dose is 500 milligrams of L-glutamine three to four times daily between meals and 50–100 milligrams of vitamin B_6 twice daily. A cautionary note: excessive doses of vitamin B_6 may cause nerve damage that is usually reversible when vitamin B_6 is stopped.

Kava Kava

A search of the medical literature on kava kava supplementation found seventeen studies for anxiety and insomnia on approximately fourteen hundred patients. Of the seventeen studies, fifteen were positive. In my experience kava kava can have a calming effect on anxiety and irritability and can also help with sleep.

Several years ago I went through a painful time of grief, where for the first time in my life I experienced panic attacks and trouble sleeping. Of all the supplements I tried, kava kava helped me the most. Kava kava is recommended by some alternative medicine practitioners to calm anxiety, promote healthy sleep, and reduce the physical and emotional effects of stress. Kava kava is thought to work by enhancing the production of GABA in the brain. It comes from the root of a South Pacific pepper tree and is commonly used as a social and ceremonial drink in the Pacific Islands. The herb is so widely used that it is thought to be, in part, responsible for the laid-back lifestyle of the islands. My patients have reported the following relief after taking kava kava: being relaxed without feeling drugged; having less muscle tension; and feeling a sense of peace and contentment, increased sociability, and initial alertness followed by a feeling of drowsiness. Do not take kava kava if you are going to drive.

Kava kava is not the type of supplement, like fish oil, that you should take every day. At most, use it for three weeks and then take a week off. Kava kava use on a daily basis may harm the liver. Kava kava has known interactions with alcohol; barbiturates; monoamine oxidase inhibitor antidepressants; benzodiazepines; other tranquilizers and sleeping pills; anticoagulants; antiplatelet agents including aspirin, antipsychotics, and drugs used for treating Parkinson's disease; and drugs that suppress the central nervous system. Kava kava can exacerbate Parkinson's disease and increase muscle weakness and twitching. Women who are pregnant or breast-feeding should not take kava kava.

Standardized dosage is 150–300 milligrams, one to three times daily as needed for anxiety or nervousness, standardized to contain 30–70 percent kavalactones. Most clinical trials have used the German kava kava extract WS 1490. It may take four weeks before you notice improvement. Kava kava should not be taken for more than three months without a two-week rest period.

Valerian

A search of the medical literature on valerian supplementation found ten studies for anxiety and insomnia. Of the ten studies, six were positive and four were negative. In my experience, valerian can be a useful sleep aid.

Many patients find valerian to be remarkably helpful as a sleeping aid. It is a well-recognized herb with antianxiety properties that is used as a mild tranquilizer, sedative, and muscle relaxant. There are about 150 species of valerian widely distributed in temperate regions of the world. The active ingredient is found in a foul-smelling oil produced in the root of the plant. The Roman physician Galen wrote about the virtues of valerian, it has been associated with the term *all heal* in medical literature of the Middle Ages, and it is also used in Chinese and Indian medicine. It was used in the United States prior to the development of modern pharmaceuticals. This centuries-old treatment for insomnia has also been helpful for symptoms of nervousness, stress, increased emotional reactivity, pain, and agitation, and it also appears to decrease seizure frequency for epileptic patients. Valerian seems to work by enhancing the activity of the calming neurotransmitter, GABA. Studies have shown valerian to be helpful for many types of anxiety disorders and for people with performance anxiety and those who get stressed in daily situations like traffic. Valerian is available in capsules, tablets, liquids, tinctures, extracts, and teas. Most extracts are standardized to 0.8 percent valeric acids. Unlike prescription tranquilizers, valerian has a much lower potential for addiction and has been used to help people who are trying to decrease their use of prescription tranquilizers or sleeping pills. (Anyone using prescription sleeping pills or tranquilizers should decrease or stop their use only under the supervision of a physician.) Sometimes valerian can cause nervousness or drowsiness, so make sure you know how your body reacts to it before you drive or do other activities that require sustained attention. Do not take valerian with alcohol, barbiturates, or benzodiazepines. Valerian is not recommended for use during pregnancy or breast-feeding. The recommended dose of valerian is 150–450 milligrams in capsules or teas.

TYPE 2: PURE DEPRESSION

I use SAMe, which was discussed in chapter 6 (see page 94).

TYPE 3: MIXED ANXIETY AND DEPRESSION

I use a combination of the treatments in Types 1 and 2. So I may use SAMe (page 94) plus GABA (see page 92).

TYPE 4: OVERFOCUSED ANXIETY AND DEPRESSION

I use supplements that boost serotonin availability in the brain, such as St. John's wort (see page 90), 5-HTP (see page 92), or inositol.

INOSITOL

A search of the medical literature on inositol supplementation found sixteen studies for a wide range of problems, including depression, obsessive-compulsive disorder, panic disorder, ADHD, Alzheimer's disease, autism, binge-eating disorder, schizophrenia, and antidepressant augmentation. The results suggest that inositol has therapeutic effects in the spectrum of illness responsive to serotonin-enhancing medication, including depression, panic disorder, and obsessive-compulsive disorder and is not beneficial in schizophrenia, Alzheimer's ADHD, or autism.

Inositol is a natural biochemical found normally in the human brain. Some scientists think it is a member of the B vitamin family. It is reported to help neurons more efficiently use the neurotransmitter serotonin. In a well-designed study of thirteen patients who suffered from obsessive-compulsive disorder, 18 grams of inositol compared with placebo significantly reduced symptoms. Spinal fluid inositol has been reported to be low in depression. Another well-designed study of 12 grams of inositol in twenty-eight depressed patients showed impressive improvement when compared with sugar pills. Since many antidepressants are effective in patients with panic disorder, twenty-one patients with this severe anxiety disorder were given 12 grams on inositol per day for four weeks. Compared with placebo, inositol was more effective with minimal side effects. Studies on inositol were not effective for all conditions. For example, it did not help schizophrenia, ADD, or Alzheimer's disease. By its actions and the conditions it helps, inositol seems to act like mild Prozac, though with fewer of the side effects. Think of trying it if you are a worrier, have trouble letting go of negative thoughts, tend to be rigid or inflexible, or hold grudges. The dose is up to 18 grams a day.

Do not take St. John's wort, L-tryptophan, 5-HTP, or inositol with prescribed antidepressants, unless under the close supervision of your physician.

TYPE 5: TEMPORAL LOBE ANXIETY AND DEPRESSION

The supplements used to treat this type include GABA (see page 92) and fish oil, discussed in the last chapter (see page 97). A higher protein, lower carbohydrate diet may also be helpful. Eight studies from Johns Hopkins researchers found that a ketogenic diet (very low carb) significantly reduced seizure frequencies in children with epilepsy. Many physicians believe that sugar is both pro-inflammatory and pro-epileptic. This kind of diet is worth a try for this type.

TYPE 6: CYCLIC ANXIETY AND DEPRESSION

As I said for severe bipolar disorder, I often think that medication is important. Having stated that, many of my patients do not want to take lithium, anticonvulsant medication, or antipsychotic medication. One dentist I treated had clear bipolar disorder, where he didn't need to sleep; had racing thoughts; and became hypersexual, hyperreligious, and spent vast sums amount of money he didn't have. He felt terrible on lithium and wanted to try natural treatments exclusively. To my surprise he responded to high-dose fish oil at 10 grams a day. I think all of my bipolar patients should take fish oil. In addition I also think some bipolar patients may benefit from a ketogenic diet, as it has antiseizure qualities and we use anticonvulsants to treat bipolar disorder.

Another type of cyclic anxiety and depression is seasonal affective disorder, or winter blues. Prozac has been found in some studies to be effective; in other studies, bright light therapy has been found to be even more effective, as has vitamin D supplementation. Vitamin D deficiencies are becoming more common across North America. It is associated with both depression and pain syndromes. Vitamin D is made in our skin from sun exposure, but because we exercise less outdoors and use sunscreen, many people even in sunny climates are deficient in vitamin D. I recommend that my patients test their 25-hydroxy vitamin D levels and, if found to be low, take a vitamin D_3 supplement or walk in the sun every day for at least twenty minutes without sunscreen.

TYPE 7: UNFOCUSED ANXIETY AND DEPRESSION

The supplement for Type 7 is SAMe (see page 94). This type is associated with overall low activity in the brain. Another natural treatment I may recommend if there has been an infection, brain trauma, or environmental toxic exposure is hyperbaric oxygen treatment, which has been found on SPECT scans to boost overall blood flow to the brain.

Knowing the type of anxiety and depression you have is critical to getting the best help. One treatment does not fit everyone and I have found this type-specific approach to be the most clinically effective way to think about and treat anxiety and depression.

| 8 |

Natural Ways to Heal

MEMORY DISORDERS, INSOMNIA, AND PAIN

In this chapter I will discuss natural treatments for memory problems and insomnia, two very common causes that impair a magnificent mind. These disorders are increasing at alarming rates. Alzheimer's disease is expected to triple by 2050, and nearly sixty million Americans have significant sleep problems.

Memory Problems

Memory problems are typically considered an issue for the elderly. In my experience as both a child and adult psychiatrist, however, I have seen memory problems across the life span. They commonly appear in children with learning disorders, in teens who are using marijuana, adults with depression and substance abuse problems, and in the cognitive decline that occurs with aging and many forms of dementia. Memory is housed in a number of different areas of the brain, especially the prefrontal cortex, which is thought to be involved with short-term memory, and the hippocampus in the temporal lobes, which are structures critical to getting memories into long-term storage. In assessing memory problems it is important to consider the following.

- Medical causes, such as low thyroid or B_{12} deficiencies
- Medications that interfere with memory such as antianxiety medicines like Xanax or painkillers like OxyContin

- Brain illnesses, such as depression or ADD
- Early stages of Alzheimer's disease
- Excessive stress (stress hormones have been found to kill cells in the hippocampus)
- Lack of sleep, sleep apnea
- Postanesthesia (some people react negative to general anesthesia and complain of subsequent memory problems)
- Environmental toxins, such as finishing furniture or painting your car in a closed garage
- Drug and alcohol abuse

Of course, the first step in enhancing memory is to fix any of the problems listed above if possible. There are a number of important supplements that have been shown to be helpful in enhancing memory, including gingko biloba, phosphatidylserine, vinpocetine, and huperzine A. Medications that have been found to help memory include Namenda, Aricept, Exelon, and Reminyl.

GINGKO BILOBA

The prettiest brains I have seen are those on gingko. Gingko biloba, from the Chinese gingko tree, is a powerful antioxidant that is best known for its ability to enhance circulation, memory, and concentration. The best-studied form of gingko biloba is a special extract called EGB 761. It will be best if this is the form you use. EGB 761 has been studied in blood vessel disease, clotting disorders, depression, and Alzheimer's disease. A comparison in 2000 of all the published, placebo-controlled studies longer than six months for the gingko biloba extract EGB 761 versus Cognex, Aricept, and Exelon showed they all had similar benefits for mild to moderate Alzheimer's disease patients.

The most widely publicized study in the United States of gingko biloba was done by Dr. P. L. Le Bars and colleagues from the New York Institute for Medical Research, which appeared in the *Journal of the American Medical Association* in 1997. EGB 761 was used to assess the efficacy and safety in Alzheimer's disease and vascular dementia. This fifty-two-week multicenter study was conducted with patients who had mild to severe symptoms. Patients were randomly assigned to treatment with EGB 761 (120 milligrams a day) or placebo. Progress was monitored at twelve, twenty-six, and fifty-two weeks, and 202 patients finished the study. At the end of the study the authors concluded that EGB was safe and appears capable of stabilizing and, in a substantial number of cases, improving the cognitive performance and the social functioning of demented patients for six months to one year. Although modest, the changes induced by EGB were objectively measured and were of sufficient magnitude to be recognized by the caregivers.

Consider taking gingko if you are at risk for memory problems or stroke or suffer from low energy or decreased concentration. The usual effective dose is 60 to 120 milligrams twice a day. There is a small risk of bleeding in the body, and the dosages of other blood thinning agents being taken may sometimes need to be reduced.

PHOSPHATIDYLSERINE

Phosphatidylserine (PS) is a naturally occurring nutrient that is found in foods such as fish, green leafy vegetables, soy products, and rice. PS is a component of cell membranes. There are reports of the potential of PS to help improve age-related declines in memory, learning, verbal skills, and concentration. Positron emission tomography studies of patients who have taken PS show that it produces a general increase in metabolic activity in the brain. In the largest multicenter study to date of phosphatidylserine and Alzheimer's disease, 142 subjects ages 40–80 were given 200 milligrams of PS per day or placebo over a three-month period. Those treated with PS exhibited improvement on several items on the scales normally used to assess Alzheimer's status. The differences between placebo and experimental groups were small but statistically significant. Effective doses of PS have been reported to be 300 milligrams per day. The types of symptoms that have improved in placebo-controlled studies of cognitive impairment or dementia include loss of interest, reduced activities, social isolation, anxiety, memory, concentration, and recall. Milder stages of impairment tend to respond to PS better than more severe stages. With regard to depression in elderly individuals, Dr. M. Maggioni and colleagues studied the effects of oral PS (300 milligrams per day) versus placebo and noted significant improvements in mood, memory, and motivation after thirty days of PS treatment.

The typical dose of PS is 100–300 milligrams a day.

VINPOCETINE

Vinpocetine has been shown in a number of studies to help memory, especially for people who are at risk for heart disease or stroke. It also helps lower high homocysteine levels, which are also dangerous to your heart and brain.

Vinpocetine is derived from an extract of the common periwinkle plant (*Vinca minor*) and is used in Europe, Japan, and Mexico as a pharmaceutical agent for the treatment of blood vessel disease in the brain and cognitive disorders. In the United States it is available as a dietary supplement. It is sometimes called a nootropic, meaning "cognition enhancer," from the Greek *noos* for "mind." Vinpocetine selectively widens arteries and capillaries, increasing blood flow to the brain. It also combats accumulation of platelets in the blood, improving circulation. Because of these properties, vinpocetine was first used in the treatment of cerebrovascular disorders and acute memory loss owing to late-life dementia. But it also has a beneficial effect upon memory problems associated with normal aging.

There is evidence that vinpocetine may be useful for a wide variety of brain problems. A 1976 study found that vinpocetine immediately increased circulation in fifty people with abnormal blood flow. After one month of taking moderate doses of vinpocetine, patients showed improvement on memorization tests. After a prolonged period of vinpocetine treatment, cognitive impairment diminished significantly or disappeared altogether in many of the patients. A 1987 study of elderly patients with chronic cerebral dysfunction found patients who took vinpocetine performed better on psychological evaluations after the ninety-day trial period than did those who received a placebo. More recent studies have shown that vinpocetine reduces neural damage and protects against oxidative damage from harmful beta-amyloid buildup. In a multicenter, double-blind, placebo-controlled study lasting sixteen weeks, 203 patients described as having mild to moderate memory problems, including primary dementia, were treated with varying doses of vinpocetine or placebo. Significant improvement was achieved in the vinpocetine-treated group as measured by "global improvement" and cognitive performance scales. Three 10-milligram doses daily were as effective or more effective than three 20-milligram doses daily. Similarly good results were found in another double-blind clinical trial testing vinpocetine versus placebo in elderly patients with blood vessel and central nervous system degenerative disorders. Some preliminary research suggests that vinpocetine may also have some protective effects in both sight and hearing.

Reported adverse reactions include nausea, dizziness, insomnia, drowsiness, dry mouth, transient hypotension, transient fast heart rate, pressure headaches, and facial flushing. Slight reductions in both systolic and diastolic blood pressure with prolonged use of vinpocetine have been reported, as well as slight reductions in blood sugar levels.

The usual dosage is 10 milligrams a day.

HUPERZINE A

Huperzine A is a remarkable compound that has been studied in China for nearly twenty years. It appears to work by increasing the availability of acetylcholine, a major memory neurotransmitter in the brain, and preventing cell damage from excitotoxins. It has been shown to be effective in improving patients who suffered with cognitive impairment from several different types of dementia, including Alzheimer's disease and vascular dementia. Huperzine A has also been shown effective to help learning and memory in teenagers. Researchers divided thirty-four pairs of junior high school students complaining of memory problems into a huperzine A and placebo control group. The huperzine A group was given two 50-microgram capsules of huperzine A twice a day, while the placebo group was given two capsules of placebo (starch and lactose inside) twice a day for four weeks. At the end of trial, the huperzine A group's memory abilities were significantly superior to that of the placebo group.

The usual dosage is 50–100 micrograms twice a day.

Insomnia

Sleep plays an important role in the formation of memory and normal learning activities. Sleep problems disrupt your energy; interfere with performance at work or school; negatively impact relationships; and compound the symptoms of ADD, anxiety, and depression. People may suffer from trouble falling asleep, frequent awakenings during the night, or waking up too early and having trouble getting back to sleep. Sleep disorders can occur transiently in response to a stress, be a chronic problem, or occur in cycles. These patterns are sometimes helpful in diagnosing the underlying problem. For example, people who have periods where they do not need more than a few hours of sleep at night combined with increased energy levels and mood may indicate the presence of bipolar illness. People who have early morning awakenings and morning fatigue with better energy as the day goes on may have a form of depression.

Insomnia is one of the most common complaints in medical practices. The number of adults in America affected may exceed sixty million. Patients have many different opinions about what constitutes insomnia and many people who believe they are not sleeping enough are discovered to be sleeping more than the average person when evaluated by a sleep laboratory. Others who complain of insomnia don't realize that they are unintentionally doing something that disrupts their natural sleep cycle. For example, they may be drinking caffeine, eating sugar late in the day, drinking alcohol or smoking, taking naps during the day, exercising vigorously late in the evening, or staying up very late into the evening, all of which disrupt sleep cycles. Untreated medical and psychiatric illnesses and some medications also disturb sleep.

Transient insomnia is something that we all have experienced. Some of the most common causes of transient insomnia are jet lag, minor stress or excitement, shift work, and trying to sleep in a new environment. This kind of acute insomnia usually goes away on its own or when the stress is resolved. Herbal teas; self-relaxation; and avoiding caffeine, alcohol, evening exercise at least four hours before bedtime also help.

Chronic insomnia is more difficult to diagnose and to treat. By far, the most common reason people develop chronic insomnia is another underlying condition that disturbs their sleep cycle. Doctors have to spend time trying to sort out whether or not a patient has secondary insomnia and, if so, what is causing it. Here is a list of some of the conditions that may cause chronic insomnia:

- Medications. Many medications, including asthma medications, antihistamines, cough medicines, anticonvulsants, and many others, disturb sleep.
- Caffeine. Coffee, tea, chocolate, and some herbal preparations contain caffeine and will disrupt sleep.
- Alcohol, nicotine, and marijuana. Although these compounds initially promote sleep for some people, as they wear off, they have the reverse effect.
- Restless legs syndrome. This jerking motion of the legs or pedaling motion can drive a person's bed partner crazy (as well as the person who has it).
- Pregnancy, PMS, menopause, and perimenopause. During many of these hormonal transition times, a woman's sleep cycle may be disrupted every few minutes.
- Thyroid conditions. Too much thyroid activity can cause people to feel revved too high.
- Congestive heart failure. This can cause trouble breathing.
- Chronic pain conditions. Pain can keep a person awake.

- Untreated or undertreated psychiatric conditions. Conditions such as obsessive-compulsive disorder, depression, or anxiety will disrupt sleep patterns if left untreated.
- Alzheimer's disease. Dementia patients often "sundown" or rev up at night and wander.
- Chronic gastrointestinal problems. Reflux causes pain and discomfort.
- Benign prostatic hypertrophy. This condition causes many trips to the bathroom at night, disrupting a full night's sleep.
- Snoring and sleep apnea, which are more common in men than in women, can adversely affect both bed partners' sleep.

After all other reasons for insomnia have been ruled out or excluded a patient can be diagnosed with primary insomnia. A doctor may also decide to send her patient to a sleep disorders laboratory for observation of their sleep cycle. Sleep labs are able to monitor patients with overnight poly-somnography and other tests that provide information about a patient's heart rate, breathing rate, oxygen levels, leg movements, brain waves, and eye movements during their sleep cycle. The results of these tests help make the diagnosis of sleep apnea, insomnia, and restless legs syndrome.

TREATMENT

Acute or transient insomnia usually responds to the practice of good sleep habits (see the section Steps to Get a Good Night's Sleep Naturally on page 117). Sometimes the practice of good sleep habits is not enough, as may be the case for some shift workers who are unable to reset their sleep cycles on demand or for people experiencing grief reactions and who may suffer from insomnia for a few weeks to a few months during the acute grief phase. People who are hospitalized are another example of those for whom the practice of good sleep habits is not enough. In these and other cases, I prescribe supplements, such as valerian, kava kava, melatonin, or medication, such as Ambien, Lunesta, or Desyrel on a short-term basis. *Chronic insomnia* requires a complex approach to treatment. Any underlying cause of chronic insomnia must be identified and treated. It is most often caused by other underlying conditions, and of these, depression and anxiety, substance abuse, psychological stress, and medication side effects top the list.

Patients who have difficulty getting to sleep frequently complain that thoughts keep them up at night. Sometimes they are anxious and therefore worry at night or obsess about problems. Other times, people say they feel fine but just can't turn off their mind and quit thinking. Nighttime thinkers often benefit from a technique called imagery distraction. Imagery distraction is an elaborate and interesting mental image developed and focused on at bedtime in order to distract the insomniac from the other thoughts that keep them awake. Patients who practice this technique fall asleep more quickly and easily than those who don't. Self-hypnosis and other relaxation techniques such as progressive relaxation, deep breathing, and meditation also help.

Natural interventions may be helpful for either acute or chronic insomnia. For some people, 400–900 milligrams of valerian root improves sleep. It also has mild anxiety-reducing and muscle-relaxing effects. Results of several double-blind, placebo-controlled trials involving valerian for the treatment of insomnia showed that patients report improvement in the quality of their sleep and a decrease in the length of time it took for them to fall asleep when they used valerian. The benefits appeared to increase after several days of use. Higher doses of valerian were associated with reports of morning sedation.

MELATONIN

Melatonin is a hormone made in the brain that helps regulate other hormones and maintains the body's sleep cycle. Darkness stimulates the production of melatonin while light decreases its activity. Exposure to too much light in the evening or too little light during the day can disrupt the production of melatonin. Jet lag, shift work, and poor vision are some of the conditions that can disrupt melatonin production. Some researchers think that being exposed to low-frequency electromagnetic fields (from common household appliances) may disrupt melatonin levels. Melatonin is involved in the production of female hormones and influences menstrual cycles. Researchers also consider melatonin levels to be involved in aging. Children have the highest levels of melatonin, which diminish with age. The lower levels of melatonin may help explain why older adults generally need less sleep. Melatonin is a strong antioxidant, and there is some evidence that it may help strengthen the immune system.

Research suggests that taking melatonin may help sleep patterns in shift workers or those with poor vision. One study found that melatonin helps prevent jet lag, particularly in people who cross five or more time zones. Melatonin is more effective than placebo in decreasing the time required to fall asleep, increasing the number of hours sleeping and improving alertness. Melatonin may be helpful for children with learning disabilities who suffer from insomnia. One study of postmenopausal women found that melatonin improved depression and anxiety. Studies of people with depression and panic disorder have shown low levels of melatonin. People who suffer winter blues or seasonal affective disorder also have lower than normal melatonin levels. Melatonin causes a surge in the neurotransmitter serotonin, which may help explain why it is helpful in both sleep and depression. Although taking melatonin does not help the primary symptoms of ADD, it does seem to help the sleep disturbances common in these children.

The best approach for dosing melatonin is to begin with very low doses. In children start with 0.3 milligrams per day, always at bedtime, and raise it slowly. In adults start with 1 milligram an hour before bedtime. You can increase it to 6 milligrams.

Steps to Get a Good Night's Sleep Naturally

- Get stimulants out of your system well before bedtime. If you take a stimulant for ADD or any other condition, try to take your last dose by early afternoon so it wears off before bedtime. Sometimes people with hyperactivity actually benefit from a stimulant before bedtime to calm them down so they can sleep. Stimulating antidepressants like Wellbutrin may need to be taken before 4 P.M. as well. Nicotine should be eliminated and caffeine should not be consumed for six to eight hours before bedtime. Caffeine is found in many foods including teas, coffee, and chocolate.

- Don't take naps! This is one of the biggest mistakes people with insomnia make. They feel tired during the day, take naps, and thereby compound their nighttime sleep cycle disruption.

- Exercise during the day is very beneficial for insomnia. However, it should be at least four hours before bedtime. Vigorous exercise late in the evening often energizes people and keeps them awake.

- Alcohol, pain medication, and marijuana also disrupt sleep. These compounds may cause initial drowsiness, but as the body metabolizes them, they interrupt sleep. Avoid trying to fall asleep using these drugs.

- Plan for transition time. Almost everyone needs time to relax and unwind before going to sleep. Put aside busy or intense work and focus on calming activities before lying down.

- Don't use your bed for anything other than sexual activity or sleeping. If you can't sleep and are not engaged in sexual or sensual contact with your partner, get out of bed. Do not work, watch TV, read, write, or lie around awake in bed.

- Move the clock. Clock watching and trying too hard to go to sleep will cause more anxiety and aggravate your problem.

- Establish a regular sleeping schedule and stay on it, even on weekends. Changing sleep patterns by staying up too late or oversleeping on weekends is enough to trigger cycle disruptions in sensitive people.

- Pay attention to your environment. Your bedroom should be comfortable. Control the temperature and light.

- Reading might help you fall asleep but don't read anything too exciting, scary, or anxiety provoking. This applies to TV watching as well.

- A mixture of warm milk, a tablespoon of vanilla (not imitation vanilla, the real stuff), and a tablespoon of sugar can be very helpful. This increases serotonin to your brain and helps you sleep.

- If sugar makes you jittery, gives you an energy boost, or if you have ADD, you need to avoid it beginning in the afternoon. You should avoid starches as well, as they turn to sugar after you eat them.

- Sound therapy can induce a very peaceful mood and help relaxation. Some people like nature sounds; others prefer soft music, wind chimes, or even fans. Our clinic makes a sleep tape with a special sound machine that produces sound waves at the same frequency as a sleeping brain. The tape is played at bedtime and helps the brain "tune in" to a brain wave sleep state, which encourages a peaceful sleep.

- Sexual activity releases many natural hormones, releases muscle tension, and boosts people's sense of well-being. People with healthy sex lives usually sleep better.

- Meditation, massage, and warm baths are also very relaxing.

I also help my patients using hypnosis and teaching them self-hypnosis. When I was an intern at the Walter Reed Army Medical Center in Washington, D.C., many of my patients wanted sleeping pills. As you can imagine, it was hard to sleep in a busy, noisy medical center. Before I gave them sleeping pills, however, I asked if I could hypnotize them first to see if that would help. Almost all of them agreed. My first professional papers came from using hypnosis for sleep. One of my patients, a decorated World War II hero, had advanced Parkinson's disease, and in a hypnotic trance his tremor went away. When I told my attending neurologist about it the next morning, he thought I was crazy. So I repeated the exercise in front of him and it became my first professional paper. When I did this for an army chaplain who was in the hospital with a heart arrhythmia, his heart rhythm normalized. When I told my attending cardiologist about what happened the next morning, he thought I was nuts, so I repeated the exercise in front of him and it became my second professional paper. Hypnosis and self-hypnosis are very powerful tools to help gain mastery over your own mind and can be helpful for sleep and other things as well. You can obtain a hypnotic audiotape from the Amen Clinics' website or go to a trained hypnotherapist.

Sleep is critical. Use the techniques listed here to help. Be persistent. If one technique doesn't work for you, don't give up. Try others.

Pain

Pain is one of the most difficult and debilitating symptoms that people suffer. Chronic pain affects everything in a negative way, such as sleep, mood, memory, and concentration. Our scans have taught me that the use of chronic pain medications, such as Vicodin or OxyContin, is harmful to brain function. Long-term use of these medications makes the brain look like people who drink too much.

Looking at these scans caused me to develop an interest in alternative treatments for pain that did not leave a toxic effect, such as fish oil, acupuncture, music therapy, and hypnosis.

From a psychiatrist's standpoint, I have also learned that pain and depression tend to go hand in hand. And that using some antidepressant medications, such as Cymbalta, or antidepressant natural supplements, such as SAMe, can be very helpful for some pain syndromes.

Another issue that came up through looking at scans is that sometimes a person's brain can get stuck on the pain.

Sam was admitted to the hospital after a suicide attempt. He was a police officer who had been in a car accident chasing a criminal. He had six back surgeries and was tired of living in pain. When I scanned his brain I found too much activity in the front part of his brain. This is the same pattern we often see with people who have obsessive-compulsive disorder or people who get stuck on negative thoughts or negative behaviors. Based on the scan I put him on the supplement 5-HTP that boosts serotonin to calm down this part of the brain, in addition to fish oil. A month later he told me that he felt much better. "I still hurt," he said, "but I don't think about the pain all the time."

Again, there are many natural ways to help the brain. Of course, you should talk to your doctor. If he or she does not know much about natural supplements, as many of us were never taught about them in school, sometimes a naturopath, a nutritionist, or a chiropractor may have information to help you.

One other thought on pain: try getting rid of all of the artificial sweeteners in your diet. When I was thirty-seven I had arthritis. My knees, hands, and fingers hurt a lot. I had trouble getting up off the floor after sitting for a while. As part of developing a brain-healthy life, I got rid of the diet sodas. Within a month, my pain went away. I don't think artificial sweeteners do that to everyone, but if you hurt, it might be something to consider.

PART TWO

A MAGNIFICENT
MIND
MAKES YOUR
DREAMS A REALITY

|9|

Ignite Your Passion

——

LIGHT UP THE BRAIN CIRCUITS THAT DRIVE SUCCESS

Passion, it lies in all of us, sleeping . . . waiting . . . and though unwanted . . . unbidden . . . it will stir . . . open its jaws and howl. It speaks to us . . . guides us . . . passion rules us all, and we obey. What other choice do we have? Passion is the source of our finest moments. The joy of love . . . the clarity of hatred . . . and the ecstasy of grief. It hurts sometimes more than we can bear. If we could live without passion maybe we'd know some kind of peace . . . but we would be hollow . . .

Empty rooms shuttered and dank. Without passion we'd be truly dead.

—JOSH WHEDON, American screenwriter and producer

Passionate living is the soul of success and the hallmark of a magnificent mind. Without passion, little of consequence happens. Passion sparks the chemical factories deep in the brain, lighting the emotional fires that turn us on. We know when we have passion, because it drives us to love, care, want, need, crave, have to have, suffer, and create. Passion is the force behind the momentum of our lives, which can be loving or hateful, money driven or charitable, magnanimous or grudging. Passion can provide the stimulus for becoming a candidate for Congress or an admired gardener.

Passion causes us to work a hundred hours a week building a business or it can keep us studying into our thirties to become a trauma surgeon. Passion may motivate some to travel hundreds or even thousands of miles each week to be in the arms of a new love or it may push others to train relentlessly for the Ironman Triathlon in Hawaii. Passion gives meaning and purpose to our lives. A magnificent mind requires directed passion, whether in raising healthy children, making a marriage amazing, thriving in your profession, or excelling at a hobby.

In the Merriam-Webster's dictionary the first definition of passion is to suffer. Do you love what you do so much so that you are willing to suffer for it? If so, you have passion. I love the brain SPECT imaging work that we do at the Amen Clinics. It is clearly one of my passions, lasting more than eighteen years. It grabbed my attention from the moment I ordered the first scan. Our work has given me tremendous joy, but I have also taken consistent, long-term grief from some of my colleagues for doing it. In the early years I was called everything from a snake oil salesman, quack, huckster, and a fraud. In 1997, after a complaint filed by one of my colleagues, I was investigated by the California Medical Board for a year for doing the imaging work in my clinic. If you do anything outside the standard of care in the medical community, the board can take away your license to practice medicine. Psychiatrists doing brain imaging work at the time was new and not part of the standard of care. Ultimately the medical board absolved me, and for a while I became one of its consultants, but it was one of the most anxiety-filled, emotionally painful years of my life. But it was my passion for the work that helped me stay the course, even in times of turmoil. Soon, it will be grounds for malpractice *not* to order brain scans in complex psychiatric cases. If I did not have passion for the imaging work, I would have given up the idea at the first sign of trouble or criticism. That would have left me as a mediocre doctor, allowing the opinions of others to run my practice and my life. Changing paradigms require passion.

Where does true passion originate? Is it in the brain, mind, society, spirit, or a combination? Why do some people have it, pushing the limits of their lives, while others are stuck in a rut of boredom and mediocrity, allowing others to direct their lives? Why does passion often get out of control and ruin lives? Can Parkinson's disease, ADHD, and addictions teach us anything about passion? Are there brain-based secrets to boosting passionate living? This chapter will explore these questions and help you develop the passion that feeds a magnificent mind.

Understanding the Seeds of Passion

As mentioned earlier, one of the most helpful concepts I learned in medical school was to always evaluate patients from a biological-psychological-social-spiritual perspective. In this model, we look at the underlying biology or physiology, psychology or mind-set, social situation or group setting, and the deeper spiritual meaning of patients' lives. By examining each of these areas you are less likely to miss important information, plus as a physician, you are not just eliminating symptoms or treating disease states, but you are nurturing and healing whole people.

It is essential in understanding passion and motivation to take a biological-psychological-social-spiritual approach and look at issues related to mind (psychology), social situation (the present moment and the groups we live in), spirit (our conscience, inner sense of knowing, and deepest sense of meaning and purpose), and biology (the physical functioning of the brain).

The Mind of Passion

The mind of passion is often influenced by significant past life events, such as the following.

- Having a mother who loved to read to you, so you developed a passion for books
- Having grown up in poverty and hating it so much that you developed a passion for security and money
- Having a lot of men give you attention for the way your body looked, so you developed a passion for working out (and maybe a subsequent eating disorder, an example of passion gone wrong)
- Having a parent be struck with Alzheimer's disease, so you developed a passion to prevent the illness in yourself and those you love
- Meeting a partner who unconsciously reminds you of a beloved parent, so you develop a passion for the relationship
- Having a child die of cancer, so you subsequently develop a passion to raise money for cancer research

There are many ways our past experiences influence our passions and drives today, from the relationships we had with our parents, coaches, teachers, and friends growing up, to the experiences we had with the sports we played or the hobbies we pursued, to our earliest sexual turn-ons, to our biggest fears and greatest joys. The factors that turned us on or off during our formative years continue to pervade and influence our lives. Significant emotional events imprinted memory traces that change the brain. If powerful enough, they can still influence your thoughts and feelings. For example, when I was in sixth grade, I performed my first comedic scene as a young Yiddish mother trying to get her toddler to eat a bowl of soup. The class laughed at just the right moments. At the end of my routine I had a warm, glowing feeling inside. It primed the pump for my desire to perform in front of others, which in turn encouraged me to be on the speech team in college, which in turn, primed me further to love presenting to groups today. As I was writing this book, I was invited to speak in front of nine thousand people in Monterrey, Mexico, at the World Conference of Spirituality, Knowledge and Integral Health in a huge arena. The experience lit up the same brain circuits primed in sixth grade.

Below is an account from one of my patients that shows how life experience can drive passion. Roger, a successful businessman, helped start a nonprofit agency that funds SPECT scans, evaluations, and treatment for people who cannot afford it, especially those who have ADD. Roger and the agency he helped to start, Recovery Assistance Foundation, have changed the lives of hundreds of people.

One of my passions is to help people with ADD. It originates from my life experiences, values, and compassion for those who are suffering when help is available. It began with our hyperactive son who was diagnosed in the first grade with ADD and treated with Ritalin, which was a godsend for helping with his focusing and impulse control problems. We were assured that he would outgrow this problem in his teen years when medication was discontinued.

In the early 1990s articles appeared that stated that ADD can be a life-long condition. This led us on a search for more information, and more important, the discovery of an expert, Dr. Daniel Amen of the Amen Clinic. We were surprised to learn that not only was our son still afflicted but the rest of the family, including me, had the inherited disorder as well. With proper treatment, I found instant help for my lack of concentration, mood swings, habit of interrupting others, and verbal raging that had gone on for years. The entire family began to understand just how much we were affected to our detriment in our personal lives and relationships.

With appropriate counsel and treatment we began to function and feel like "normal" people. Understanding how much we had struggled with a real handicap, rather than a character defect, led to new feelings of self-worth. The total effect was life changing!

Going from suffering to a solution turned me into an evangelist for finding a way to get help for people who needed it. Working together with Gaylen and Linda Bronson, we started Recovery Assistance Foundation, which has now changed the lives of hundreds of people.

The Social Context of Passion

Passion also occurs in the context of the present moment or the current social situation or group you find yourself in. For example, if you have recently fallen in love, most things in life revolve around your new relationship. New love, as we will see, is as powerful as cocaine. If, on the other hand, you have recently split up from your significant other, your passion may be about moving on, Internet dating, or if you are ill fated, hating your ex or getting back together with him though you know he doesn't want you anymore. If you have children a certain age, the passions may revolve around their activities or helping them get a great education. After retirement you may develop a passion for travel. If struck by an illness, passion may be focused on survival. Passions are influenced not only by our past lives but also by the issues and people we face right now, our current relationships, stresses, and physical and emotional health issues. The speaking opportunity in Mexico gave me the passion to learn at least some Spanish to prepare for my lecture.

The Spirituality of Passion

Our spiritual beliefs are intimately involved with passion. Your beliefs in a higher power, how you see yourself in the universe, your level of conscience, your overall sense of meaning and purpose, all contribute to the passions you develop. New evidence is emerging that the brain is hardwired for God.

When I was asked to speak in Mexico by psychiatrist Jose Castillo Ruiz, one of the conference organizers, he told me that I could not talk about sex. He had read and used several of my books in his clinical practice, including *Healing ADD* and *Healing the Hardware of the Soul.* My book *Sex on the Brain* had been recently published and I was in the middle of a publicity tour when he invited me to speak at the conference, so I wanted to talk about it in my lecture.

"We are a very Catholic, conservative country," he insisted. "Better to stick to safer topics." He was very clear. Stay away from sexual topics and controversy.

At noon on the day of the conference, I gave my lecture in the Monterrey Arena, to thousands of people, on my book *Healing the Hardware of the Soul.* Just months before Beyoncé, Gwen Stefani, and Andrea Bocelli had been on the same stage. I was inspired by the opportunity. It was the largest group I had ever spoken to live. My conference hosts were wonderful. Beforehand everyone kept asking me if I wasn't going to be nervous speaking in front of so many people. "No," I replied, "when you love your work, the passion overrides anxiety." I did have them, however, help me with my Spanish. I started my lecture by saying in Spanish, *"Queridos amigos mios. Viva Monterrey,"* to a large cheer from the audience. "My dear friends, hail Monterrey." My lecture was great fun and well received. I behaved myself and did not talk about sex.

Late in the afternoon I was on a panel with a psychiatrist from Harvard and four religious mystics from around the world. They were from the Catholic, Jewish, and Islamic faiths. I had no idea ahead of time what questions we would be asked. Dr. Castillo Ruiz told me not to worry, that they would be asking us questions from the audience. Being seated onstage at a long table in front of thousands of people with the arena darkened and the bright lights flooding our faces was a strangely isolating experience. I felt alone with my thoughts.

The first question was about the feeling of mysticism and spiritual experience. I would go last. The mystics all talked about the ecstasy of mystical experience. Three of the religious men compared it to sexual experiences. One said that the Song of Solomon, an erotic love story, was the holiest book in the Bible. I started to get nervous. The door to talk about spirituality, sexuality, and the brain was wide open. Did I dare go through it? A priest from Spain, Father Santiago Guerra, talked about St. John of the Cross, a Carmelite religious mystic from his country in the sixteenth century, who wrote religious poetry detailing his mystical experiences in a highly sexualized way.

> *Upon my flowering breast*
> *which I kept wholly for him alone,*
> *there he lay sleeping,*
> *and I caressing him . . .*

When the breeze blew from the turret,
as I parted his hair,
it wounded my neck
with its gentle hand,
suspending all my senses.

I abandoned and forgot myself,
laying my face on my Beloved;
all things ceased;
I went out from myself,
leaving my cares.

—St. John of the Cross from *The Dark Night of the Soul*

As it got near my turn, I wrote several notes. Then I looked at Dr. Castillo Ruiz, who was engrossed in the dialogue. I knew he did not expect me to remain silent. When it was my turn, the moderator asked me if there was a neuroscience connection to spiritual experience.

Hesitantly I started, "According to some researchers, the right side of the brain, especially the area of the temporal lobe, underneath your temple and behind your eyes"—with my right hand I pointed to that area on my head—"has been implicated in spiritual experience. Michael Persinger, a research psychologist from Laurentian University in Canada, noted that when he gave low volt electrical stimulation to this area people had religious or spiritual experiences. They often felt the presence of God or a supernatural being in the room." I made eye contact with Dr. Castillo Ruiz, who was sitting in the front row. He smiled at me when our eyes met. Safe so far. "Okay," I thought to myself. "Here goes."

"Religious experience and sexual experience, just like the type discussed by my mystic colleagues, occur in the same general area of the brain." Dr. Castillo Ruiz now looked nervous.

"In a fascinating study from Finland, using brain SPECT technology to look at blood flow and activity patterns, the same study we use in our clinics, the outside of the right temporal lobe also lights up when women have orgasms, when they are brought to sexual ecstasy. Every other part of their brain decreased in activity during orgasm. It was only the right temporal lobe, or 'God area,' that lit up. In my new book, *Sex on the Brain,* I theorized that sexual ecstasy, in fact, can be a spiritual experience. Haven't you ever wondered"—here I paused for a few seconds—"why she cries 'Oh God, oh God' when you make her happy? I have wondered. Why doesn't she cry, 'Oh Daniel, oh Daniel,' when I am the one doing all the work?"

As I was talking, my words were being simultaneously translated into Spanish. I wondered if the audience would understand the meaning of what I was saying. Then a moment later as I heard the translator chuckling in my ear, the arena roared with laughter. Dr. Castillo Ruiz laughed as well and also looked relieved.

"Great lovers," I continued, "often use similar techniques as religious leaders to induce a state of romantic ecstasy, such as music, candles, poetry, and communion. Passionate loving is a godly experience. Spirituality and sexuality and the brain are tied together with passion. Great lovers induce mystical experiences." The connection between spirituality and sexuality may be one of the reasons we see so many religious leaders get themselves into trouble with sexual issues. If similar areas of the brain are involved, it takes healthy functioning of the brain's supervisor, prefrontal cortex, to keep impulses in check.

I have seen religious passion dramatically change people's lives in a positive way. When I was nineteen years old I became involved with Teen Challenge, a Christian group whose mission was to help drug addicts. Started on the streets of New York City by Assembly of God minister David Wilkerson, he dealt with the homeless, prostitutes, and criminals who were addicted to hard-core drugs like cocaine, heroin, or methamphetamine. I witnessed many drug addicts completely change after they gave their lives to Christ. They began to heal by making a spiritual commitment, becoming part of a church, and reading and applying the Bible to their lives. The passion of their beliefs overtook their drive to use drugs.

If, like me, you grew up in a deeply religious home, you often define passion outside of yourself, as making a positive difference in the world. This can lead you to serve others, or it can leave you in an emotional bind, deeply conflicted and ambivalent, especially if you are not honest with yourself about what you truly love and want. Many people have a passion to serve God and make a positive difference in life, while at the same time they have a burning desire for connection and sexual gratification. Lying to yourself about your passions can get you into trouble. It is better to be honest about your passions and motivations and find healthy ways to satisfy them, rather than repress them so much they come out in unhealthy ways.

The Brain of Passion

Ultimately, passion is felt, processed, and directed in the brain. We are hard-wired for passion. There are neural circuits that, when activated, move us off the sofa toward our psychological, social, and spiritual goals. It is important to understand four brain systems that work together to form the passion and motivation circuit in the brain. Three have been discussed before:

- Prefrontal cortex (PFC)—Helps with judgment, impulse control, and supervising and controlling our passions
- Deep limbic system (DLS)—Involved with mood, emotional tone, and emotional memory
- Basal ganglia (BG)—Integrate feeling and movement, also involved with drive and pleasure
- Ventral tegmental area (VTA)—Produces the neurotransmitter dopamine, which is involved with saliency or how important something is to do. When something is highly salient we must do it.

Dopamine is the chemical activated by passion and love. Love is a drug and works in the same place in the brain as cocaine, the BG. A study by anthropologist Dr. Helen Fisher demonstrated dopamine's connection to new love. Her research group recruited forty subjects who had just fallen in love—twenty who stayed in love and the other half who had recently split up. She put these people into an MRI tube with a photo of their sweetheart and one of an acquaintance. Each subject looked at the sweetheart photo for thirty seconds, then, after a distraction task, at the acquaintance photo for another thirty seconds. They switched back and forth for twelve minutes. The result was a picture of a passionate brain. There was increased activity in the right VTA. This is the part of the brain where dopamine cells project into other areas of the brain, including the BG, part of the brain's system for reward and motivation and the limbic system, involved with emotion. The sweetheart photos, but not the acquaintance photos, caused this to happen.

Psychiatrist Nora Volkow, director of the National Institute of Drug Abuse, performed studies in which she tagged cocaine with a radioactive isotope to see where it worked in the brain. It lit up the BG, part of this reward circuit. Interestingly, the ADHD drug Ritalin did the same thing. The reason cocaine is addictive and Ritalin typically is not is that cocaine has greater power and is in and out of the brain quickly, causing people to want more.

Ritalin has a weaker response that lasts longer. Yet both cocaine and Ritalin increase motivation. Cocaine may increase motivation for sex, while Ritalin often increases motivation to get your homework finished.

In a healthy brain, there is good emotional control by a competent PFC but also plenty of emotion, drive, and saliency from the DLS to get things done. Figure 9.1 shows a healthy passion circuit. Healthy dopamine levels can drive passion, especially in the context of good activity in the PFC, which acts as the reins so you do not get out of control. Low levels of dopamine are associated with certain problems that rob us of motivation, such as Parkinson's disease, or cause erratic inspiration, such as in ADHD. Addictions occur when passion circuits take over control. These conditions are very instructive in our search for understanding the brain's role in passion and how to modulate it.

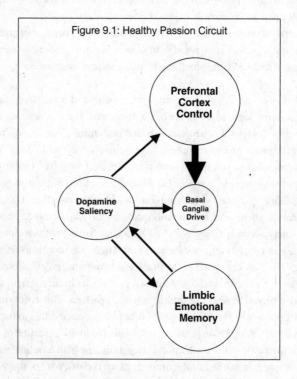

Figure 9.1: Healthy Passion Circuit

Prefrontal Cortex Control

Dopamine Saliency

Basal Ganglia Drive

Limbic Emotional Memory

The Passion Thief: Parkinson's Disease

First described by the English physician James Parkinson in the early 1800s, Parkinson's disease is a chronic, progressive disease that is linked to a destruction of the dopamine-producing cells in a part of the BG known as the substantia nigra. Initially, Parkinson's disease is a movement disorder characterized by a resting tremor, muscle rigidity, slowness, impaired balance, and a shuffling gait. As it progresses, the face becomes unable to express emotion and people often become depressed and unmotivated.

Several years ago I received a call from one of my childhood friends. His father, Carl, had been diagnosed with Parkinson's and was experiencing personality changes. The family was very concerned about him. Until his retirement, Carl was an accomplished, active, talkative, kind man. Now, all he wanted to do was stay home. He had no motivation and wanted his wife to completely wait on him while he watched television all day long. He particularly liked scary movies, Jerry Springer, and Dr. Phil, which shocked his family. When I asked him about these shows, his emotionless face came to life, his eyes lit up, and his smile became broad. He liked the fighting and the drama. They were exciting to him. They made him feel alive. Parkinson's disease took this sweet, considerate, brilliant man and turned him into a complete stranger to his family. These were shows he would never have watched before. Now, he thrived on watching people throw chairs, loved learning about siblings who were having sex with each other, and enjoyed watching Dr. Phil chew people out for not choosing the right behavior.

There is more to the dopamine story. In a sad twist of fate, several of the medications used to treat Parkinson's disease by increasing dopamine availability in the brain, including Mirapex and Requip, have come under fire for increasing pleasure or reward sensations too much, causing people to have affairs or start compulsive gambling. Dr. Max Wells alleged in court that his medication caused a gambling addiction that made him a habitual high roller at Las Vegas casinos where he lost $7 million by late 2005 and another $7 million by January of 2006. Dr. Wells had originally been taking Mirapex for his Parkinson's, but when he noticed his occasional recreational gambling had become more serious, he told his doctor that he thought that drug might be the cause. His doctor changed his medication to Requip and increased the dosage. Although Wells then began running up massive gambling losses, amassing some $1.2 million in debts, his wife remained unaware of the problem since she was not present when the losses occurred. When Dr. Wells finally told his wife about the losses, the problem was brought to the attention of his physician. As soon as Requip was stopped, so did the compulsive gambling. The behavior changes seen in some Parkinson's disease patients whose therapy includes dopamine boosters can be wide ranging. On the mild side, some start buying lottery tickets and nothing more. Others, however, have been known to develop serious obsessive-compulsive disorders as well as aggressive sexual impulses, overeating, medication abuse, or pathological gambling. A balance of dopamine is best; too little and there is no motivation, too much and we can go nuts.

Erratic Inspiration: ADHD

Parkinson's disease usually occurs after the age of fifty. An example of a low dopamine state that starts early in life and often persists into adulthood is ADHD. First described by English physician George Still in 1902, ADHD is characterized by short attention span, distractibility, disorganization, procrastination, and poor internal supervision or judgment. It is often, although not always, accompanied by hyperactivity and impulsivity. Dopamine gene abnormalities are common in ADHD and medications that increase dopamine availability in the brain, such as stimulants like Ritalin or Adderall, are used to treat it. In addition, ADHD is associated with low activity in the prefrontal cortex. Low dopamine levels are associated with low PFC activity as well. When the VTA does not produce enough dopamine, it cannot drive the BG-PFC circuit into appropriate action.

The hallmark symptom of ADHD is difficulty paying attention. But interestingly, people with ADHD do not have trouble paying attention to everything. They struggle with regular, routine, everyday attention, such as for schoolwork, homework, paperwork, or chores, the stuff that makes life work. They die in boring lectures and are pained by long meetings, and traditional church services seem like they go on forever. However, for events that are new, novel, highly stimulating, interesting, frightening, passionate, or filled with love, people with ADHD can often pay attention just fine. These areas have their own intrinsic dopamine. Again, love is a drug. This phenomenon often fools parents, physicians, and bosses.

An ADHD teenager may be struggling in school getting mostly C's, D's, or F's, while in one or two classes he is thriving. A parent, seeing the erratic grades, often makes the wrong assumption and gets upset at the teen, saying, "I know you are smart. Look at the A in history. You are just lazy in your other classes." Yet if the teen loved history or his history teacher, the love supplied the dopamine for his increased performance. He needs love or excitement to pay attention.

Likewise, many physicians make the same fundamental mistake in diagnosing ADHD. They ask parents if children have the attention span to watch

TV or play video games. Some children with severe ADHD can watch TV or play video games for six hours straight. When the parents say yes, the physician dismisses the diagnosis. When considering ADHD in teens or adults, doctors ask if they can pay attention. Almost all say yes. The insightful ones will say, "Yes, if I am interested!" The physician will then dismiss the idea of an ADHD diagnosis even when flagrant problems are present. It is critical to ask about specific attention for regular, routine everyday tasks and to ask those around the ADHD person. You often get a very different answer.

At work, employees who have ADHD often pose a frustrating challenge for supervisors. Many people with ADHD are bright, social, and insightful. They often excel at sales or creative jobs. Yet when asked to do simple paperwork or complete a project on time, the ADHD employee struggles. Unknowing, supervisors see the behavior problems as willful and insubordinate and often terminate potentially great employees.

Many people with ADHD are conflict or excitement seeking. Without enough dopamine to boost their brains, they use external stimuli, such as fighting with siblings, parents, or lovers; stirring up trouble at work; going to scary movies or to strip clubs; engaging in serial Internet dating; exposing themselves to risky sexual practices; or edgy driving to light up their lives. I once treated an ADHD man who was a professional race-car driver. He said he never felt more alive than when he was on the starting line of a race.

I often see this pattern in teenage girls with ADHD who come to one of my clinics after a suicide attempt from feeling devastated over the loss of a romantic relationship. The next week they often feel better because someone new has shown interest in them. The following week they may be even better still because they have hooked up with the new guy. Then the trouble begins. The next week there is often fighting and turmoil in the new relationship. And the following week she is often devastated because they broke up. Yet the next week she may have a new guy on her radar, so she feels better, and the cycle starts again. Whether the behavior is luring, hooking up, fighting, or breaking up, the effect on the brain is the same. There is drama and stimulation. When the pattern is uncovered and people become aware (in Sigmund Freud's language, making the unconscious conscious), healing can start, as long as appropriate stimulation is given to the PFC with proper treatment.

Passion Circuits Out of Control: Addictions

Addictive disorders also teach us about passion and motivation. These disorders cause people to feel and act out of control. They work on the same circuitry in the brain as love but in a very destructive way. The drugs or behaviors that light the passion circuits are strangely reinforcing and grab a person by the throat, whether it is alcohol, drugs, sex, gambling, or eating. Robert Downey Jr., who struggled with a prolonged, severe drug addiction, once said it was like having a loaded gun to your head, demanding you to stop, then doing it anyway, despite the consequences. You would rather risk death than to be without the high.

According to Minneapolis sex addictionologist Mark Laaser, Ph.D., "the arousal template" underlies many addictions. In this model it is important to understand the first addictive experience. Cocaine addicts often say they are, unsuccessfully, chasing their first high. Gambling addicts usually have one big win that flips the switch and the chase for the next big win is on. Sex addicts often have a powerful first experience that they start pursuing with great energy and motivation. If the experience was unusual they may even develop a fetish or paraphilia.

When low activity in the PFC accompanies a powerful arousal template, people lose control over their behaviors. Low activity in the PFC can be from a brain injury, ADHD, environmental toxin, or sedating substance such as alcohol. Figure 9.2 demonstrates what happens during an addiction.

Love is a drug, whether it appears in the form of a specific history teacher, Jerry Springer, Dr. Phil, alcohol, cocaine, women's running shoes, or horror movies. When someone who struggles with low dopamine levels is in a job or relationship they love, they have fewer problems at work. I have even seen ADHD people need less medication for jobs they are passionate about, rather than jobs that bore them. I often tell my ADHD patients to choose professions they love, rather than ones they think will make them a lot of money, as they will be more likely to be successful. Love for God can help break an addiction, as we saw with Teen Challenge. In the context of a healthy PFC, the secret to passion is to do what you love. How do you find what you love? What are the steps to discovering your passions?

Maximum Fun: Lighting the Passion Circuits in a Healthy Way

On the crystal clear, breezy shores of Lake Tahoe in early August, my nephew Matt married his high school sweetheart, Charly. They were in their early twenties, finishing their last years of college and starting a life together they hoped would last forever. As the upbeat ceremony finished, rather than play the traditional wedding recessional song, Matt and Charly walked out of the service to the theme music from Rocky. Matt was the champion. He got the

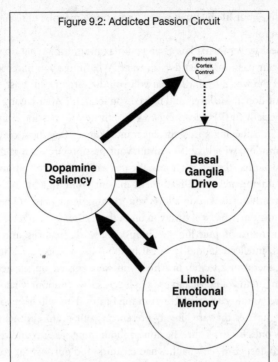

Figure 9.2: Addicted Passion Circuit

In this diagram you see the PFC is weak, so it has little control over unbridled passions that drive behaviors. Addiction actually changes the brain in a negative way, making it harder to apply the brakes to harmful behaviors. In the non-addicted brain, the PFC is constantly assessing the value of incoming information and the appropriateness of the planned response, applying inhibitory control as needed. In the addicted brain, this control circuit becomes impaired through drug abuse and loses much of its inhibitory power over the circuits that drive response to stimuli deemed salient.

girl of his dreams. Later, as I sat with my family at the reception, looking out at the deep blue lake as the sun sparkled diamonds of light on the water, Dusty, the best man, got up to give a toast. He read from his notes. He said all of the usual things best men say at weddings. Then he turned to Matt and said, "You once told me that you start each morning by thinking of the maximum amount of fun you can have that day, then spend the next sixteen or so hours making it happen. I have never forgotten what you said. Maximum fun. You live your life just that way. I know being married to Charly will be maximum fun."

In a healthy way, what has given you maximum fun? What do you love? What is your passion? What do you want? What must you have? What will you travel the world to find? What will you die for? In your past, what has raised your dopamine levels and moved you forward? After having a healthy brain, especially the PFC, learning how to activate your passion circuits is the next step in achieving a magnificent mind. You activate these circuits with intense emotion, with love. To activate your passion circuits it is important to know what has turned you on in the past. This will help you understand the arousal templates that already exist in your brain. In addition, knowing what currently turns you on allows you to gauge your present level of passion and imagine what will turn you on in the future.

For each area of your life—relationships; work; finances; and physical, emotional, intellectual, and spiritual health—list at least three to five instances, general or specific, in which you were turned on, excited, or felt maximum fun in your past and present life. Also, write about what you think would give you those same feelings in the future. This will help you see the passion templates that are already present in your brain and help you develop new ones for the future. Be honest about things like sex and recreation, but also go deeper to see what has had meaning and purpose for you as well. At the risk of too much exposure, here is my list for relationships.

RELATIONSHIPS

Past:
1. Falling in love, kissing my first love for hours
2. Being part of a big family, family gatherings, playing together
3. Competing at tennis, table tennis, basketball, anything

Present:
1. Being in love, making love, being close, talking for hours
2. Being a parent, encouraging, teaching, protecting, helping
3. Cultivating friendships from all over the globe, being helpful to those I love
4. Being part of a big family, family gatherings, playing together

Future:
1. Being in love, physical and emotional closeness and connection

2. Being a parent and grandparent, encouraging, teaching, protecting, helping
3. Being part of a big family, family gatherings, playing together
4. Having friends all over the globe, finding mutual support and caring

The first time I did this exercise, it was clear to me that my passions are about being connected, sexual, playful, and helpful, where I am a lifelong learner and living a life that matters to make this planet a better place. As you search for the match to light the passion circuits in your brain, it is essential to specifically define what success means to you. My goals are likely not your goals, and your goals will not be someone else's. Success is a personal definition, and it may change over time as you go through different stages of life. Specifically, how do you define success? This is of critical importance, because as we will see, your brain tends to make happen what it focuses on.

| 10 |

Make Your Own Miracles

USE YOUR BRAIN TO DEFINE YOUR DREAMS
AND MAKE THEM A REALITY

If you go to work on your goals, your goals will go to work on you.
If you go to work on your plan, your plan will go to work on you.
Whatever good things we build end up building us.

—JIM ROHN, author and motivational speaker

Your brain is the most powerful organ in the universe. It has the ability to direct your life in a positive way or create a living hell. To harness your brain's power it needs direction and vision. It needs a blueprint. You are more likely to be successful on your own terms if you define success clearly, specifically, in writing, with detail.

As the passion circuits supply the emotional fuel for your life, the prefrontal cortex (PFC) is the steering wheel and the brakes. The PFC has been called the executive brain and is the chief executive officer (CEO) of your life. Like a great CEO, the PFC adds direction and helps you stay the course, despite whatever obstacles are put in your path. When the PFC is healthy, we are thoughtful, goal directed, focused, exhibit good judgment, and can control our impulses. When it is low in activity we tend to get distracted, scattered, and follow the whims of the moment rather than our goals. We also have trouble controlling our passions, which may get us accused of sexual harassment, in debt from a spending frenzy, or a drunk-driving arrest. When the PFC works too hard, we micromanage our lives and get little accomplished. One simple way to help the PFC manage our lives better is to have clear, passionate, written goals—goals that sustain and motivate.

How Do You Define Success?

Given that this book is about optimizing the brain to be your best in life, it is important to have a clear definition of what success means to you. Most people want to be successful without knowing exactly what that means. When pushed to define success, most equate it with happiness, wealth, recognition, independence, friendships, achievement, or inner peace—all vague concepts. Even most dictionaries define success in ways that have little specific meaning: common phrases used are "a favorable result; the gaining of wealth, fame, etc.; or a successful person or thing." Does this mean that success is ambiguous? Not at all. It simply means that it is a very personal thing and needs to be defined in the context of individual lives. What may be one person's success might be another person's failure. Defining success depends on many factors. Here are several to consider.

1. DEVELOPMENTAL STAGE OF LIFE

Success for a seventeen-year-old is often having enough money for a car, making the sports team, and having a date on most Friday nights. For someone in his early twenties it may mean having maximum fun. A person in his thirties may measure success by being on the right career track, having a home and a mortgage he can afford, and being able to give his kids the piano or dancing lessons they want. These examples are both markedly different from the way a sixty-five-year-old might look at success. To him success might involve security, health, contentment with his life, and being able to share the joys of his children and grandchildren.

2. FAMILY BACKGROUND

Family of origin is one of the most important influences on how people define individual success. Family values, traditions, religious orientations, and goals serve as the backdrop against which success is often measured. Success in one family may mean little, or even failure, in another. For example, one family might put a high emotional value on education and academic accomplishment, while another family might focus on athletic success. Some families may define success in group terms, for the married couple or for the family as a whole, while others have more individual definitions.

Success messages are given to children even before birth. It is not uncommon to hear parents voicing aspirations for their children during the mother's pregnancy. As the child grows, these messages may be subtle: excitement when a child pretends to be a doctor or picks up his first football or apathy when he bangs on the piano or takes an interest in classifying bugs. Or the messages may be overt: ridicule when a good student brings home four A's and three B's, indicating acceptance only comes with perfection, or praise when a child dates the culturally acceptable person and disdain when he does not.

Initially, most children are very interested in getting their parents' attention, and they are constantly on the lookout for ways to gain favor. If the parental messages are too harsh, however, it is not uncommon to find children defining success in ways opposite to the ideas of their parents, setting up conflict. Unfulfilled goals or dreams of parents are also transmitted to children. A parent who always wanted to go to college but could not afford it may put a strong emphasis on education. A mother who felt trapped or tied down by her marriage and children will encourage her daughters to have careers and make something of themselves, so as not to repeat her unhappy scenario.

Several other important factors originate from family background. These include identification with parents or grandparents; the wish to please, hurt, or compete with parents; and the desire to give their children things they felt lacking in their own childhoods. Someone raised in the turmoil of an alcoholic home might define success in terms of having a loving family life and being able to give his children the stability and emotional security he never had. Competition with siblings or friends is often an important factor in how a person defines success. You may define your success based on the thoughts and actions of others.

Clinically, I have found that if a child grows up in an approving and loving environment, success is much easier to find in whatever way he chooses to define it. But if a child grows up in a household where the parents were never satisfied no matter how hard the child tried, success is likely to be defined in unreachable terms.

3. PSYCHOLOGICAL MAKEUP

How a person is put together psychologically also has a great impact on how he views success. Character structure, inner life, relationships, psychological health, and brain health interact to give him feelings of contentment or turmoil. A person who has a need to be loved and admired will feel more successful with fame and achievement as opposed to wealth. Someone who is a loner will feel more successful with individual accomplishments than group ones. Likewise, an antisocial character will feel more successful breaking the law and getting away with it rather than living by the rules.

One of the most successful people I have met was a patient of mine who had a serious psychotic illness—chronic schizophrenia. Most aspects of a schizophrenic's life are affected by this devastating illness. For Beth, however, it was different. She sought the treatment she needed, took responsibility for taking her medicine and keeping her therapy appointments, and trusted the husband who loved her. Success for her was different than it is for most people. It was defined as staying out of the hospital and being able to raise her children in a sane environment, one that was different from the torture of her own early youth. I never saw her more proud than the day she walked into my office and said she had gotten a job all by herself at a doughnut shop.

Success is individually defined according to the circumstances of your life. In the process of realizing your dreams it is critical to define success for yourself, as specifically as possible. Here are nine rules to keep in mind.

Rule 1: Your Success Is Defined Only by You

Most people look to others for examples of success. Statements like "He must be successful because he is a surgeon" (or "drives a BMW" or "lives in a rich neighborhood") are very misleading. Unless you know how other people define success, you have very little idea whether they consider themselves successful. It's clear from my clinical work that many, many people who others would classify as "successful" are unhappy. They lack the feeling of success. Only we can author our own success and we need to personally define its parameters.

Along a similar line, if you let someone else define your success, you're likely to be unhappy. You may even feel as though you are living out someone else's life, not your own. Katie, a patient of mine, lived this example.

Katie worked at her father's publishing company. She was very good at her job and was loved by her supervisor and co-workers. Yet she felt unhappy. She had wanted to be a grammar school teacher ever since the fourth grade. She entered college majoring in primary school education. However, her father talked her out of teaching. Low pay, disruptive kids, and waning social status for teachers were the reasons he gave her. He told Katie that she should enter his business, as she had the possibility of taking it over one day. Katie followed her father's advice, but she always felt unfulfilled in her job and found that she longed to work with kids in a classroom. In fact, she arranged her schedule to start at 10 A.M. so she could volunteer at a local school. She even spent her vacations tutoring at the school. When her father discovered what she was doing, he felt regret. He told her to go teach. He had followed his passion. He wanted the same thing for her.

Rule 2: Success Is a Feeling

Success is nothing until you feel it. I once heard a story about three umpires on how they call balls and strikes. The first one said, "I call them the way I see them." The second umpire said, "I call them the way they are." And the third one said, "They ain't nothing until I call them."

Success is a feeling, a perception on your part. Most people think of success in terms of symbols, not feelings. In the final analysis, however, it is how we feel about where we have been and where we are going that is the ultimate measure of our success in life.

We all know of people who had all of the success symbols—social status, wealth, possessions, outstanding achievements, admiration—but who considered themselves failures. The symbols did not prevent Elvis Presley, Marilyn Monroe, Jimi Hendrix, River Phoenix, John Belushi, Robert Downey Jr., Owen Wilson and countless other so-called successful people, from feeling like failures who needed drugs or alcohol or who turned to self-destruction to be rid of the painful feelings. I call this the empty success syndrome—the outward appearance of success without any of the positive feelings on the inside. A word of caution: sometimes feelings lie to you. If all evidence points to success in your life, but you feel unsuccessful or like an impostor, there may be a problem with your thinking.

Rule 3: Success at Any Price May Not Be Success

Since success is a feeling, the means by which the symbols of success are obtained may be important. For most people (not everyone), the ways in which they reach their goals have an impact on how they feel about themselves in the process. If goals are reached in ways contrary to individual belief systems, conflicts over the reality or value of the success may arise. For example, if an executive made it to the top by using his friends as stepping-stones, he may feel loneliness later on that could ruin his feelings of accomplishment. Or consider the situation of someone who gets ahead by lying or cheating. People who build a career on a foundation of dishonesty may temporarily enjoy their achievement, but after a short while they are likely to feel doubt about their ability and self-worth and end up feeling more like criminals than success stories.

Rule 4: Success Is a Process

Success is not a static entity, a gold watch at the end of thirty years, or a paper published in the *New England Journal of Medicine*. It is a process of defining and redefining, struggling toward and reaching the goals you set for yourself. It is the day-to-day feeling that accompanies your efforts that drives you on.

Most people think of success as an end point, the pot of gold at the end of the rainbow. The end of the rainbow, however, may be a dangerous place to be. There are many examples of people who reach their pinnacles only to develop serious illnesses or depression shortly thereafter. Executive promotion depression has been known to behavioral scientists for some time. This occurs when a person has reached his major goal in work, say, to become a company's CEO, and then becomes depressed. Unless he immediately sets new goals for himself, the feeling of "is this all there is?" may set in, leading to depression.

More insight into the dangers of reaching goals comes from the research of Dr. E. K. Gunderson and Dr. Richard Rahe, who correlated life events with the development of physical illness. Surprisingly, they found that not only did stresses like death of a spouse, divorce, job loss, and detention in jail correlate with greater physical illness, but so did positive events like marriage, outstanding personal achievements, graduating from college, job promotions, and retirement.

If success is viewed as a goal to be reached, what happens after that? Feelings of success live only for a short while after goals are reached. The ultimate satisfaction comes from attaining, not just from attainment. Successful people are not there; they are in the process of getting there, wherever there may be for them.

Rule 5: Success Occurs in Steps

No one is born with the feeling of success. In fact, we are all born a bit confused and soon learn that we are very small in a very big world. It is hard to have much sense of self-esteem and mastery when you have to crawl or walk along the furniture to get anywhere. With loving and encouraging parents, however, our sense of mastery grows day by day, not in leaps or giant steps, but in small baby steps. Hopefully, we will make progress, but there will always be days when we slip back a step or two. With support, we learn that these setbacks are part of the process, and we continue along the road of self-development.

Early successes bring positive feelings, which encourage children to want to do more to obtain more positive feelings. If the child gets enough positive feelings about himself, he will begin to believe in his abilities and be able to achieve, because it feels good to be successful. This process does not happen overnight and will not change overnight. Expecting to find success in instant solutions (instant wealth, relationships, recognition, or achievement) invites lifelong disappointment. Success, like learning to walk, is a process that occurs in tiny steps.

Rule 6: Success Is a Balancing Act

Balance is just as important to feelings of success as to a ballet dancer. We all have a personal life that no one else sees, a relational life with others, and a work life. It is very possible to feel successful in one of these areas while feeling like a failure in the others. Very few people I know have it all. But if your life becomes too unbalanced, you may find that your non-success areas drain energy from those areas you feel good about. Balance, perspective, and trade-offs are necessary for success. What good is it to make all the money in the world if the person of your dreams leaves you?

You decide how much weight to give to each area of your life. This varies for all of us, and it will even be different at different stages in your life. When you think about defining success, don't allow yourself to become unbalanced.

Rule 7: Success Can Be Learned

Success is not something that you're born with or something you inherit. It is something that comes from a healthy brain that is properly encouraged and programmed. In *Secrets of Successful Students* I describe how I went from being a mediocre high school student to summa cum laude in college. Looking back, the transformation was not a big mystery. No one in grammar school or high school ever really taught me how to study. Nor did I have much motivation or confidence to succeed. When I learned the secrets of great students and developed the maturity and passion to succeed, I was able to make it happen. Likewise, success in any endeavor occurs through a series of steps. After tending to your brain's health, determine what steps you need to do in order to be successful. In particular, see what others have done in situations similar to yours.

Rule 8: Defining Success Too High or Too Low Will Derail You

If you aim too high you'll quickly feel overwhelmed and your goals will dissolve into daydreams. Expecting to make a million dollars on your first real estate deal after attending a seminar or expecting your chronically conflicted marriage to turn around in three weeks of marital therapy only sets you up for failure. Change, success, and fulfillment take time. On the other hand, if you aim too low, your patience and endurance may run out before you get the positive feelings necessary to motivate you to go on. The best way to start defining and experiencing success is by setting up reasonably realistic goals that can be obtained in a foreseeable period.

Rule 9: Success Is Having the Ability to Be Honest with Yourself

To feel successful, you must be able to be honest about the things that are really important to you. Whether it has to do with acquiring money, changing careers, becoming involved in a new relationship, or discarding a destructive one, being truthful with yourself is the only way to allow the inner sense of contentment and success to exist without feeling like an impostor. Persistent dissatisfaction and frequent mind changes are clues that you aren't being honest with yourself.

Honing Your Individual Definition of Success

The following questions are designed to help you clarify exactly, at this point in time, what success means to you. Remember that success is a process, and the answers to these questions will change over time. On a separate piece of paper, answer the questions as honestly as you can, and be prepared to be surprised by your responses.

This rest of this builds on itself. Answer the questions in sequence. It will take some time to complete, and the information it will generate is crucial to helping you define your goals for success. When you finish, go over your answers at least twice to reflect on their significance. Make it count!

1. Rank the following ten items in order of their importance to you (1 = most important, 10 = least important).

    ____Happiness
    ____Fun
    ____Wealth
    ____Health
    ____Fulfilling relationships
    ____Fame
    ____Individual accomplishments
    ____Legacy
    ____Making a difference in the lives of others
    ____Faith in a higher power

2. With the above ranking in mind, what are you now doing to accomplish or enhance the first five items you placed on the list? Success is a process. What are you doing to help that process along?

3. Think of yourself lying in your coffin at the end of your life. What was really important to you in your life? What really mattered to you? At the end of your life, what has value for you? This has always been one of my favorite questions. It helps put your life into a lifelong perspective. When you start with the end in mind, the present moment becomes much more important.

4. Are you giving enough time and effort to those people or things that really matter to you? Or are you unconsciously spending the bulk of your time on things of lesser personal value?

5. What developmental period of life are you in (adolescence, young adulthood, middle age, etc.)? How have your personal goals changed from the previous period? How do you think they'll change ten years from now? Thinking ahead prevents events like midlife crises, empty nest syndrome, and so on.

6. List ten instances in which you felt most competent, ten instances in which you felt most confident, ten instances in which you felt most connected to others, and ten instances in which you felt the most joy in your life.

7. Name five people whom you look up to and admire. Describe the specific traits you admire and the ways you would like to be like them.

8. Name five people you know whom you do not admire. Describe the specific things about them that turn you off. Be as specific as you can.

9. List five experiences in which you felt like a failure.

10. List five experiences in which you felt successful.

11. In defining goals, there are three major areas of your life to examine:

    a. relationships (with spouse or lover, children, family, friends)

    b. work/finances (your job, school if you are a student, or tasks at home if you're a housewife, current and future finances, etc.)

    c. personal life (the part of your life that applies just to you outside of relationships or work: physical and emotional health, spirituality, interests, intellectual growth, etc.)

How significant/important is each to you? Rank each of them on a 1- to 10-point scale, giving 10 points to areas that are all-consuming and 1 point to areas that have little significance to you.

Relational life ____

Work/Financial life ____

Personal life ____

How much time do you give to each area? Does this reflect its importance to you?

Answering these questions will also help you answer the questions "What do you want? What matters most?" When you know what you want, you can then go take active steps toward accomplishing your goals. You mind makes happen what it sees.

Your Brain Makes Happen What It Sees

Jenny, age thirty-two, was a bus driver for the city in the Bay Area. She came to see me in her work uniform, looking very sad, and eight months pregnant. As she sat down on the sofa in my office she had tears running down both her cheeks. Her family and boyfriend had just disowned her and she felt isolated, alone, and confused.

"How can this happen?" she started. "How can I look and feel pregnant but not be? How can I make my own breasts larger? Have no periods? Have this belly?" Her voice raised as she put her hand on her distended abdomen. "How is this possible? Am I crazy?"

Jenny had been together with her boyfriend for four years. They were planning to get married when she believed she became pregnant. For the past two years she had wanted to be pregnant. Even though her initial pregnancy test was negative she was convinced that she was. All of the signs were there. The test must have been wrong, she thought. She had morning sickness and even thought she felt the baby move. As she believed she was getting closer to delivery date she went back to the doctor who, after running more tests, told her she was definitely not pregnant.

The weekend before she got the news from her doctor, her family had just given her a baby shower. The family, initially excited, now felt duped. They told her they did not want anything more to do with her. Her boyfriend, not knowing what to think, moved out.

Jenny had a condition known as pseudocyesis, or false pregnancy. Believing she was pregnant, even though she wasn't, her brain sent the signals to the rest of her body to make the symptoms of pregnancy occur. Pseudocyesis has been known since antiquity. Hippocrates wrote of twelve women who "believed they were pregnant" in 300 B.C. In 1923 John Mason Good coined the term from the Greek words *pseudes* (false) and *kyesis* (pregnancy).

As I explained her condition, Jenny initially looked confused. Over time, however, she began to understand the power of her brain. After a family meeting, and several sessions with her boyfriend, she reconnected with the people she loved.

Believing she was pregnant even though she wasn't, her brain changed the whole shape and function of Jenny's body. Likewise, seeing fear in your future, even where there is none, can make you feel so panicked you end up in the emergency room. Seeing your husband or sweetheart leaving you can make you act so insecure, clingy, and dependent that it is more likely you will be left.

Negative thoughts can make negative things happen, while positive thoughts can help you reach your goals. The expectation of success is a very powerful force by itself. Skilled physicians have known for centuries that positive expectations play a crucial role in the outcome of many illnesses. Until 100 to 150 years ago, the history of medical therapeutics was largely that of the doctor-patient relationship and the placebo effect (placebos being inert substances that have no physiologic effect on the problem). Actually, most of the treatments by physicians in times past would have been more harmful than beneficial to the patient, if it weren't for the recuperative powers of the human organism supported by the belief in the healing powers of the physician's prescriptions. The benefits of the placebo effect are determined by the expectations and hopes shared by the patient and the doctor. Action, ritual, faith, and enthusiasm are the vital ingredients. After studying the psychotherapeutic process Johns Hopkins psychiatrist Jerome Frank,

M.D., concluded that the belief of the therapist in his treatment and the belief of the patient in the therapist were the most important factors in a positive outcome to therapy.

Although a placebo is a substance that is considered pharmacologically inert, it is by no means "nothing." It is a potent therapeutic tool, on the average about one half to two thirds as powerful as morphine in relieving severe pain. It is now recognized that one third of the general population are placebo responders in clinical situations relating to pain, whether the pain is from surgery, heart disease, cancer, or headache. It is very clear that placebo responses are not simply a result of the patient fooling or tricking himself out of the pain. Placebo administration can produce real physiologic changes. Some of the physiologic pathways through which the placebo effects work have been identified. In a study done by a University of California research team, it was found that the placebo effect of pain relief in dental patients could actually be blocked by administering these patients naloxone, a drug that neutralizes morphine. From this study and others, it has become clear that the belief in pain relief stimulates the body to secrete its own pain relieving substance, called endorphins, which act in the same manner as morphine, only they are much more potent. In a recent study, doctors at Houston's Veterans Affairs Medical Center performed arthroscopic knee surgery on one group of patients with arthritis, scraping and rinsing their knee joints. On another group, the doctors made small cuts in the patients' knees to mimic the incisions of a real operation and then bandaged them up. The pain relief reported by the two groups was identical. In a brain imaging study, researchers found that when placebo worked for depressed patients, brain function also changed in a positive way. Change your beliefs; change your brain.

Tell your brain what you want and match your behavior to get it. If your mind takes what it sees and makes it happen, it is critical to visualize what you want and then match your behavior over time to get it. Too many people are thrown around by the whims of the day rather than using their prefrontal cortex to plan their lives and follow through on their goals.

One-Page Miracle

One of the most powerful yet simple exercises I have designed is called the One-Page Miracle (OPM). It will help guide nearly all of your thoughts, words, and actions. It is called the OPM because I've seen this exercise quickly focus and change many people's lives.

Directions: On one sheet of paper, clearly write out your major goals. Use the following main headings: Relationships, Work/Finances, and Myself. Under Relationships write the subheadings Spouse/Lover, Children, Extended Family, and Friends. Under Work/Finances write Short Term and Long Term. Under Myself write Physical Health, Emotional Health, Spirituality, and Character. Self is that part of you outside of relationships or work. Often it is the part of you that no one sees but you.

Next to each subheading succinctly write out what's important to you in that area; write what you want, not what you don't want. Be positive and use the first person. Write what you want with confidence and the expectation that you will make it happen. Keep the paper with you so that you can work on it over several days or weeks. After you finish with the initial draft (you'll frequently want to update it), place this piece of paper where you can see it every day, such as on your refrigerator, by your bedside, or on the bathroom mirror. In that way, every day you focus your eyes on what's important to you. This makes it easier to match your behavior to what you want. Your life becomes more conscious and you spend your energy on goals that are important to you.

I separate the areas of relationships, work, and self in order to encourage a more balanced approach to life. Burnout occurs when our lives become unbalanced and we overextend ourselves in one area while ignoring another. For example, in my practice I see that a common cause of divorce stems from a person's working so much that little energy is left over for his or her spouse.

Here is an example I did with one of my patients who came to see me after a head injury at the insistence of his wife. Tony is a program developer at a local production company. He is married with one child. Since the injury he had significant impulse control problems, spent too much money, and was irritable at home.

After you look at the example, fill out the OPM for yourself. If you have PFC challenges, this exercise will be very helpful for you. If you don't have challenges in this part of your brain, this exercise will still help keep you focused on what's important in your life. After you complete this exercise put it up where you can see and read it every day. It is a great idea to start the day off by reading the OPM to get focused for the day.

Tony's One-Page Miracle
What Do I Want for My Life?

RELATIONSHIPS—To be connected to those I love
> **Spouse/Lover:** To maintain a close, kind, caring, loving partnership with my wife. I want her to know how much I care about her. I want to act in a way that makes her feel less worried about me.
> **Children:** To be a firm, kind, positive, predictable presence in my child's life. I want to help her to develop into a happy, responsible person.
> **Extended Family:** To continue to keep close contact with my parents and siblings, to provide support and love
> **Friends:** To take time to maintain and nurture my friendships

WORK—To be my best at work, to be the best program developer I can be, while maintaining a balanced life. Specifically, my work activities focus on taking care of my current projects, doing activities targeted at obtaining new programs, and giving back to the community by doing some charity work each month. I will focus on my goals at work and not get distracted by things not directly related to my goals.

FINANCES—To be responsible and thoughtful and help our resources grow
> **Short Term:** To be thoughtful of how our money is spent, to ensure it is directly related to my family's and my needs and goals. Since the injury my judgment has not been the best, so I will check with my wife before I spend more than fifty dollars.
> **Long Term:** To save 10 percent of everything I earn. I pay myself and my family before other things. I'll put this money away each month in a pension plan for retirement.

MYSELF—To be the healthiest person I can be, which is even more essential since the injury
> **Physical Health:** To take care of my body on a daily basis, exercise, eat well, get good sleep, take a vitamin and fish oil, and the other supplements Dr. Amen recommends for me
> **Emotional Health:** To feel stable, positive, and grateful
> **Spirituality:** To live close to God, attend church regularly, and pray daily
> **Character:** To be honest, thoughtful, kind, and trustworthy, to live with integrity

MY ONE-PAGE MIRACLE
What Do I Want? What Am I Doing to Make It Happen?

RELATIONSHIPS
Spouse/Lover: _____
_____

Children: _____
_____

Extended Family: _____
_____

Friends: _____
_____

WORK
_____
_____
_____

FINANCES
Short Term: _____
_____

Long Term: _____
_____

MYSELF
Physical Health: _____
_____

Emotional
Health: _____
_____

Spirituality: _____
_____

Character: _____
_____

Once you clearly define what you want, meditate and focus on it, you're ready to make your goals and desires part of your daily life. By developing specific nerve pathways for your desires, the planning and steering part of your brain, the PFC, will help you realize your dreams. Your OPM now becomes the guidepost for all of your thoughts, feelings, and actions. It is the road map of your life. As you now know what you want, it is critical to move your behavior toward your goals and away from things you do not want. Consistent, positive, congruent effort is essential to success. Clearly, this takes a healthy brain, especially in the PFC. Let your brain help you design and implement your success in life. Work toward goals that are important to you. Many other people or corporations are happy to decide what you should do with your life. Use the OPM to help you be the one who has the primary say. Your brain receives and creates reality. Give it some direction to help make your life what you want it to be. Teach yourself to be focused on what's important to you. This auxiliary PFC will help you keep your life on track.

| 11 |

Know When to Apply the Brakes

STRENGTHEN YOUR BRAIN'S INTERNAL CONTROLS

The art of leadership is saying no, not yes. It is very easy to say yes.

—TONY BLAIR

On a recent trip to Maui, I watched a fascinating interaction between an assertive four-year-old, redheaded girl in pigtails and her mother. I was having lunch at a café overlooking the Maalaea Harbor at the Maui Ocean Center. It was a warm, serene day, with a light tropical breeze. The sea was calm. Then, in a flash, a storm erupted at the table next to me. Reaching for her camera, the mother accidentally knocked over a glass of ice water. Her little girl squealed with excitement, probably because she was the one who usually spilled the drinks. The mother was obviously embarrassed. As she started to mop up the water, the little girl gleefully started to play in it with both hands. Sternly, the mother told her to stop and put her hands down at her sides. But the little girl wanted to play in it, so she didn't listen the first time. The mother repeated her warning, this time with a consequence attached. "One more move toward the water," the mother said, "and I am taking away your baby dolly." This caused the girl to retreat quickly. Her baby doll, also with red hair, was more important to her than the momentary pleasure. I had seen her playing with the doll before the water incident. After a few seconds, however, I could see the temptation of the water was starting to build in the little girl's brain. The tables were made of a rough stone top and the water formed little pools with the ice floating like miniature ships. It just seemed like too much fun. The little girl sheepishly looked at her mother to see if she was watching. When she saw that her mother was distracted with the cleanup effort, the girl slowly started to move her stretched out little fingers toward the water. It reminded me of the struggle between good and evil we all face. Do I inhibit my impulses and do what is right? Or do I do what I want in the moment? Which one would win on this gorgeous Maui day, I wondered? There were competing interests. Maximum fun or maintaining possession of a beloved baby dolly? "She is only four," I thought to myself. "Her (PFC) has barely started its long trek toward maturity." As it turned out, the mother mopped up the water with the help from an attentive waiter and the little girl was saved from her impulses. Her dolly's freedom was safe, at least for the moment.

Unfortunately, we are not all so lucky. At some point our mothers let us go and we are left alone with our impulses. What we do with them is a major determinant of our success or failure in life. Being successful is as much about inhibiting actions as it is about starting or maintaining them. A car without brakes is a death trap. A life without brakes, even with great passion, is likely to end early in failure. Passion is important to fuel our success, while clear goals help steer us in the direction we want to go. To stay on track we also need good brakes to modulate our movements, to slow us down when we are going too fast, to stop us when we get the urge to take a detour or go in the wrong direction. Weak brakes cause us to crash, while brakes that are too sticky impede our progress. This chapter will discuss a critical function of the PFC in regard to a magnificent mind—the ability to say no and control our impulses.

Prefrontal Cortex—Master Brakes

As discussed earlier, the PFC is involved with higher functions, such as planning, forethought, and impulse control (see Figure 11.1). The PFC also helps us to modulate emotions, keeping us from getting too high or too low. As it does not fully develop until we are in our midtwenties, we see children and teens being much more emotional. When I walked through the door at home after a day at work when my children were little they would run to greet me with wide open arms and lots of excitement. When they were disappointed, they might cry crocodile tears. As they got older, their emotions were under much better control, plus I was not nearly as exciting to them as teenagers.

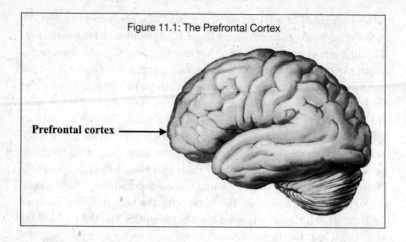

Figure 11.1: The Prefrontal Cortex

Prefrontal cortex ———→

When there is damage to the PFC, people often lose tight control over their emotions. James Brady, President Reagan's press secretary, offers a dramatic example. On March 30, 1981, when John Hinckley attempted to assassinate President Reagan, Mr. Brady was shot through his frontal lobes. Not only did he suffer paralysis, but he also had personality changes and became more emotional. His highs were too high and his lows too low. He said during an interview on television that when he was a little sad, he might start to weep uncontrollably or if he heard something that was slightly funny he might start to laugh as if it was the funniest thing he had ever heard.

Healthy activity in the PFC is associated with conscientiousness; abnormally low PFC activity is associated with carelessness, inconsistency, troubled decisions, and impulsivity. In reviewing 194 studies researchers from the University of Illinois at Urbana-Champaign found that increased death rates were associated with such impulsive behaviors as tobacco use, diet and activity patterns, excessive alcohol use, violence, risky sexual behavior, risky driving, suicide, and drug use. A healthy PFC is essential for a long and successful life. Abnormalities in the PFC can be the result of inherited conditions, such as ADHD, or be the result of damage from brain injuries or toxic exposure. It can also result from poor training or overly permissive parents.

The Short Pause: How Weak Brakes Sabotage Our Lives

Saying no to the urges of the moment is often more important than saying yes, even to positive actions. It takes only a moment, a pause, to reflect on the consequences of our actions to see if they are in our overall best interests. When the little girl paused before she gave in to the urge to splash water all over the table, she was allowed to keep her doll. When you pause before saying yes to the urge to cheat on your spouse, you are more likely to keep your marriage intact. When you pause before saying yes to the urge to tell off an irritating customer, you are more likely to keep your job. When you pause before taking money illegally out of the company coffers, you are more likely to stay out of jail. When you pause before saying yes to volunteering for a project or taking on work that is not directly related to your own goals, you are more likely to stay focused and be successful. Having the short pause, to think through an intended comment or action to decide if the behavior fits your goals, is a PFC function and a major key to success.

Impulsivity, an inability to inhibit behavior, is at the core of much of the personal failure I have witnessed over the past three decades as a psychiatrist. I have seen many people who exhibited impulsive behaviors, such as murderers, robbers, rapists, pedophiles, wife beaters, child abusers, compulsive gamblers, sex addicts, drug and alcohol addicts, bulimics, road ragers, thrill seekers, unfaithful spouses, and countless others. I saw a ten-year-old boy who impulsively tried to jump on a moving train, imitating scenes from movies, only to slip as he tried to grab the ladder and have both legs amputated by the large steel wheels as he fell underneath the train. I saw a man who impulsively stabbed others for no reason. I saw him only when he was shackled. And, I saw a woman who would get in cars with men she didn't know to have a good time, just because she was invited.

Thoughtless words and actions, again and again, have caused harm to careers, relationships, and how we feel about ourselves. Impulsivity is at the root of many political scandals, sexual harassment issues at work, and fiscal irresponsibility on the job or at home. Let's look at each area listed in the One-Page Miracle to see how impulsivity can sabotage lives.

RELATIONSHIPS

People who struggle with impulsivity often say thoughtless, hurtful things that negatively affect their relationships. Many of my patients with ADHD, for example, play this relational game I call "Say the First Thing that Comes to Your Mind." Some even wear it as a badge of pride. "I am brutally honest," they say. I usually reply that it is usually not helpful. Healthy relationships require tact. They require us to inhibit the first thoughts that come to mind. Once, I walked into my waiting room to greet an eight-year-old patient. I was about ten minutes late for the appointment. When she saw me she said, "Well, it's about damn time." Her mother looked horrified and apologized for the little girl's comment. Living with ADHD loved ones myself, I knew comments like that were just part of the terrain. This game causes many, many problems. When you just say the first thing that comes to mind, you can hurt someone's feelings or give away secrets that were entrusted to you. One of my patients was given the task of bringing a friend to his surprise birthday party. On the way to the party my patient inadvertently started talking about how much fun they were going to have at the party. When he saw the look on his friend's face he was horrified that he had ruined the surprise.

In addition to saying thoughtless, hurtful things, weak brakes are also associated with frequent interruptions. When someone who struggles with impulsivity gets a thought in his head he feels like he has to say it, rather than waiting for the other person to finish her thought. He believes his point is so important that he just can't wait. Once, in a couples session, when I pointed this behavior out to a woman whose husband was very frustrated by their poor communication, she said she had to say what was on her mind or she would forget it. It also meant that she wasn't listening to him. I gave her some paper to write down the thoughts she was afraid she'd forget, so her husband could complete a thought.

Other types of impulsivity that hurt relationships include:

- Calling people bad names
- Lashing out in anger
- Throwing tantrums
- Exhibiting unpredictable behavior
- Answering cell phones or text messages in the middle of having an important conversation
- Having affairs
- Saying yes to more projects at work that take you away from home
- Becoming involved with Internet pornography when you know it hurts your spouse and takes sexual energy away from her
- Lashing out, hitting, or belittling children when they irritate you

Impulsivity often ruins work relationships and job potential. Saying thoughtless, hurtful things to co-workers, vendors, or customers has gotten many people terminated. Stealing, sexual indiscretions, drinking on the job, using Internet access at your workplace to look for another job are just a few examples. Impulsivity behind the wheel has caused drivers their lives.

WORK/FINANCES

As an employer, I have often thought about doing brain scans on the people I hire. I have never made a hiring decision based on a scan, but sometimes I wish I had. Eventually, most people who work at the Amen Clinics get scanned, either out of curiosity or because they are going through a difficult time, such as postpartum depression or have suffered a head injury. The results have been very consistent. The people who have worked for me who had low PFC activity tended to get into the most trouble, by being late, saying thoughtless, hurtful things to co-workers or patients, making careless mistakes, procrastinating on their tasks, or getting into trouble with the law. They also tended not to last long.

I once treated a doctor who was fired from his county mental health job in San Francisco. It usually takes a lot to be fired from these jobs because psychiatrists are hard to find. One day he had a patient at 1 P.M. When his clinic administrator called him at 1:30, because he still had not arrived at the clinic, he told her that he was playing golf in Oregon. He had forgotten about the appointment. That was the last straw. He was fired. A scan revealed he had very low PFC activity.

Finances are often ruined by impulsivity. One of my first patients came to me thirty thousand dollars in debt. She knew her husband would be furious. She had a shopping addiction that she felt she couldn't control. I have seen many patients in trouble with the IRS because they did not plan for their taxes. The IRS does not care if you have a brain problem as the reason for delinquency. Its agents tend not be impulsive but rather compulsive.

SELF

Impulsivity hurts our emotional, physical, and spiritual lives. It is often involved in many psychiatric disorders, such as ADHD, addictions, and temper problems, which erode self-esteem. It is involved in eating disorders like bulimia and obesity. "I'll just have one or two bites of the chocolate cake," for some, turns into eating the whole cake. Impulsivity causes us to give up too quickly when exercising or meditating (I'll do it later), and is often involved in sin, which I define as doing what you know is wrong, according to your conscience.

When the Brakes Come Off: Prozac, Crazy Sex, and Costa Rica

Sometimes impulsivity can be triggered by taking a medication that lowers your PFC. Kimberlee was hurting. She was going through chemotherapy for thyroid cancer and felt overwhelmed, tired, and depressed. In her mind, at age twenty-six, she was supposed to be healthy. She was supposed to be at her best. Yes, she had struggled from an eating disorder in her teens and early twenties, but she thought that she had gotten beyond it. Now this nightmare. The hopelessness, lack of energy, and beginning weight gain from the thyroid dysfunction were too much to bear. She started purging again and thought her life was over. Who would ever want her, bulimic, fat, depressed, and with cancer? She was a woman who was desired for her looks. She had long, thick, flowing, dark red hair; soft peach skin; high cheekbones; the face of an angel; and what others would think, but never her, a perfect body. None of that mattered in this moment. Kimberlee felt anxious, panicky, sad, and hopeless. She couldn't sleep but spent days fretting in bed. On the advice of a worried friend, she saw a local psychiatrist. Kimberlee was hesitant to see the doctor, but she was so tired of feeling bad.

After filling out a few pages of information and spending forty-five minutes with the doctor, Kimberlee left the office with a prescription for Prozac at a fairly high dose. She wondered how he could know much about her in that short period of time. He mentioned something about situational depression and the need for the high dose of Prozac to deal with the eating disorder. The appointment was a whirlwind and she was unsure about all that he said. She did remember his saying that the medication had few side effects and she should start to feel better in a week or two. With the hope of feeling better she started the medication.

Within a few days she started to feel much better. Her energy improved and she started to feel optimistic once again. She started going out with her friends and became more social. "How strange," she thought. "I feel great because of a little green and white capsule." Over the next few weeks she felt better than she ever had. Her worries were dissolved and she looked forward to new adventures.

She went with friends for an evening of fun at the Beverly Hotel in Los Angeles. There she met an interesting fifty-year-old man, Mark, who was obviously captivated with her. He invited her to his home in the Hollywood Hills. Within three days Mark invited her to go with him on a trip to Costa Rica. To her own surprise, she agreed, which was completely out of character for this woman who had been fairly shy her whole life. When she questioned her own judgment about going to a foreign country with a man she had just met, she thought, "What the heck, it is time to start living."

She had a great time on the trip. Mark was fun and uninhibited. She felt as though her depression and worries were from a lifetime ago. One night in a bustling Costa Rica strip club after a few glasses of wine, Kimberlee found herself feeling so good that when Mark put his hand on her inner thigh it sent eclectic sexual feelings to her inner pelvis and up her spine. She leaned into Mark, moaned encouragement, and kissed him passionately. Feeling her responsiveness, Mark brought his hand between her legs and stimulated her directly. With her eyes closed, Kimberlee was totally focused on the pleasurable feelings. Her sounds of satisfaction started to fill the club. Soon everyone's eyes were turned toward her as she came to orgasm. When she breathlessly became aware of her surroundings, she became embarrassed and started to feel horrified by her very public behavior.

Mark did not turn out to be a good guy for Kimberlee. He left Costa Rica early the next morning, leaving a plane ticket on her nightstand. Feeling ashamed of herself, she boarded a plane to Miami on her way back to Los Angeles. On the first leg of the flight she sat in first class. When the pilot walked by her seat, he smiled at her. Kimberlee was too tired and too upset to care. The stewardess in first class told her that the pilot would love to meet her. After several attempts to say no, Kimberlee agreed to have a drink with him at the Miami airport.

They hit it off and drank several glasses of wine and talked for hours. When he invited her to his hotel room, she went. They had passionate, intense sex all night. On her flight home the next day, she began to hate the person she was becoming. What happened to her judgment? Her morals? Her good sense?

Connecting the change in her behavior to starting Prozac, she stopped the medication and on the advice of a friend came to see me at the Amen Clinics. When I saw Kimberlee it was clear that the Prozac had disinhibited her. It took the lid off of her judgment and impulse control, as well as her internal moral compass. When we performed SPECT scans of her brain off the Prozac, they showed us that, in fact, Prozac was the worst possible choice for her. Her scans showed low activity in her PFC. Her internal supervisor was weak and could not control the passions of the moment. It could not see long-term consequences.

Prozac and medications like it, called selective serotonin reuptake inhibitors, increase the availability of the neurotransmitter serotonin in the brain, which helps to calm the brain. Prozac is most effective for people

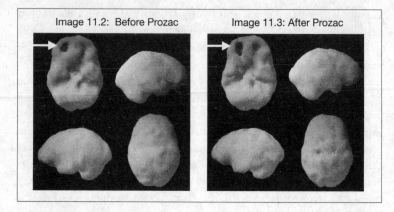

Image 11.2: Before Prozac   Image 11.3: After Prozac

whose PFC works too hard, causing them to be inflexible, worried, obsessed, and rigid. When Prozac works, it helps calm the PFC to help people feel more relaxed, happier, and less anxious. If the PFC is already characterized by low activity, however, giving Prozac to someone like Kimberlee lowers her PFC even further, thereby disinhibiting her and causing serious problems in her life. Kimberlee needed her PFC stimulated, not relaxed. How would the doctor know unless he looked? Images 11.2 and 11.3 show a depressed woman's brain before and after Prozac. Notice the marked decreased PFC activity.

As I wrote in *Sex on the Brain,* the brain is a sneaky organ. All of us have weird, crazy, sexual, stupid, unhelpful, dishonest, hurtful, even violent thoughts. Thankfully, our PFC inhibits these sneaky thoughts and prevents us from saying them or acting upon them. When this part of the brain works right we can laugh at or dismiss these sneaky thoughts. When there is dysfunction, damage, or disease to this part of the brain, these hurtful, embarrassing thoughts surface in our behavior.

Subtle Ways That Weak Brakes Can Sabotage Success

In Jim Collins's best-selling book, *Good to Great,* the hedgehog concept is one of the major principles behind why companies go from good companies to great ones. The concept is about razor-sharp focus. The idea for this principle came from Isaiah Berlin's famous essay "The Hedgehog and the Fox" that divided the world into hedgehogs and foxes, based upon an ancient Greek parable: "The fox knows many things, but the hedgehog knows one big thing." Those who led less effective companies tended to be foxes, never gaining the clarifying advantage of a hedgehog, being instead scattered, diffuse, and inconsistent. Too often business, family, or personal leaders are involved in too many activities and get distracted by the excitement of the moment, which takes time and attention away from their primary goals.

In a similar way, General Electric's legendary CEO Jack Welch became famous for a particular business strategy. If the company was not No. 1 or No. 2 in a market and could not get there in a short period of time, he sold or closed the business unit, even if it was making money. He wanted the company to achieve total focus on what it did right to optimize their efforts. During his twenty years of leadership at General Electric, Welch increased the value of the company from thirteen billion dollars to several hundred billion. Weak brakes impair our focus and get us involved in many different things that have little to do with our goals.

A lack of clear focus and being distractible causes us to say yes to trivial or less important activities, which robs time and energy from more important ones. Raccoons with shiny objects come to mind. I had two pet raccoons growing up. Whenever these furry, masked creatures saw something shiny they had to explore. This is where our new technology is scattering our attention and focus. As we pop on the Internet to do our work, many of us must first check out our news pages, see who has e-mailed us, turn on the music and download a song or two, see if our Internet dating sites have produced anyone interesting, and then get ten instant messages from friends who are also on. It often takes people half an hour or more to get to their work. Many also leave their e-mail notifications on while working, so they are constantly interrupted. These interruptions erode our brakes.

Strengthen Your Brakes

Whenever you give in to your impulses and lose your focus, you actually weaken the PFC's control over your life and make the behaviors more likely to occur again. When you resist negative behaviors you strengthen the PFC and your own self-control. Resisting the temptation to waste time or engage in activities that are worthless or harmful makes you stronger. Repetitively doing positive activities makes them more likely to occur. Disciplined behavior increases discipline.

Psychiatrist Lewis Baxter, in a series of breakthrough experiments at UCLA, found that when he prevented obsessive-compulsive-disordered patients from engaging in their senseless repetitive thoughts or behaviors it actually changed the brain's function in a positive way, working in a way similar to medication. Changing your thoughts and behaviors changes your brain. Give in to useless behaviors and you are more likely to keep doing them. Engage in more useful behaviors and you will be more likely to continue them. Your moment-by-moment actions program your brain's actual function.

It starts early in life. As I mentioned earlier, when you allow a child to whine to get their way, you actually teach the child's brain to whine. When you give in to a temper tantrum, you teach the child's brain to have more tantrums as a way to get what he or she wants. Giving in to bad behavior disinhibits behavior and weakens the PFC, as the child does not have to exercise any self-control. The brain is like a muscle, and the more one uses it, the stronger it gets. The brain, also like muscles, has memory. Giving a child clear, consistent, reasonable consequences for negative behavior while reinforcing positive behaviors enhances development in the PFC. So many behavior problems in children are due to erratic or absent parenting. The lack of effective parenting sets children up to have problems their whole lives. Parents act as a child's PFC until his or her own PFC develops. Strengthening the brakes starts early. In a similar way, providing employees with adequate supervision, feedback, consequences, and reinforcement helps them perform better at work. Of course, too much supervision, or micromanagement, lessens productivity.

Here are five things you can do to increase your brakes, PFC, and impulse control.

1. Work on developing a great brain. Enhancing brain function makes everything in your life easier, including impulse control. Exercise, good nutrition, new learning, taking a multiple vitamin and fish oil supplement are all strategies to help overall brain health. Along the same lines, stop any behaviors such as excessive alcohol use, lack of sleep, smoking, excessive TV, or video games. Also, treat any conditions that negatively affect the PFC, such as ADHD, depression, or brain trauma.

2. Read your One-Page Miracle every day. Ask yourself repeatedly throughout the day if your behavior is getting you what you want. Do your words and deeds match your desires? This exercise helps develop clarity and decreases unwanted or useless behaviors. Remember, your One-Page Miracle needs to be your goals and desires, not someone else's. As such, they are most likely to motivate you to stay on track

toward your goals, but you must make them a part of your daily life. Your brain needs to see them every day. If you know that you want a kind, caring, loving relationship with your spouse, then even when you are stressed or irritated you are likely to act in ways that are helpful to your relationship.

3. Develop razor-sharp focus. Get rid of the things in your life that do not fit your goals. One of my friends, Timothy, an entertainment attorney who represents authors, complained that he did not have time for his family. He had a three-year-old daughter, Larissa, who adored her father but had recently been acting up. Her mother said she was having more tantrums during the day and appeared sullen. Larissa complained she wanted to see her daddy more, but he usually got home after she went to bed. Timothy struggled with guilt but also felt the need to build his business. There were too many things happening at work that he felt he could not let go. Knowing that I was a child psychiatrist, he wondered if she had ADHD or another behavior problem. After hearing the story, I thought that she might just be missing her daddy, like she said. I did the One-Page Miracle exercise with Timothy. Clearly, his wife and daughter were very important to him. Then I asked him to be aware of all his activities at work for a week. Keeping detailed notes on his activities each day, he could tell he was wasting time: he walked to the coffee shop twice a day for drinks, three or four times a week he went to lunch with friends, and he constantly took phone calls from colleagues who had questions about their businesses. In defining his work goals, I asked him what were the most important things for him to be doing at work. What were the tasks and activities that built and sustained his business? He wrote three things:

- Take great care of my current clients.
- Develop new clients.
- Spend 10 percent of my time in pro bono work.

I suggested that anything unrelated to these three goals he needed to let go. He understood the concept of total focus. He could bring his coffee to work (preferably decaf), he could limit lunch with friends to once a week, and he could allow his voice mail to screen calls from his nonpaying clients. Within a month, he was coming home earlier and spending more time with his wife and daughter. Larissa's behavior dramatically improved. Spend time on the things that matter.

4. Know that saying no is okay. Too often, people feel anxious about saying no to someone. Many people, like me if I am not careful, are people pleasers. It bothers us when someone is upset with us, so we work hard to please others. We do not want to upset anyone. Somehow we believe that their unhappiness reflects badly on us. One concept that has helped me personally in this area I actually learned from my friend Timothy in the above story. He taught me to think in terms of "short-term pain versus long-term pain." About the time I was helping him with Larissa, my oldest daughter asked me for another puppy. I had always had trouble saying no to her, but we had three other animals at home. When I discussed the situation with Timothy, he said, "Do you want short-term pain or long-term pain?" As he explained it, a puppy was potentially a fifteen-year decision, while saying no to Breanne was a disappointment that would likely last hours, days, or (worst-case scenario) weeks. It made so much sense, so the puppy found another home.

   The principle of short-term pain versus long-term pain has helped me in many areas of my life from weight loss to relationships. When I look at the ice cream and feel hungry, I ask myself, "Is the hunger I'm feeling now (short-term pain) worth courting obesity, a condition that runs in my family (long-term pain)?" At work, if I need to fire an employee who is not working out, I often think short-term pain (the discomfort of letting someone go) versus long-term pain (the continuing hassles of having to deal with an ineffective employee). Whenever you find yourself in a quandary about what to do with an uncomfortable situation, just ask yourself, "Short-term versus long-term pain?"

5. Learn the phrase "I need to think about it. If I want to do it, I will get back to you." So many of my patients have trouble saying no, and they impulsively say yes and end up taking on more than they can do, distracting them from their goals. Sometimes they take on so many things that they end up doing nothing. When you are not sure what to do, you do not necessarily have to tell people no. A better answer frequently is "I have to think about it." Or "I need to talk to my board (or staff or spouse)." Give yourself time to make decisions about time. Then ask yourself whether the new task or request fits the goals you have for your life. Two quotes from Oprah Winfrey can be helpful to drive this point home.

One of the biggest lessons I've learned recently is that when you don't know what to do, you should do nothing until you figure out what to do because a lot of times you feel like you are pressed against the wall, and you've got to make a decision. You never have to do anything. Don't know what to do? Do nothing.

I didn't want to say "No" because I didn't want people to think I'm not nice. And that, to me, has been the greatest lesson of my life: to recognize that I am solely responsible for it, and not trying to please other people, and not living my life to please other people, but doing what my heart says all the time.

Use these five tips to gain more control over your PFC and impulses; developing total focus will get you much closer to your goals and overall happiness.

Embrace the Truth

LIBERATE YOURSELF FROM THE LIES POLLUTING YOUR BRAIN

We have met the enemy and he is us.

—POGO POSSUM

You can't empty your mind of thoughts. You might as well try to empty the ocean of its water. Thoughts just keep coming back, it seems. That's the way of it. But thoughts aren't a problem if they're met with understanding.

—BYRON KATIE, *A Thousand Names for Joy*

A number of years ago I wrote an article for *Parade* magazine called "How to Get Out of Your Own Way." After the article was published my office received over ten thousand letters asking for more information about self-defeating behavior. CNN heard about the response and asked me to be on one of its shows. At the time, I had never been on TV, but I agreed to do it because I thought it might help spread the news of my work. In the green room waiting to go on, I had a panic attack. I couldn't catch my breath, my heart raced, and I wanted to run out of the studio. Fortunately, the little voice in my head started to laugh at me and said, "You treat people who have this problem. What do you tell them to do?"

"Breathe! Slow down your breathing." People who have panic attacks breathe too fast; by slowing down your breathing you start to get control over yourself. I did that and felt calmer.

Next I thought, "Don't leave. If you leave the studio, you will never come back and the fear will take control of you and you will never be on TV again." So I didn't leave.

Then I thought, "Write down the first three thoughts in your head to see if you're scaring yourself. If you are, talk back to those thoughts." My first thought was "You are going to forget your name." Now that was funny, because why would an interviewer have to ask the name of an invited guest? The second thought was "You are going to stutter," and the third thought was "Two million people are going to think you are an idiot." I chuckled to myself. No wonder I wanted to run out of the studio. My brain was playing a horror film with me as the main victim.

Fortunately for me, I knew how to talk back to these thoughts. You do not have to believe every thought you have. Thoughts lie. They lie a lot. Just because you have a thought has nothing to do with whether or not it is true. I had been teaching my patients something I call ANT therapy for years. ANT stands for "automatic negative thought," and like ants at a picnic, the ANTs in your head can ruin your day. In ANT therapy, whenever your feel sad, mad, or nervous, you write down the thoughts going through your mind and evaluate whether or not they are true. If they are not true, talk back to them. You do not have to believe or accept every thought you have. You need an internal ANTeater on patrol.

So, in the CNN studio in Los Angeles, I took out a piece of paper, just like I would tell my patients to do, and did the ANTeater exercise. I drew two lines vertically down the paper, dividing it into three columns. In the first column I wrote down the thoughts, unedited as they occurred in my brain. In the second column I wrote the type of ANT it was. In my work, I have described nine different types of ANTs (see box on page 172). In the third column, I killed the ANTs by talking back to them. Were you good at talking back to your parents when you were a teenager? I was excellent. In the same way, you need to learn to be good at talking back to the lies you tell yourself.

So in the first column I wrote the initial thought: "You are going to forget your name." In the middle column I wrote, "Fortune-telling," because I was predicting the worst, the most common ANT among people who have panic attacks. In the third column, I wrote, "Probably not. I have never forgotten my name. But if I do, I have my driver's license in my wallet." Playing with the thoughts help to see how absurd they can be.

Below the first ANT I wrote out the second one: "You are going to stut-

---

SUMMARY OF NINE DIFFERENT TYPES OF ANTs

1. Always Thinking: Overgeneralizing a situation and usually starting thoughts with words like *always, never, everyone, every time*
2. Focusing on the Negative: Preoccupying yourself with what's going wrong in a situation and ignoring everything that could be construed as positive
3. Fortune-telling: Predicting the future in a negative way
4. Mind Reading: Arbitrarily believing you know what another person thinks, even though they have not told you
5. Thinking with Your Feelings: Believing your negative feelings without ever questioning them
6. Guilt Beatings: Thinking with words like *should, must, ought,* or *have to* that produce feelings of guilt
7. Labeling: Attaching a negative label to yourself or others
8. Personalization: Allowing innocuous events to take on personal meaning
9. Blame: Blaming other people for the problems in your life

---

ter." In the middle column I wrote, "Fortune-telling," because I was still predicting disaster in the future. And in the third column I wrote, "Probably not. I usually don't stutter, but if I do there will be people who stutter in the audience who will now have a doctor they can relate to." Having fun with the thoughts helps you disarm them.

Then I wrote the last thought: "Two million people will think you are an idiot." In the middle column I wrote, "Fortune telling." Again, I was predicting the worst. In the third column, I wrote, "Maybe so." Then next to it I wrote three numbers, 18-40-60, which stands for a rule I teach my patients, called the 18-40-60 rule, which says that when you are age eighteen you worry about what everyone thinks of you, when you are age forty you don't give a damn what anyone thinks about you, and when you're age sixty you realize no one has been thinking about you at all. People spend their days worrying and thinking about themselves, not you.

This five-minute exercise helped me relax and I was able to go on the television show and do well. If I would have run out of the studio, I would have likely never gone back and it would have dramatically changed my life and career.

Negative Thoughts Change Your Brain and Your Life

Do not let your thoughts prevent you from having a magnificent mind. Learn how to talk back to them. The ANT technique described above is not hard. I once taught it to a nine-year-old boy who suffered from terrible anx-

MAGNIFICENT MIND AT ANY AGE | 173

iety and depression. After several weeks he told me he was feeling much bet-ter. He said, "It's an ANT ghost town in my head."

Here is an example from his ANT therapy. He worried incessantly that his mother would die and leave him alone. This is not an uncommon worry for children who suffer with anxiety disorders. We did the ANT exercise to-gether in my office.

ANT	Type of ANT	ANTeater
My mother will die and leave me alone.	Fortune-telling	I have no way of knowing that. My thoughts are making me sick. She could live a very long time.

Internal logic is one of the most important brain skills we will ever need. It is the ability to tell ourselves the truth, to be completely honest and logical with ourselves. It is a course we should have all taken repeatedly, like English or math, starting in the third grade. Yet nowhere are we ever taught how to question our own thoughts, how to correct the erroneous words and images that circle in our minds, torturing and tormenting our souls. So much trouble is stirred up by the lies we tell ourselves and few people know how easy it is to correct them.

Nearly all of us have suffered an inordinate amount of fear, anxiety, ter-ror, and depression as a result of the unquestioned thoughts generated by our brains. Thoughts that are downright lies. It is hard to be effective direct-ing a life, a family, or a business with distorted negative thinking patterns. Yet in my experience, most people walk around infested by ANTs, and they don't have the skills needed to rid themselves of these pesky creatures. They have no idea that the source of their suffering is within their own synapses.

How you think moment by moment plays a primary role in how you feel. Predominantly negative thoughts cause you to feel bad, while positive or hopeful ones help you to feel good. In this chapter, I will give you a thinking tune-up. I will teach you how to tell yourself the truth to improve brain function and your overall sense of well-being. To start, here are five simple facts to help you begin to manage your thoughts and emotions.

FACT 1

Did you know that every time you have a thought your brain releases chem-icals? That's how your brain works. You have a thought, your brain releases chemicals, an electrical transmission goes across your brain, and you become aware of what you're thinking. Thoughts are real and they have a real impact on how you feel and how you behave. Like a muscle, the thoughts that you exercise become stronger and become the thoughts you rely on and believe, good or bad.

Every time you have an angry, unkind, hopeless, helpless, worthless, sad, or irritating thought, your brain releases negative chemicals that make you feel bad. Think about the last time you were mad. How did your body feel? When most people get angry, their muscles become tense, their hearts beat faster, their hands start to sweat, and they may even begin to feel a little dizzy. Your body reacts to every negative thought you have.

Every time you have a happy, hopeful, kind, optimistic, positive thought, your brain releases chemicals that make you feel good. Think about the last time you had a really happy thought. How did you feel inside your body? When most people are happy their muscles relax, their hearts beat slower, their hands become dry, and they breathe slower. Your body also reacts to your good thoughts.

Mark George, M.D., when he worked at the National Institutes of Mental Health, demonstrated this phenomenon in an elegant study of brain function. He studied the activity of the brain in ten normal women under three different conditions: when they were thinking happy thoughts, neutral thoughts, and sad thoughts. During the happy thoughts, the women demonstrated a cooling of their emotional brain and they felt better. During the sad thoughts, he noticed a significant increase in the emotional brain's activity, which is consistent with depression. Your thoughts matter.

FACT 2

Your body reacts to every thought you have. We know this from polygraph or lie detector equipment. During a lie detector test, a person is hooked up to equipment that measures the following.

- Hand temperature
- Heart rate
- Blood pressure
- Breathing rate
- Muscle tension
- How much the hands sweat

The tester then asks questions, like "Did you do that thing?" If the person did the bad thing his body is likely to have a "stress" response and it is likely to react in the following ways.

- Hands get colder.
- Heart goes faster.
- Blood pressure goes up.
- Breathing gets faster.
- Muscles get tight.
- Hands sweat more.

Almost immediately, his body reacts to what he thinks, whether he says anything or not. Now the opposite is also true. If he did not do the thing the tester asked about, it is likely that his body will experience a "relaxation" response and react in the following ways.

- Hands will become warmer.
- Heart rate will slow.
- Blood pressure goes down.
- Breathing becomes slower and deeper.
- Muscles become more relaxed.
- Hands become drier.

Again, almost immediately, your body reacts to what you think. This not only happens when you're asked about telling the truth, your body reacts to every thought you have, whether it is about work, friends, family, or anything else.

FACT 3

Thoughts are very powerful. They can make your mind and your body feel good or they can make you feel bad. Every cell in your body is affected by every thought you have. That is why when people get emotionally upset, they actually develop physical symptoms, such as headaches or stomachaches. Some physicians think that people who have a lot of negative thoughts are more likely to get cancer. If you can think about good things you are more likely to feel better.

Think of your body as an ecosystem. An ecosystem contains everything in the environment, including water, land, cars, people, animals, vegetation, houses, landfills, and so on. A negative thought is like pollution to your system. Just as pollution in the Los Angeles Basin affects everyone who goes outside, so too do negative thoughts pollute your mind and your body.

FACT 4

Unless you think about your thoughts, they are automatic or "they just happen." Since they just happen, they are not necessarily correct. Your thoughts do not always tell the truth. Sometimes they lie to you. I once treated a college student who thought he was stupid, because he didn't perform well on tests. When he was tested, however, we discovered that he had an IQ of 135, very bright. You don't have to believe every thought that goes through your head. It's important to think about your thoughts to see if they are helping you or hurting you. Unfortunately, if you never challenge your thoughts, you just believe them as if they were true.

One negative thought, like one ant at a picnic, is not a big problem. Two or three negative thoughts, like two or three ants at a picnic, become more irritating. Ten or twenty negative thoughts, like ten or twenty ants at a picnic, may cause the couple to pick up and leave the picnic.

FACT 5

You can learn to eliminate ANTs and replace them with positive thoughts that are not "pie in the sky" thinking but rather true, real, accurate thoughts that give you peace, encouragement, and a fair assessment of your current situation. This skill alone could completely change your life if you embrace and practice it. Once you learn about your thoughts, you can choose to think good thoughts and feel good or you can choose to think bad thoughts and feel lousy. That's right—it's up to you! You can learn how to change your thoughts and change the way you feel. One way to learn how to change your thoughts is to notice them when they are negative and talk back to them. If you can correct negative thoughts, you take away their power over you. When you just think a negative thought without challenging it, your mind believes it and your body reacts to it.

Whenever you notice these ANTs, you need to crush them or they'll ruin your relationships, your self-esteem, and your personal power. So here is the exercise: Whenever you feel sad, mad, or nervous write out the automatic thoughts in your mind. Then ask yourself if any of them are ANTs, if any are distorted. What type of ANTs are they? Then kill each ANT by talking back to it. You do not have to believe every thought you have! In fact, if you do, they will surely make you sick.

The Work: Another Technique

As I wrote earlier, a number of years ago I went through an emotionally painful time in my life after I lost someone important to me. I felt terrible for almost nine months, despite all of the emotional management skills I had developed over the years. I had trouble sleeping, felt sad and anxious, and suffered crushing chest pain. Hard as I tried, I couldn't get the other person out of my head. In my search for healing I read at least fifty books about grief. None of them made a bit of difference until I read *Loving What Is* by Byron Katie.

In this very wise book, written with her husband, accomplished author Stephen Mitchell, Katie, as her friends call her, described her own experience suffering from suicidal depression. She was a young mother, businesswoman, and wife in the high desert of Southern California. She became severely depressed at the age of thirty-three. For ten years, she sank deeper and deeper into self-loathing, rage, despair, constant thoughts of suicide, and paranoia. For the last two years, she was often unable to leave her bedroom and care for herself or her family. Then one morning in 1986, out of nowhere, Katie woke up in a state of amazement, transformed by the realization that when she believed her thoughts, she suffered, but when she questioned her thoughts, she didn't suffer. Katie's great insight is that it is not life or other people that make us feel depressed, angry, abandoned, and despairing but our thoughts that make us feel that way. In other words, we live in a hell of our own making, or we live in a heaven of our own making.

Katie developed a simple method of inquiry—the Work—to question our thoughts. It consists of writing down any of the thoughts that are bothering us or any of the thoughts in which we are judging other people, then asking ourselves four questions, and then doing a turnaround. The goal is not positive thinking but rather accurate thinking. The four questions are:

1. Is it true? (Is the stressful or negative thought true?)

2. Can I absolutely know that it's true?

3. How do I react when I believe that thought?

4. Who would I be without the thought? Or how would I feel if I didn't have the thought?

After you answer the four questions, you then take the original thought and completely turn it around to its opposite, and ask yourself whether the opposite of the original thought that is causing your suffering is not true or even truer. Then, turn the thought around and apply it to yourself (how does the opposite of the thought apply to me personally) and to the other person, if one is involved in the thought (how does the turnaround apply to the other person).

When I personally started to do the Work I immediately felt better. I was more relaxed, less anxious, and more honest in dealing with my own thoughts and emotions. Katie and Stephen have since become friends and I have shared their insights with almost all of my own friends and patients. You will notice that there are similarities between the Work and ANT therapy. The Work is also powerful, easy to learn, and very effective.

For example, I had a mild-mannered, charming patient named Nile who loved his girlfriend very much. She was beautiful, brilliant, passionate, and generous. But the downside of their love affair was that the girlfriend's bad moods suddenly manifested as intensely and unpredictably as tornadoes. When his girlfriend was on a tear, she lashed out at Nile, finding fault with everything from his earning power to his taste in clothes. Accusing him of selfishness and of taking her for granted, she often made his life miserable. Understandably, Nile lived in constant apprehension and stress. Whenever his girlfriend had a temper tantrum, he suffered from headaches and stomach pains. Nile's thoughts about his girlfriend were literally making him sick!

In one part of his mind, Nile knew it was time to end the relationship. But he felt powerless to break things off because another part of him still loved his girlfriend.

I had Nile begin the Work with the statement "I do not want to break up with my girlfriend."

Well, when I asked him if this was true, he immediately said, "No, I have to leave her because this relationship is making me sick."

Okay. But did he know this to be absolutely true? "I have the psychiatrist bills to prove it," he joked. "But seriously, sometimes it feels like I'm losing my mind."

And how did he react when he thought "I do not want to break up with her"?

"My hands start sweating, I feel tense all over, I'm stressed out."

I invited Nile to turn the thought around and find three examples to see if this were more true than the original stressful thought.

"I do want to break up with my girlfriend," he started. "I'm tired of walking on eggshells all the time. And I'm sick of churning out stomach acid whenever she flips out. Even though I love her, she's bad for my health and I think I deserve better," he concluded.

Asking the four questions and doing the turnaround helped Nile realize that he was breaking up with his girlfriend in order to reclaim his peace of mind, health, and autonomy. When he eventually told her that he had to end the relationship, Nile felt a huge burden had been lifted from his life. His headaches and stomachaches stopped and he started dating again, with a stronger sense of self.

If you want to know yourself, write down your stressful thoughts, four questions, and the turnaround about someone else. Point the Work toward others in the beginning, and you will soon see that everything outside you directly reflects your own thinking. Yes, your thoughts are all about you, and very often, they are completely disconnected from your reality, or "what actually is." This strategic form of thinking and questioning your thoughts directly puts a close-up lens on the reality of your life, which is always a good thing, because the truth can set you free.

Truth in the Courtroom of Your Mind

One of the other exercises many of my patients have found helpful in quelling the critics in their heads and boosting their self-esteem is one I call "Truth in the Courtroom of Your Mind." It takes a bit of effort, but you are worth the time it takes. Do the following steps.

1. Take a piece of paper and draw out a courtroom scene. Include the judge, prosecuting attorneys, defense lawyers, defendant, court reporter, witness stand, and jury box. This is a drawn representation of the voices in your head.

2. Choose a crime that you mentally accuse yourself of. It can be anything you feel guilty about, or anything you've actually done of which you're ashamed.

3. Put yourself on trial. Actually begin to write out the dialogue of a trial. Have opening statements by the prosecutor and the defense. Call witnesses. Raise objections. At first, notice the strength of your internal prosecuting attorney; after all, he's had practice accusing you all these years. However, as you write out the trial, you'll begin to notice the lies your prosecutor tells in the courtroom. He distorts the truth to make you look worse.

4. Strengthen your defense attorney. Instead of the wimp he has been, make him stand tall and defend you with eloquence instead of silence. Hire the best lawyer in the world to help defend you. You're worth it.

5. Repeat this exercise several times, until you have sufficiently strengthened your defense attorney.

Some have written two pages of dialogue, but I have one patient who wrote forty pages. Do what helps you. One person who performed this exercise wrote, "This is fun. I hired a whole gang—Clarence Darrow, Daniel Webster, Melvin Belli, Bella Abzug, Johnnie Cochran, and Perry Mason. Then I gave the prosecution Hamilton Burger, who has never won a case, and a guy I used to know who became the worst lawyer ever to pass the bar. Every time old Burger is about to make a point, my old friend trips him up. He forgets to file papers and summon witnesses too."

After you've tried this exercise several times on paper, begin to set up this scenario in your head: Identify your accusing voices (can you match them up to your accusers of the past?), and identify and strengthen those voices that root for you and defend you. Our prosecuting attorneys can also work in our best interest. They do that by bringing up important issues we need to look at, but they do it in such a way as to help us learn from our mistakes rather than beating us up for them. The commentary these inner voices provide on our actions can either enhance or sabotage our chances for success. Train your inner voices to work in your own best interest. After all, they are your voices; put them under your control.

The Truth About Gratitude

When you bring your attention to the things you are grateful for in your life, your brain actually works better. Psychologist Noelle Nelson and I did a study on gratitude and appreciation. She was working on a book called *The Power of Appreciation* and had her brain scanned twice. The first time she was scanned after thirty minutes of meditating on all the things she was thankful for in her life. Then she was scanned several days later after focusing on the major fears in her life. After the "appreciation meditation," her brain looked very healthy. On the day of her "fear-based meditation," Noelle took the exercise very seriously. One of her fears was about what would happen if her dog got sick and she couldn't work. She had a string of frightening thoughts.

"If my dog got sick, I couldn't go to work because I would have to stay home to care for him."

"If I didn't go to work, however, I would lose my job."

"If I lost my job, I wouldn't have enough money to take my dog to the vet and he would likely die."

"If the dog died, I would be so depressed I still wouldn't be able to go back to work."

"Then I would lose my home and be homeless."

After these thoughts I scanned her brain. Her frightened brain looked very different from her grateful brain. Rather than look healthy, she had seriously decreased activity in two parts of her brain. Her cerebellum, in the back part of the brain, completely shut down. The cerebellum, also called the little brain, is known to be involved in physical coordination, such as walking or playing sports. New research also suggests that the cerebellum is involved in processing speed, like clock speed on a computer and thought coordination or how quickly we can integrate new information. When the cerebellum experiences low activity, people tend to be clumsier and less likely to think their ways out of problems. They think and process information more slowly and they get confused more easily. When I saw this finding, I thought that this was why negative thinking is involved in athletic slumps. If an athlete thinks he will fail, likely he will. I now had proof that negative thinking actually shuts down the coordination part of the brain. The other area of the brain that was affected was the temporal lobes, especially the one on the left. The temporal lobes are involved with mood, memory, and temper control. Problems in this part of the brain are associated with some forms of depression and also dark thoughts, violence, and memory problems. In Noelle's scans, when she practiced gratitude, her temporal lobes looked healthy. When she frightened herself, her temporal lobes became much less active. Negative thought patterns change the brain in a negative way. Practicing gratitude literally helps you have a brain to be grateful for.

Here is the exercise: Write out five things you are grateful for every day. The act of writing helps to solidify them in your brain. In my experience, when depressed patients do this exercise daily they actually needed less antidepressant medication. Other researchers have also found that people who express gratitude on a regular basis are healthier, more optimistic, make more progress toward their goals, have a greater sense of well-being, and are more helpful to others. Doctors who regularly practice gratitude are actually better at making the correct diagnoses on their patients.

When you tell yourself the truth, your brain works better and you feel and act happier. Using the ANTeater exercises and the Work, along with having a competent internal defense attorney and focusing on gratitude, are essential skills to keep your brain healthy and encourage success in everything you do.

| 13 |

Get Unstuck

___

ENHANCE YOUR BRAIN'S ABILITY TO CHANGE AND ADAPT

He who rejects change is the architect of decay.

—HAROLD WILSON

The bend in the road is not the end of the road unless you refuse to take the turn.

—Anonymous

Doing something the way that it has always been done does not mean you will be successful doing it the same way going forward, even if you were wildly successful doing it that way in the past. Business consultant Tom Peters writes that we are in the greatest change revolution perhaps of the last thousand years. Change will be the norm, not the exception. To be successful in the coming world environment, it is critical to be mentally flexible and to change as change is needed. Minds trapped in the past, or even minds trapped in the present moment, will be left behind.

Trouble Getting Unstuck

In 2005 fisherman Jim Peterson was eighty miles off the coast of Newport, Oregon, when the engine of his sixty-year-old wooden troller became stuck in reverse. Even though he tried and tried, the gears would not shift. Far from his home port of Coos Bay, Jim weighed his options: wait hours for the Coast Guard to tow him home, wait for help from other fishermen, or drive the boat all the way back in reverse. Jim decided not to wait. "It was odd," he told the *Register-Guard* of Eugene, "watching the wake roll out the front windows. Like watching a movie in reverse." More foreign still, Jim said, was trying to steer the thirty-eight-foot boat. "It was like backing up a truck towing a trailer, with extra motion underneath." Getting home was a thirty-nine-hour ordeal, three times the normal time it should take.

Being stuck in reverse, obsessing about the past, or being unable to shift mental gears in the present is extremely common among people who struggle in relationships, at work or within themselves. Change is very hard for them. The brain, like a car or a boat, has gear-shifting mechanisms. When an engine is stuck in first, it uses excessive energy, whines loudly, and doesn't get very far. When an engine is stuck in reverse it can be downright dangerous. Smooth shifting is a prerequisite to an easy ride. In a similar way, when your brain gets stuck you use too much energy, whine loudly, and do not make much progress in your life. Trouble shifting your attention can lead to disastrous results and inhibits change.

Through the decades of both my clinical practice and business work I have seen people's brains get stuck in many different ways, often involving being stuck in the past, present, or future. Healthy change becomes impossible. Here are some examples.

- Being stuck in the past—Holding grudges, being unforgiving, holding on to emotional pain or regrets, having unresolved grief or trauma, and exhibiting low self-esteem from repetitively judging their own past behavior. In business, tightly holding on to the ways a company has always done things, even though they may be outdated or harmful.
- Being stuck in the present—Being oppositional and argumentative; have to have their own way; are uncooperative and selfish; and feel trapped in a difficult relationship, stressful job, an addiction, or an obsession. In business, being rigid or unyielding in policies or procedures.
- Being stuck in the future—For individuals, worrying, being fearful, predicting the worst, and exhibiting insecurity. In business, not taking appropriate risks for fear of failure, seeing fear in the future, and being overprotective.

When you are stuck in a position, you are not moving your life forward. Business, family, and personal success require change, flexibility, and the

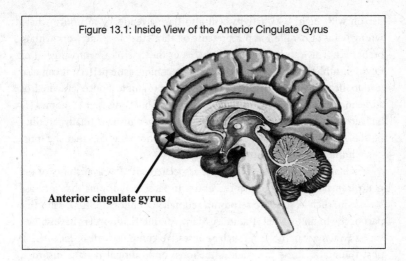

Figure 13.1: Inside View of the Anterior Cingulate Gyrus

Anterior cingulate gyrus

ability to transition. Being able to move fluidly through your life is an ability of a magnificent mind. This ability, in part, involves a section of the brain we have discussed earlier, called the anterior cingulate gyrus, or ACG, the brain's gear shifter (see Figure 13.1).

It is involved with cognitive flexibility and helps people shift their attention from task to task or idea to idea. When this part of the brain is healthy people are able to see options to situations, they are able to go with the flow, change as needed, and move easily from idea to idea. They are more likely to be inclusive and cooperative with others. When the ACG is low in activity, people struggle with attention. Low ACG activity has been found in brain imaging studies in people with ADHD. When the ACG is damaged or hurt some people develop a syndrome called akinetic mutism, which is associated with low motivation and less verbalization or speech. When the ACG is high, people have trouble shifting attention and tend to get stuck on negative thoughts or repetitive behaviors. Getting stuck is associated with being inflexible, rigid, oppositional, argumentative, having trouble with transitions, worrying, holding grudges, and even struggling with obsessive thoughts or compulsive behaviors. People with high ACG activity struggle with transitions and hate when things do not go as expected. Other people often feel diminished or controlled in the presence of those with high ACG activity.

The ACG is also involved with error detection. When it is healthy, people will notice when things are wrong or out of place and work to fix them. When the ACG works too hard, anything out of place will drive them nuts. A person with high ACG activity will also have a tendency to notice what's wrong in his or her life and put pressure on those they love and work with to be perfect. This can be a healthy trait, as in the case of a neurosurgeon or Olympic athlete, where it is essential that techniques are perfect. It can also lead to life ruin when it gets out of control. For example, I once saw a neurosurgeon who was technically a genius at work but a disaster at home. He badgered his wife and children to be perfect. When his wife finally left him, he stalked her. He could not get her out of his head and felt that she must come home in order for him to feel okay.

High activity in the ACG has been associated with low availability of the neurotransmitter serotonin in the brain. In fact, medications that increase serotonin, such as selective serotonin reuptake inhibitors (SSRIs), calm this part of the brain on SPECT studies. Many psychiatric disorders have shown excessive activity in the ACG, such as obsessive-compulsive disorder (OCD), post-traumatic stress disorder, addictions, oppositional defiant disorder, obsessive-compulsive personality disorder, autistic spectrum disorders, and certain forms of depression. SSRIs have been used in all of these disorders with varying levels of success. Even though these might seem like a wide variety of problems, they share a common underlying mechanism—getting stuck, being rigid, being unable to change, and having trouble shifting attention. People with OCD get stuck on awful obsessive thoughts or repetitive behaviors, such as checking, counting, or washing; people with posttraumatic stress disorder get stuck on past hurtful events; people with addictions get stuck on their drug; people with oppositional defiant disorder get stuck on arguing and saying no; people with obsessive-compulsive personality disorder get stuck on needing to have their way; people with autistic spectrum disorders often get stuck on rituals; and people with certain forms of depression get stuck on their failures from the past.

Examples of being stuck in rigid thought patterns and behaviors are all around us. Maybe there are even some in your own life. Here are some brief examples of what a "stuck" person might say.

- I hate being divorced (eight years later).
- I have to have it my way.
- You hurt me years ago and I'll never forget.
- I won't ever forgive you.
- It'll never be the same.
- I'm always worried.

- I can't get bad thoughts out of my head.
- Do it my way.
- I can't change. This is the way it should be done.
- It's your fault.
- I don't agree with you.
- No. No. No. I won't do it. I don't want to do it. You can't make me do it.
- I have a lot of complaints about you.
- I've never hated anyone more than you.
- This will never change.

People who live or work with people who tend to get stuck often say things such as:

- Nothing ever gets forgiven or let go.
- She brings up issues from years and years ago.
- Everything has to be the way she wants it.
- He can't ever say he's sorry.
- She holds on to grudges forever.
- He never throws anything away.
- She's rigid.
- If things aren't perfect he thinks they are no good at all.
- I don't help her because I have to do it exactly her way or she goes ballistic.
- He argues with everything I say.
- She tends to be oppositional.
- He doesn't like to try new things.

Let's look at three detailed examples of how getting stuck prevents people from fulfilling their dreams.

Philip, age eight, was brought to see me by his mom and dad because of his extreme tantrums. They could go on and on, sometimes for hours. The week before his appointment, the parents surprised Philip by taking him to Disney World for his birthday. Philip had always loved the Magic Kingdom and his parents thought he would have a blast. The one mistake they made, however, was surprising him. Philip had a very rigid brain. He needed things to be a certain way or he would become very upset, sometimes to the point of violence. He needed to know what to expect and time for transition. When they pulled the family car into the Simba parking lot at Disney World Philip threw a three-hour tantrum. They could not console or settle him down and ended up going home. His birthday was ruined. I sat in amazement as I listened to the story. Not that I hadn't heard many stories like it in the past, but just the week before I had seen another child who had the exact same tantrum at Disney World. Mickey was losing his touch, I thought. Looking at Philip, I asked why he got so upset. He said he didn't know. I asked him if he liked Disney World. He said yes. I asked if he was sure. Again, he said yes. I then told him it was okay not to like Disney World. It is expensive, and there are long lines, and lots of people. Philip looked at me like, "Poor Dr. Amen. He just doesn't get it." Then he said, "I like Disney World and have no idea why I flipped out."

I diagnosed Philip with Asperger's syndrome, a high functioning autistic spectrum disorder characterized by rigid thinking patterns. His brain scan showed intense increased activity in his ACG. Autistic spectrum disorders are characterized by cognitive and emotional inflexibility. People with an autistic spectrum disorder get stuck on negative thoughts and behaviors, much like patients who have OCD. Often, they appear as if they have to have things their way. On the surface they appear selfish. Yet it is not selfishness that is the problem, it is inflexibility. Their brain gets stuck.

Christine and Tim had been married for five years when they came to see me. They were fighting nearly every week, sometimes about money or sex, sometimes seemingly about nothing at all. In evaluating the couple it was clear that they were both rigid and inflexible. They both wanted their way, with little compromise. I had seen this pattern many times before. Christine was a nurse who had grown up in an alcoholic home and had struggled with anxiety, depression, and excessive worry. At home, she had a place for everything and was upset when things were not where they were supposed to be. *Neat freak* was a term she had heard many times in her life. Tim was a trial attorney who was financially successful but difficult to be around. He went through many assistants, was argumentative at home and work, and appeared to Christine as narcissistic and self-absorbed. The first few sessions I had with them I felt like a referee in a boxing ring. They both postured to get one up on each other and only saw things from their own perspective. Both had trouble listening and had a long list of complaints they had to discuss. People like Christine and Timothy wear out the typical marital therapist. I was the fourth marital therapist they saw. But I had a secret weapon. Looking at both of their scans, it was clear that the ACG worked way too hard. In some important ways they were both like Philip: rigid, inflexible, and needing their way. To be helpful to this couple, it was imperative to balance their brains or they were destined to be unhappy or divorced, not only in this marriage but in the others to come. Seeing their scans, they understood the dilemma and both became cooperative with treatment. A better brain is connected to a happier marriage.

Les had to be the boss at work. He could never work for anyone else. It was always his way or the highway. He had sold his wholesale grocery business to a larger company for a healthy sum of money but left after eight months, even though he had agreed to stay on for three years. It was a big loss financially, but Les couldn't stand always fighting with his new management team. Whenever they disagreed with him, he thought they were idiots; he argued incessantly and worried about the company. The management team thought Les had an irrational arrogant streak and viewed him as oppositional, a poor listener who struggled to get along. Les was also divorced and estranged from his only son. His ex-wife often told him that he was selfish and that he would hold on to grudges and hurts for years and years. After leaving his company, Les became depressed and was referred to our clinics by his sister who was also our patient. His scan, like Philip's, Christine's, and Tim's, showed too much activity in the ACG. He was rigid, inflexible, worried, and alone.

These three cases are blatant examples of being stuck, manifested tantrums, fighting, and self-sabotage. Let's look at two more subtle examples of how getting stuck can cause trouble.

Wilson, a young information technology administrator for a medical insurance company, was struggling in his marriage. He and his wife were having more frequent disagreements and seemed to be growing apart. Wilson worried about their future together. At work, he was becoming more and more distracted. He could not get the problems at home out of his head. Initially, his company supervisors saw him as a rising star—bright, hardworking, and a real asset to the morale and profitability of the company. Lately, they started to wonder if they made the right choice by promoting Wilson, as several important tasks were left undone. Through their employee assistance program, they suggested Wilson see me. Rather than viewing the referral negatively, which many employees do initially, I found Wilson to be open and interested. He was worried about his marital problems and wanted help to resolve them so he could get the anxious thoughts out of his head. I taught him how to eliminate the repetitive negative thoughts, be more present at work, and increase the communication with his wife. Getting stuck on these stressful thoughts almost cost Wilson his promotion. His open spirit saved him.

One of my close friends, Kerry, got a new job as the chief financial officer for a group of surgery centers across Southern California. She was very excited about her new position. Kerry tended to be a worrier, and if you saw her home the word *anal* might cross your mind, which is not all that uncommon for accountants. After about six months into her new job, Kerry started to appear stressed. In dealing with a group of physicians, she often found that they were argumentative, oppositional, and rigid. She took their negative comments personally and would dwell on them for weeks. I could see that the initial excitement about the job had been slowly draining out of her. On one of our walks, we discussed her worries at length. By all outward accounts they loved her at work. After a few months she had been given a substantial raise and more responsibility. She was in charge of several new projects to grow the business. She had never worked for physicians before. I told her that *M.D.* stands for "minor deity," and that many physicians tend to be "cingulate," argumentative and rigid, especially in dealing with their families and staff, although not their patients, because they see them as providing their livelihood and purpose in life. About an hour into our walk, we got to the bottom line. Even though a doctor would say something negative to her once, in Kerry's head she heard the comment five hundred times. It was as though her mind was repeatedly hitting the replay button of the negative comment. This was Kerry's issue, not her employers. Understanding the culture of her workplace and, more important, how her own brain was sabotaging her, she was able to relax and have more fun at work. She learned that she did not have to hit the replay button; in fact, doing so was hurtful to her. I told her of a spin-off from the serenity prayer that I often use myself.

> *God, grant me the serenity*
> *to accept the people I cannot change,*
> *the courage to change the one I can, and*
> *the wisdom to know that person is me.*

Making Unconscious, Brain-Driven Behavior Conscious

Over the years, I have seen hundreds of people who had too much activity in the ACG. Often, they would struggle with change, get stuck on negative thoughts, and need to do things a certain way or they would be upset. They also tended to be argumentative and oppositional, which can be a challenge in a psychotherapy session. Part of my job is to notice behavior patterns and feed them back to my patients.

Lindy had the cingulate from hell. She was the CEO of a local software company and had a child with Asperger's syndrome. She was brilliant, attractive, and very successful on the surface. Underneath her pretty exterior, she was chronically stressed, and had trouble in relationships. After her third divorce she came to see me. I remember one therapy session with Lindy where I felt that no matter what I said she would argue with me. I had been seeing her for about three months and it was like she was wearing Teflon. Everything I said just bounced off her. Nothing would stick. A bit out of frustration I said, "It seems like no matter what I say you argue with me."

What do you think Lindy said next?

"No, I don't," was her reply.

I smiled, "That's how it seems to me."

"But I don't do that!" she quickly shot back.

"I know you say that," I said with a more serious look. "But if you want to get better, I want you to think about what I am saying."

"I don't do that," she said even more emphatically.

It is usually not very helpful to argue with patients, especially ones who get stuck, but I felt that I needed to press this point.

"If you want to get better, this is what I would like you to do."

She opened her mouth in protest, but I raised my hand for her to let me finish.

"If you want to get better, I want you to watch yourself this week. See if it is not your automatic tendency, in most situations, to argue with people. See if you are not always arguing with others in your head and that you tend to form the opposite opinion of what people say automatically, no matter what they are saying."

"But I don't do that," she protested one last time.

"Just watch it this week." With that we ended our session.

The next week as Lindy sat down in my office, she started, almost with excitement, "I do that! My mind is always arguing with people. How weird."

"Do you want to do that?" I said.

"What do you mean?" she asked.

"Do you want to be a chronically difficult person who argues with everyone?"

"No." She appeared sad. This was a hard realization.

"Your brain's automatic tendency is to argue and oppose. It is unconscious. When the anterior cingulate gyrus works too hard, people tend to get stuck in opposition or negative thoughts and behaviors. But obviously, that drives away the people you love. They get tired of the conflict, unless, of course, they need it."

She was finally listening with an open mind and not arguing with me.

"If you want to correct this problem, before you say no to someone or start to argue with them, I want you to ask yourself, first, before you say anything, what you really think about the situation and if it fits your personal goals to argue, oppose, or say no."

This is the essence of making unconscious, brain-driven behavior conscious and will driven. This is the essence of mental health and a major factor in success. Do you operate from your goals rather than your brain's natural tendency to argue, oppose, or seek sameness? When you understand your own brain's vulnerabilities ask yourself if your behavior matches your desires and goals. If you find that you are argumentative, oppositional, or impulsive, take a step back before you respond and ask yourself the question, again and again, Does my behavior get me what I want? If it does, then you are living a conscious life and not reacting out of the realm of your unconscious.

Greasing the Gears

Balance is needed in your ACG. It is critical to shift gears as needed. Otherwise you end up throwing tantrums, fighting with the people you love, making stupid financial decisions, making mistakes at work, or feeling tormented by hurtful comments from less than thoughtful people. Shifting gears too hastily will make you distracted and unable to stay on the path toward your goals when things get tough. We need a healthy balance so we can stay on track but also be able to take the turns when they come up along the roads of our lives. Here are seven steps to help you be more flexible without compromising your ability to stay focused on what is important to you.

1. BALANCE YOUR BRAIN

If you or someone you love tends to resist change, gets stuck on negative thoughts or behaviors, or is rigid and oppositional, it is likely the brain needs a boost of the neurotransmitter serotonin. There are both natural and pharmaceutical ways to enhance this important chemical, including aerobic exercise, nutritional and supplement strategies, as well as SSRI medications.

Exercise can be very helpful in calming worries and increasing the brain's flexibility. Exercise works by increasing brain levels of L-tryptophan, the amino acid building block for serotonin. L-tryptophan is a relatively small amino acid and has trouble competing against the larger amino acids to enter the brain. During exercise the larger amino acids are utilized to nourish muscle tissue, which causes a relative decrease in the availability of these larger amino acids in the blood stream. As such, L-tryptophan can compete more effectively to enter the brain and raise brain serotonin levels. In addition, exercise helps your energy and may distract you from the bad thoughts that tend to loop. One of the best things to do when you are upset and cannot get thoughts out of your head is go for a run or a long, fast walk or to play tennis.

There are two ways that food can increase serotonin levels. According to MIT researchers, carbohydrate-containing foods such as pastas, potatoes, bread, pastries, pretzels, candy, and popcorn temporarily increase L-tryptophan levels in the blood, resulting in more L-tryptophan available to enter the brain where it is converted to serotonin. The calming effect of serotonin can often be felt in thirty minutes or less by eating these foods. The problem, of course, is that you will want to duplicate this positive feeling and use these foods repeatedly, which is not healthy. Cerebral serotonin levels can also be raised by eating foods rich in tryptophan, such as turkey, peanut butter, eggs, green peas, potatoes, and milk. Many people unknowingly trigger cognitive inflexibility or mood problems by eating diets that are low in L-tryptophan. For example, high-protein, low-carbohydrate diets that I recommend for low dopamine states (related to prefrontal cortex underactivity) often make cingulate problems worse.

In the short run, when someone is upset with you or stuck in her position, give her a cookie. In a few minutes, she may be more flexible. If you wanted to be a bit Machiavellian, you could use food at business meetings to manipulate the environment. If you need people to pay better attention at meetings, serve more protein-based food, such as nuts and cheese. If you want them to be less contentious and more cooperative, serve cookies.

Nutritional supplementation can also be helpful, such as 5-hydroxy-tryptophan, inositol, and St. John's wort, discussed in chapters 6 and 7.

My friend and colleague Barry Chaitin, who is the chair of the department of psychiatry at the University of California–Irvine, talks about patients who have sticky thoughts and that medications such as Prozac are like grease for their gear shifters, helping them to be more flexible. SSRI medications, such as Prozac, Zoloft, Paxil, Luvox, Celexa, and Lexapro, can be very helpful in calming overactivity in this part of the brain. Because of side effects and cost, I tend to recommend exercise, dietary interventions, and natural supplements first, but it depends on the severity of the clinical situation.

2. NOTICE WHEN YOU'RE STUCK, DISTRACT YOURSELF, AND COME BACK TO THE PROBLEM LATER

One of the most helpful ways to overcome being stuck on negative thoughts or behaviors is to notice when you're stuck and distract yourself. Becoming aware of circular or looping thoughts is essential to gaining control over them. Whenever you find the thoughts "circling the wagons" (going over and over), distract yourself from them. Get up and do something else. Distraction is often a very helpful technique. It gives you power or a measure of control in the situation. Some of my ACG patients find it helpful to make a list of all the things they can do to distract themselves when they get harassing thoughts. Here are some examples:

- Sing a favorite song.
- Listen to music that makes you feel positive.
- Take a walk.
- Do a chore.
- Play with a pet.
- Do structured meditation.
- Focus on a word and do not allow any other thoughts to enter your mind.

If you allow repetitive thoughts to go over and over they get worse and have more power over you. If you actively distract yourself from them or block them, over time they lose their control over you and become less and less.

3. THINK THROUGH ANSWERS BEFORE AUTOMATICALLY SAYING NO

As mentioned, many ACG people have an automatic tendency to say no. Fight the tendency. Before answering questions or responding to requests in a negative way, take a breath and think first whether or not it is in the best interest of the situation to really say no. Often it is helpful to take a deep breath, hold it for a few seconds, and then slowly exhale, just to get extra time before responding. For example, if your spouse asks you to come to bed and make love, take a deep breath before responding that you're tired, sick, too busy, or not in the mood. Use the time during the deep breath to ask yourself whether or not you really want to deny your partner; determine if it's in your best interest to say no and continue doing what you're doing or if it's in your best interest to get close to your partner. The automatic no has ruined many relationships. Take enough time to ask yourself if saying no is really what you want to say.

4. WRITE OUT OPTIONS AND SOLUTIONS WHEN YOU FEEL STUCK

Whenever you feel stuck on a thought, it is often helpful to write it down. Writing the thought down gets it out of your head. When you see a thought on paper, you can deal with it in a rational way. When these thoughts cause sleeping problems, keep a pen and paper near your bed to write them out. After you write out a thought that has gotten stuck, generate a list of the things you can do about it and the things you can't do about it. For example, if you are worried about a situation at work, such as whether or not you'll get the promotion, do the following:

- Write out the thought: "I'm worried about whether or not I'll get the promotion at work."
- Make a list of the things you can do about the worry.
  - I can do the best job I can at work.
  - I will continue to be reliable, hardworking, and creative.
  - I will make sure the boss knows I desire the promotion.
  - In a confident (not bragging) way, I will make sure the boss knows about my contributions to the company.
- Make a list of the things you cannot do about the worry.
  - I cannot make the decision for the boss.
  - I cannot want the promotion any more than I do.
  - I cannot will the promotion to happen. Worrying will not help.
  - I cannot make the promotion happen, although I do have lots of influence on the process by my attitude and performance.

Use this simple exercise to unlock the thoughts that keep you up nights feeling tense.

5. SEEK THE COUNSEL OF OTHERS WHEN YOU FEEL STUCK
(OFTEN JUST TALKING ABOUT FEELING STUCK WILL OPEN NEW OPTIONS)

When all of your efforts to rid repetitive thoughts are unsuccessful, it is often helpful to seek the counsel of others. Finding someone with whom to discuss the worries, fears, or repetitive behaviors can be very helpful. Through the years, I have used mentors to help me through some of the problems I've had to face. Other people can be a "sounding board"; they can help you see options and provide a reality check for you.

6. WHEN DEALING WITH OPPOSITIONAL PEOPLE, DON'T OVERREACT TO THE OPPOSITION

Don't try to convince someone else who is stuck. If you're locked in the middle of an argument, take a break! Take ten minutes, ten hours, or even ten days. One of the best marital suggestions I give couples is "Learn how to go to the bathroom." When you can see that your partner is beginning to get into cingulate territory and is starting to go over the same point again and again, excuse yourself and say you have to go to the bathroom. If you're in a repetitive, negative argument with somebody, and you distract yourself, you're often able to come back later and work it out.

I learned long ago not to try to argue with people who had ACG problems. When another person is "stuck" on a thought or behavior, logical reasoning is often ineffective in swaying their opinion. One of the best techniques I've found to deal with those who get stuck is as follows: I will briefly make the point I want to make. If I can tell the other person is getting locked in to his position, I try to change the subject and distract him away from the topic at the moment. Distraction allows time for the other person's subconscious mind to process what I said without having to lock in on it or fight it. Often, when we come back to the issue, he'll have a more open mind to the situation. Here's an example.

Jackie came to see me for marital problems. Her husband traveled and was unable to attend many of the sessions. In the individual sessions, I saw that Jackie frequently became locked in to her position and left little room for alternative explanations for behavior. Her husband complained of the same thing. He said that she would go on and on for hours and not listen to anything he said. As I realized this was her pattern, I used the brief "attack and retreat" model I described. When she complained about her husband's not paying attention to her, I wondered aloud if it wasn't because he felt she didn't listen to his opinion. Immediately, she said I was wrong. She said that she was a very good listener. I didn't argue with her but went on to something else for a while. The next session, Jackie talked about listening more to her husband. Because I hadn't engaged her in a prolonged battle, her subconscious was able to hear and process what I said.

This is often a very helpful technique for teenagers. Many teens argue and oppose their parents as part of the natural individuation process. I teach parents to get out of struggles with their teenagers by briefly making their points and moving on to other topics. Important issues can be revisited at later times.

7. EMPLOY PARADOXICAL REQUESTS

Remember "reverse psychology"? Once a treatment for difficult patients, it works with ACG folks too. But you need to be sly about it. When employing reverse psychology, a person basically asks for the opposite of what he or she wants. When you want a kiss from a naturally oppositional two-year-old, say, "I don't want a kiss." The next moment they are begging to give you a kiss. When you want someone to help you with a chore say, "You probably wouldn't want to help me with this chore." Family therapists have developed whole paradoxical treatment prescriptions to deal with resistant couples. Basically they tell the couple to do the opposite of what they really want them to do. The therapist bets on the couple's resistance to suggestions. For example, if the couple is having problems spending time together and finding time for sex, the therapist would tell them not to spend any time together and definitely to avoid sex. Many couples would find after these paradoxical suggestions that they would start to spend more time together and make more love regularly and passionately than they had in years.

Paradoxical suggestions and interventions have been used as therapeutic prescriptions by psychotherapists for many years. These interventions have gone under many names, such as "anti-suggestion," "negative practice," "paradoxical intention," "the confusion technique," "declaring hopelessness," "restraining change," "prescribing a relapse," and "therapeutic double-blind." Basically, they involve suggesting the opposite of the desired response. It is my contention that they probably work best on ACG clients. A common paradoxical suggestion given to people who have trouble sleeping is "Stay awake as long as possible when going to bed." Psychologists Ascher and Turner treated male patients who could not urinate in public restrooms because of anxiety by instructing them to go to public restrooms and go through the entire procedure of urinating (standing in front of the urinal, unzipping their pants, and taking out their penis) but to refrain from urinating. With repeated trials they were able to overcome their fear of urinating in public. Milton Erickson, one of the fathers of modern hypnosis, used this technique successfully on many clients. He explicitly instructed one client who did not wish to self-disclose to withhold information until he was ready to provide it and no sooner.

On a personal level, whenever you want a cingulate person to do something for you it is best to make it look like it is his or her idea. Do not ask for many things directly, as you are likely to be disappointed. Ask for the person's input. Get her feedback. Get her to commit to doing certain things, before telling her that it is a requirement. Here are some examples.

- If you want someone to meet you for dinner, it is often best to ask about what time is good for her as opposed to telling her to meet you at a certain time.
- If you want a hug, it is often best to say something like "You probably wouldn't want to give me a hug."
- If you want him or her to go to the store with you, say something like "You probably wouldn't want to go with me."
- If you want someone to finish a report by next Thursday, say, "You probably can't finish the report by next Thursday."
- If you want a child to comply with a request without giving you a problem, say, "You probably wouldn't be able to do this without getting upset, would you?"

These seven steps will help you develop more flexibility, another key component to a magnificent mind.

| 14 |

Develop Mental Toughness

——

CULTIVATE A RESILIENT BRAIN

*If I had a formula for bypassing trouble, I wouldn't pass it around.
Wouldn't be doing anybody a favor. Trouble creates a capacity to
handle it.*

—OLIVER WENDELL HOLMES

*People are like stained-glass windows. They sparkle and shine
when the sun is out, but when the darkness sets in, their beauty is
revealed only if there is a light from within.*

—ELISABETH KÜBLER-ROSS

Chris had struggled with anxiety and trouble breathing when he first
came to see me. He was sixteen years old and had a condition known as
Goldenhar syndrome, which meant he was born without his left jawbone.
He had undergone twenty-one operations to fix his deformity, which included bone grafts from his own body. His face was severely scarred like an
old railroad yard. The sense of panic started when he was on the operating
room table being intubated for the last two surgeries. His mother, Maria,
was concerned, as Chris had been a very resilient boy, and she brought him
to see me. He had at least two more surgeries to go. A few sessions of relaxation training and hypnosis easily cleared up his anxiety.

As I got to know Chris, I came to believe that despite his anxiety reaction, which didn't occur until his twentieth surgery, he was the healthiest person I had ever met. He was president of his tenth-grade class. He was a straight-A student and had a girlfriend he adored. He also had very clear goals for his future and a great attitude, despite the multiple surgeries and distorted face. After his anxiety abated, I continued to see him for a few months without cost. I felt driven to understand why he was so healthy, despite his circumstances. I had other patients, who had not faced nearly his stress and challenges but who were emotional wrecks nonetheless. For the most part, psychiatrists study illness, not mental health. I came to believe that there were four reasons for Chris's resilience.

First, Chris's mother never allowed his illness to be an excuse for anything. Maria was loving but firm. Inside, Chris's illness deeply pained Maria. Like all good mothers, she hurt for her son, but early in Chris's illness she realized that babying him would only handicap him and she would have none of it. He still did chores, he was expected to excel at his schoolwork, and he participated with other kids even when they made fun of him. She helped him rehearse what to say when they were cruel, which they were. When the other kids found that Chris did not get upset by the teasing, but expected it and laughed along with them, they stopped teasing and befriended and admired him. Their petty complaints seemed small compared to what Chris endured. Second, because of Chris's behavior, he had a strong peer group. His group of friends often came to the hospital to see him after his surgeries and he spent a lot of time with them. He was a good friend. Third, Chris was an optimist. In listening to his speech, he almost always saw the upbeat side of issues. He did not see his condition as a handicap. When we talked about it, he said, everyone has something. "This is my problem," he said. "At least I do not have cancer or something that will kill me." Lastly, I did not need a SPECT scan to know that Chris had a great brain. He was flexible, goal oriented, focused, passionate about his life, and positive and honest in his thinking. I often wish I could bottle Chris's attitude and give it away to my children, patients, and even take a dose or two myself.

Psychiatrist Robert Pasnau, past president of the American Psychiatric Association, once said at a lecture to the residents in my training program that coping requires three things: information, a sense of control, and self-esteem. Chris clearly had high self-esteem. He also knew what was happening; he was very informed about his condition and what must be done. His anxiety started when he felt as though he was losing control. He was not supposed to be aware of being intubated (this is where a metal tube is placed in your throat to keep your airway open for breathing during the anesthesia and surgery). The anesthesiologist had not given him enough medication on the twentieth surgery, and he was aware of the tube in his throat and felt panicky and out of control.

How Childhood Sets Up Resilience or Vulnerability in the Brain

Evidence from both animal and human studies shows that children who experience extreme, uncontrollable stress, such as physical or sexual abuse, are more likely to suffer from anxiety and depression and are more vulnerable to stress later in life. At birth there is substantial flexibility in the brain's ability to respond and adapt to stressful events. Some research suggests that there may be a critical period in the first few weeks of life, during which time traumas are particularly harmful to the brain's ability to handle stress. Studies of humans who survive child abuse have found changes in the functioning of the brain circuits responsible for handling stress. A study of women who were abused as children found that they had an increase in their stress hormones compared with those who were not abused. Long-term exposure to stress hormones has been found to kill cells in the hippocampus, part of the limbic brain deep in the temporal lobes, involved with memory, learning, and emotion. Smaller hippocampal volumes are found in people with depression and chronic stress disorders. Early abuse or stress can cause longstanding changes in brain circuits associated with resilience and learning. Women who are abused are more likely to stay with men who are abusive, in part because of their own anxiety, erratic memory, and low self-confidence. These findings suggest that child abuse can lead to long-term changes in the brain and may help to explain why mistreatment is passed down generation after generation.

An interesting twist on the research, however, occurs when children are exposed to milder, more manageable forms of stress. It appears that these stresses actually aid in building resilience. Some stress, it seems, is good, even important. This is known as stress inoculation, based on the analogy to vaccinations against infections. The theory is that when a person is presented with a mild form of an infectious disease, he or she develops immunity by learning how to fight it off. Children who are faced with and overcome moderately stressful events, such as family moves, parental illnesses, or loss of a friendship, are better able to deal with adversity later in life than people who were never exposed to trouble as children. Children who learn to cope with stress seem to have a better ability to deal with hardships over the long term. In one study, teenage boys who survived stressful childhood events experienced less overt signs of stress, such as increased heart rate and blood pressure changes, when performing challenging tasks compared with their counterparts who had not struggled with earlier trouble. Research on animals lend credence to the stress inoculation theory and provides insight into its brain mechanism. Young monkeys separated from their mothers for one hour every week (a manageable stressor) experienced acute distress during the separation periods, and temporarily increased levels of cortisol, the stress hormone. Later in life, however, the same monkeys demonstrated lower anxiety and lower baseline cortisol levels than monkeys who had never been separated from their mothers. Furthermore, these stress-inoculated monkeys demonstrated improved performance on tests that measure prefrontal cortex function. Poor control of prefrontal cortex function has been associated with depression and impulsivity in humans.

It seems that it is the amount of early stress that matters. Too much is clearly a problem, but too little leaves you without the skill to manage trouble later on. This research highlights an important point. *Try not to protect your children from every hardship they may face.* As a father of three children, I never wanted my children to suffer, yet if I did everything for them and never allowed them to experience stress, they would not develop the ability to deal with the hardships that inevitably come their way. It would be as though I never vaccinated them against stress. Likely, this is why Chris did so well. His mother never allowed his handicap to be used as an excuse. Even when he was stressed by being teased by the other children, he had to keep dealing with it and therefore learned how to deal with it. Social skills are now his strength.

Ten Ways to Boost Resilience

All of us have adversity in our lives. All of us have faced physical, emotional, financial, work, and relational stresses. Self-doubt, fears, failure, loss, anger, and disappointment reach into all of our experiences. It is during these times, when we are stressed or pushed to our own personal limits, that our behavior defines our character. Over the past decade, research on resilience, on people like Chris, has grown, giving important clues to why some people persevere and others give up. In this chapter I will synthesize this research and show you ten ways to boost your own ability to bounce back when adversity strikes.

1. Gather information.
2. Develop a personal sense of control.

3. Build self-esteem.
4. Keep your pleasure centers healthy.
5. Clear up past traumas.
6. Face your fears.
7. Strengthen your ability to deal with adversity.
8. Use positive emotions, especially laughter.
9. Rely on a moral compass.
10. Nurture social support.

1. GATHER INFORMATION

Psychologist Abraham Maslow noted that what you do not know has power over you, whereas knowledge brings choice and control. Most of us handle adversity better when we know what we are up against. Chris knew what needed to be done for his face, so he was better able to handle the inevitable pain. Not knowing what to expect increases anxiety and decreases resilience.

At no other point in history has information been more readily available than it is right now. Immediate information abounds on everything from financial stress, marital struggles, child rearing, post-traumatic stress disorder, depression, and work challenges. Amazon.com lists nearly two million books, and Yahoo! and Google are the constant companion for so many of us. Still, many people sabotage themselves by not accumulating enough information on their challenges. There are a number of reasons people do not become adequately informed, including failing to ask the appropriate questions, not knowing how to gather accurate information, magical thinking that says, "I should know all," and fear of the truth.

Asking the right question is the most important step to getting the right answer. It is a sign of curiosity and indicates a willingness to learn. The fear of appearing stupid, however, often prevents questions and stifles learning. How many times have you wanted to ask a question, yet when it came to saying the words, fear of embarrassment kept your mouth shut? How many times have you not gotten the information you needed because of the fear that you would be a nuisance to the other person? You may be the victim of misconceptions. Many people see those who ask questions as interested and willing to learn, not stupid. Second, many people feel good if they can help others and enjoy sharing their knowledge. If you're bothering them, you will probably be able to tell and you can ask them another time. Even better, you can start by asking if this is a good moment for them to answer a question. In business, if you do not have all the information you need to do your job, but you are afraid to appear stupid by asking questions, think of how much worse you'll feel when it's discovered you're not doing the job right. Most supervisors wish to teach because they, like most of us, get satisfaction from helping others to do something well, especially if they're held responsible for the kind of job you do.

There is no doubt in my mind that the failure to ask questions and gather information damages many relationships. When we are confused about others' behavior or think we may have gotten the wrong information from them, it is crucial to clarify the meaning of their behavior. Without clarification, our assumptions take over, and little things may turn into monsters. The worst thing that can happen when you ask a question is that someone may refuse to answer it, give you an answer you don't like, or make you feel stupid for asking. I think ignorance is worse than those three things. You can lessen the chances of a negative response by asking questions in an appropriately respectful way at the right time. But when you have questions, *ask them*! They will get you more information, which will bring you closer to your goals and help you manage difficult times and situations.

Expecting yourself to know something without being taught is what psychiatrists call magical thinking. It is like a person who has never been somewhere before refusing to ask for directions when he is lost. This magical thinking of "I should know the answers" occurs in many situations. I see it most frequently with parents who expect themselves to be good parents of difficult children despite never having had a role model to teach them. Pride is often an excuse to cover ignorance. Be kind to yourself and don't expect more from you than is reasonable. If you don't know something, admit it and find the answer to it.

Another reason people don't ask questions or become informed is that they are afraid of the answers. I see this most commonly in people who marry after knowing each other for only a few weeks. They are generally tired of being alone and want to be in a relationship so badly that they leave common sense behind. Ignorance, they think, is better than information. But this usually backfires. Often, hidden information surfaces, and one or both parties feel betrayed. Some are too eager to trust before finding out if a person is trustworthy. This may also be true in business or personal issues when something is wanted so much that denying reality is preferable to denying the opportunity to obtain the desired goal. The following statements summarize the importance of information:

• What I do not know has power over me, whereas knowledge brings choice and control.

- Information is power.
- My fear of being ignorant overcomes my fear of asking questions.

2. DEVELOP A PERSONAL SENSE OF CONTROL

A man can fail many times, but he isn't a failure until he begins to blame somebody else.

—JOHN BURROUGHS

The perceived degree of personal control that you have over a stressful event plays a key role in determining whether the event will lead to subsequent vulnerability or resilience to stress. In one animal study, rats exposed to uncontrollable and unpredictable shocks developed exaggerated fear responses and heightened anxiety states; animals subjected to predictable shocks from which they could escape did not develop this learned helplessness. Furthermore, rats that learned to have control over a stressor (by learning to escape predictable shocks) were less likely to develop learned helplessness when they were subsequently exposed to unpredictable shocks. This finding in rats supports the observation in humans that learning to manage one stress enhances subsequent resilience to many other unrelated stresses. For those people who experienced severe early life stresses, it is critical to know that they may be more vulnerable to the effects of stress, and to become resilient they would be wise to work hard to strengthen their brain's ability to resist stress.

In my clinical experience, this sense of control is one of the most important factors in managing stress and succeeding in life. You can tell when people feel out of control, because they blame others for their situation in life. When something goes wrong at work or in their relationships, they often find someone to blame. Fight this tendency. It makes you a victim with little to no control over your own life.

Additionally, people who lack a personal sense of control often live in the past. You will hear them saying, "If only I had done so and so, things would be different."

If only:

I didn't marry that good-for-nothing husband of mine.
I finished school.
My parents hadn't gotten divorced.
The company hadn't changed hands.
I had made that sale.

I hadn't forgotten my diaphragm.
I'd chosen a different career.
I had rich parents.
Etc., etc., etc.

The past continues to haunt these people even when it has no relevance. A tremendous amount of emotional energy is invested in things that cannot be changed. I had a patient, Kathy, who had an encyclopedia of "if onlys." "If only I finished college." "If only I hadn't married David." "If only we didn't live in Washington, D.C." "If only I could find a good day care center." "If only we lived in a different neighborhood." And on and on. When I pointed out to her how much energy it must have taken to come up with this list, Kathy said, "If only I didn't worry so much." I was about to pull out my hair with her. But after several months she learned to rechannel that energy into "What do I want now and how do I get it?" This is a much healthier approach to life.

Never forget that your success starts and ends with you. You want it. You define it. You go after it. You achieve it, or you don't. Only you are personally responsible for how your life turns out. Many other people will try to take responsibility for you, like your parents, your spouse, your friends, or your co-workers, but in the final analysis, they can only influence how your life progresses, they cannot control it. Only you can.

Once you fully realize this most important ingredient of success, your life will never be the same. You will stop blaming others for your failures and disappointments and start working on changing yourself to be the kind of person you want to be. As long as you can blame someone else for why things aren't the way you want them to be, you can comfortably avoid change. After all, "it's their fault." However, when you have no one to blame but yourself, you are more likely to seek change. Not many people feel comfortable saying, "It's my fault."

Now, it is true that life is not fair. We are all dealt a different hand of cards in life. Some hands are very good; some hands are very, very bad. The obstacles we have to overcome are not the same for each person. It is, however, what we do with the hands we are dealt in life that determines how we feel about ourselves, not the initial hands themselves.

Eric Fromm, M.D., summed up the concept of personal responsibility in his book *Man for Himself* when he wrote, "Man must accept responsibility for himself and the fact that only by using his own power, can he give meaning to his life." You have the power. It is up to you how you use it.

There is an interesting side effect to taking personal responsibility for your life. The more you realize that you're in control of your own life, the more you realize that you cannot control anyone else's life. You become more independent, while at the same time you stop believing you can change other people. You realize only they can do that. Efforts directed toward changing your parents, your spouse, or your boss stop, leaving you more time and energy to work on yourself. Success takes a lot of time and energy.

Personal responsibility and self-control are clear hallmarks of a successful person. Without these, you see yourself as a victim of the world and you are unable to take or accomplish any more than the world is willing to give. Personal responsibility dictates that "if it's to be, it's up to me." It's accepting that you are human and bound to make mistakes. But when you make them, you learn from them, and you look toward creative problem solving rather than looking for someone to blame. Taking personal responsibility for your life takes supreme courage and can be painful at any age. But the payoff is independence and freedom.

Researchers have demonstrated that it is possible for a person to change the way he perceives himself in the world; i.e., victims can take more control. These "thinking" exercises will work to strengthen your sense of personal responsibility if you commit yourself to completing them. The only person you sabotage by not completing these exercises is you. Are you worth it?

For the next week, be aware of your thoughts when something goes wrong—a mistake is made, you have a problem, you have an accident, any situation in which you have a tendency to blame someone else. After you identify an incident such as this, fill in the sheet below. Do this for at least three separate incidents.

EXAMPLE

1. What happened? I got a speeding ticket.

2. What was my first response to the situation? Was it to find someone else to blame? "I wasn't going that fast. They must have set up a speed trap."

3. Why is it important to blame someone else? How does that help? "If I can blame the police officer, then it is easy to first try to talk him out of the ticket. If that doesn't work, it is then okay for me to be nasty to him."

4. Am I uncomfortable if I can't find someone to blame? "Yes. That means it's my fault. And who likes to admit anything is their fault?"

5. Is it okay for me to make a mistake in this instance? "No. My insurance will go up, because this is my third ticket in a year."

YOUR TURN:

1. What happened?

2. What was my first response to the situation? Was it to find someone else to blame?

3. Why is it important to blame someone else? How does that help?

4. Am I uncomfortable if I can't find someone to blame?

5. Is it okay for me to make a mistake in this instance?

You can learn to talk back to your automatic "blaming others" habit of thinking. I've set up a double-column technique to help you retrain your thoughts. In the first column, write down your automatic thought when a problem comes up, and in the second column, write down a rational response. Here are some examples to help you get started.

Blaming Others	Personal Responsibility Response
I'm late for my appointment. It's my wife's fault I overslept.	I can't honestly blame my wife because I overslept and am late for the appointment. If being on time is important to me, I will set the alarm to ensure I get up and accept responsibility for my timeliness.
I told the staff to rotate the merchandise and the job isn't done. They never do anything right. Their failure to follow orders is the reason sales are down.	When I notice the staff hasn't completed a job, it's my responsibility to follow up on it, so they learn to do their jobs completely. The reduction in sales probably has nothing to do with the staff not following orders. Sales fluctuate every day.

| My husband always makes me feel unhappy because he acts so nastily toward me. | My husband cannot make me feel anything without my permission and cooperation. If my husband acts nastily to me, I can choose to talk to him about it; I can make it clear to him that if he doesn't change his ways, he'll lose me; I can end the relationship; or I can continue to feel miserable. It's my responsibility how I choose to feel and how I allow other people to treat me. |

YOUR TURN:

Blaming Others	Personal Responsibility Response
1.	_____
2.	_____
3.	_____

Each time this week you catch yourself blaming others for something that is happening to you, *stop.* Immediately stop the blaming. Think about how you contributed to the situation, and immediately work on ways to solve the problem. Refuse to spend any more energy looking for scapegoats. Look to yourself and others for answers, for ways to solve problems. Stop blaming yourself; stop blaming others. It is wasted energy.

Every time you're tempted to blame someone else but don't, give yourself a big pat on the back. You're on your way to taking control of your life.

3. BUILD SELF-ESTEEM

He that respects himself is safe from others; he wears a coat of mail that none can pierce.

—HENRY WADSWORTH LONGFELLOW

How you feel about yourself is paramount to how you manage the stresses in your life. Having healthy self-esteem is akin to being on good terms with yourself. It is believing that you are worth working in your own best interest.

It is believing that you can have a positive impact on others and that you are worth others having a positive impact on you. Self-esteem helps you manage and survive when devastation hits you. It is the internal voice that is on your side and gives you the encouragement to press on, even when things look bleak. Without a positive sense of self, any accomplishments, no matter how big or small, will be negated by an accusing inner voice that keeps repeating you're no good, erasing any feelings of success. Self-esteem is a cornerstone of resilience.

A fifty-year Harvard study turned up some startling truths about self-esteem. Begun as an effort to understand juvenile delinquency, the study followed the lives of 456 teenage boys from inner-city Boston. Many of the boys were from broken or impoverished homes. When they reached middle age, one fact stood out: regardless of intelligence, family income, ethnic background, or amount of formal education, those who had worked as boys, even at simple household chores, enjoyed happier and more productive lives than those who had not. These results are not difficult to explain. George Valliant, M.D., psychiatrist in charge of the study, said, "Boys who work in the home or community gained competence and came to feel they were worthwhile members of society. And because they felt good about themselves, others felt good about them as well." People who felt best about themselves as adults were made responsible for themselves as children. Children do, so they believe they can do: they believe in themselves.

Important people contribute to a child's self-esteem, particularly parents, friends, grandparents, teachers, and coaches. Children often idealize important adults and develop an image of the ideal person they'd like to be. Initially, the ideal persons are often the parents. It is common to hear four- and five-year-old children say they want to be like their mommies and daddies. As they grow, the ideal person often becomes a composite of many admired and respected people. The closer their sense of themselves is to their image of those they admire, the greater their self-esteem. The greater the distance between their sense of themselves and their image of the ideal person, the lower their self-esteem.

The way we talk to ourselves, our inner voice, is the day-to-day indicator of our self-esteem. We all have many voices inside our heads commenting on our daily thoughts and behaviors. These voices are a synthesis of the strong voices we've heard throughout our lives. If the parental voices we heard were positive, chances are our inner voices will be the same. If they were harsh and negative, it is likely that we'll talk to ourselves in a punitive way. When our self-esteem suffers, our inner voices often take on the quality of a "Critics

Committee," which runs a nonstop dialogue on how we could have done things better. These voices can often be recognized as specific voices from the past if we take the time to examine them. If you notice the Critics Committee tormenting you, revisit the exercises in chapter 12, especially "Truth in the Courtroom of Your Mind" (see page 179) to excise these negative thoughts.

4. KEEP YOUR PLEASURE CENTERS HEALTHY

One of the biggest buffers against severe emotional trauma is a healthy brain. When the brain works right, all of the other coping mechanisms can engage to help you weather the emotional storms that hit you. In particular, when the pleasure centers deep in the brain are healthy, and able to experience happiness and joy in the midst of trouble, it will be easier to get up once you are knocked down. Caring for this part of the brain is involved in both lasting happiness and resilience.

The pleasure centers, discussed earlier, are made up of the ventral tegmental area, basal ganglia, and other limbic areas of the brain. They are responsive to several neurotransmitters, particularly dopamine. When dopamine is low, as with Parkinson's disease, there is a high incidence of depression and low motivation and it is harder for sufferers to experience joy. To keep these areas healthy, it is important to engage in meaningful and pleasurable activities on a regular basis. Do work you love and make time for fun with those you love. These activities prime pleasure's pump and help these centers stay healthy.

Equally important, be careful not to wear out your pleasure centers through drug abuse or too many repetitive behaviors, such as Internet gambling, pornography, compulsive shopping, or even excessive Internet dating. In his brilliant book *Thrilled to Death: How the Endless Pursuit of Pleasure Is Leaving Us Numb,* pioneering psychologist Archibald Hart discusses how the modern-day trend of constantly needing excitement and stimulation is depleting us of joy. Instant and text messaging, e-mail, Internet, video games, music downloads, emotionally charged movies, and television all vie for our attention. We are requiring more and more stimulation in order to pay attention at all, in order to feel happiness or joy. Teenagers at a computer often have ten instant messaging conversations going at once. The first time I saw my teenage daughter doing this, I wondered how she could really pay attention to any of the conversations she was having. Television commercials are another example of how technology is driving our attention and constantly pushing on the pleasure levers in our brain. A thirty-second commercial forty years ago had ten three-second scenes. The same commercial in 2007 has thirty one-second scenes, driving us to need more stimulation in order to pay attention and numbing us out.

The constant use of video games, so common among our children, teens, and young adults, is another potentially serious source of the problem. Many people play for hours at a time, to the detriment of their responsibilities, and some even go through withdrawal symptoms when they are not allowed to play or stop. A brain imaging study published in the journal *Nature* helps to explain why. While a group of people played action video games, researchers took positron emission tomography scans to see which parts of the brain video games activated. They saw increased activity in the basal ganglia, where dopamine works. Other researchers have discovered that cocaine and methamphetamine also work in this part of the brain. Video games bring pleasure and focus by increasing dopamine. The problem is that the more dopamine released during video games, the less that is available later on to do regular life tasks, such as schoolwork, homework, or chores. Many parents have told me that the more a child or teen plays video games, the worse he does in school and the more irritable he tends to be when asked to stop playing. I saw the negative effects of video games in my own house. Video games came into our home when my son was ten years old. Initially, I thought they were very cool. I never had exciting games like these when I was a child. But over the next few years I saw that he was spending more and more time with the games and less time on his work. He would also argue when he was told to stop playing. I decided that the games had to go. We have all been better off since. We have to be careful not to use technology to numb ourselves out, so that we can experience happiness and pleasure, especially when we need it during times of stress.

Work to keep the pleasure centers healthy. Here are some simple guidelines.

- Treat any illnesses, such as depression, that interfere with pleasure center function.
- Curb the use of constant stimulating activities, such as gambling, shopping, pornography, Internet use, scary movies, and high-risk activities.
- Exercise, especially doing something you love, such as dancing or playing tennis.
- Make time to laugh, since humor enhances the pleasure centers without wearing them out.

- Connect meaningful activities and pleasure, such as volunteering for activities you love.
- Develop appreciation and gratitude.
- Look for pleasure in the little things in your life, such as a walk with a friend, a great meal, or a meaningful church service.

5. CLEAR UP PAST TRAUMAS

Unresolved traumas from the past make us more vulnerable to future stresses. Carrying haunting memories sensitizes us to anything that is likely to remind us of the prior experience and robs us of resiliency. For example, Jenna had to file bankruptcy in her midtwenties owing to her diagnosis with thyroid cancer. Her medical bills were more than she could ever imagine paying. Twelve years later, she still was extremely anxious about money. She worked long hours as a nurse and was barely getting ahead. Money was a big issue in her relationships with men. They often thought she was overfocused on financial issues, which scared them away. It wasn't until she got help for her financial fears that she was able to act more rationally and optimistically about her finances.

In my experience, when there are unresolved traumas, a psychotherapeutic treatment technique called eye movement desensitization and reprocessing (EMDR) can help extricate them from your brain. The focus of EMDR is resolving or eliminating the emotional distress arising from difficult childhood memories or traumatic events, such as automobile accidents, assaults, natural disasters, or combat trauma. I have also found it helpful for dealing with past failures in sports that drive anxiety and prevent peak performance.

EMDR was developed by psychologist Francine Shapiro beginning in 1987. While walking around a lake, she noticed that a disturbing thought disappeared when her eyes spontaneously started to move back and forth from the lower-left to the upper-right visual fields. She tried it again with another anxiety provoking thought and found that the anxious feeling went away. In the days that followed she tried the technique with friends, acquaintances, and interested students and found the technique helpful in relieving anxiety. She then went further to work with patients and developed a technique that is now used worldwide and is a standard technique used by the Department of Defense for combat veterans who suffer from post-traumatic stress disorder.

The mainstay of EMDR involves clients bringing up emotionally troubling memories while their eyes follow a trained therapist's hand moving horizontally back and forth. Following a specific protocol, the clinician helps the client identify the images, negative beliefs, emotions, and body sensations associated with a targeted memory or event. Through the therapy, positive statements and beliefs replace the negative ones. The believability of this new thought is rated while the client thinks of the disturbing event. The goal of EMDR treatment is the rapid processing of information about the negative experience and movement toward an adaptive resolution. This means a reduction in the client's distress, a shift in the client's negative belief to positive belief, and the possibility of more optimal behavior in relationships and at work. It is important that EMDR be done by a trained therapist. You can contact the national EMDR International Association at www.EMDRIA.org for more information and a list of certified EMDR therapists.

To be resilient, it is essential to clean out the closet in your head of past or current traumas. That way, they no longer control your present or future behavior.

6. FACE YOUR FEARS

Facing your fears is a key component of resilience training. Allowing fear to take hold and put down roots in your brain ensures they will control you later on. People who suffer from posttraumatic stress disorder, for example, avoid many aspects of their lives, such as people, places, events, and opportunities, as these may serve as reminders of the trauma. Subsequently, the conditioned fear is solidified in the brain rather than extinguished. In contrast, people who are resilient are more adept at facing and managing their fears. They use their fears as a guide to understand threats and decide what to do. When you face your fears, you are likely rewiring your brain to have control over it. When you hide from your fears, they begin to control you. In simple terms it means getting back on the bicycle once you have fallen off, getting another job after being fired, or becoming involved in a new relationship after a messy divorce.

7. STRENGTHEN YOUR ABILITY TO DEAL WITH ADVERSITY

Failure is not fatal. It is part of learning and growing. One of my personal heroes is Abraham Lincoln. He had many successes in his life but also faced many tough challenges. He lost his mother at age nine and he did not have a good relationship with his father. His marriage was turbulent and he lost two of his children to death. He suffered from several bouts of depression, even being suicidal at times. He hated how he looked and once said if he ever met anyone as ugly as himself he would shoot the wretch to put him out of his misery. He was elected to the legislature in 1834 but also lost several elections, including twice to the U.S. Senate. He was elected president in 1860, but his early years in the White House were extremely turbulent. There were many Northern defeats at the start of the Civil War and he was constantly criticized. His early losses and defeats perfectly placed him to be able to withstand failure. If he had been successful in all his endeavors, he would have never been able to withstand the pressures of the presidency. He remains perhaps the greatest American leader of all time. His failures, losses, and struggles prepared him for ultimate success.

In a similar way, Michael Jordan, perhaps basketball's greatest player ever, has said, "I have missed more than 9,000 shots in my career. I have lost almost 300 games. On 26 occasions I have been entrusted to take the game winning shot . . . and missed. And I have failed over and over and over again in my life. And that is why . . . I succeed." Failure is not fatal. Not trying is!

Failure is a part of everyone's life. No one starts out walking in life; it is months before we even learn how to crawl. It is not failure that holds people back but their attitude toward failure and their fear of it. Toddlers don't give up when they fall; they take their bruises and try again. Anyone who has had small children knows that despite many failed attempts at mobilization, most children go very quickly from crawling to walking to running to climbing up to places they shouldn't. It is arrogant to think that we are perfect and we will never fail. We are not programmed with the answers; we learn them. We get the right answers by learning processes and observing our errors along the way. Successful supervisors do not get angry when their employees make mistakes. They say, "Don't be afraid to make mistakes; learn from them. Just don't make the same one twice. Observe what you do and you'll always improve."

How supervisors deal with the mistakes of their employees often determines the quality of the employees. When people go to work expecting to be yelled at or belittled, their fear and anger get in the way of their doing the best they can. When they go to work knowing that they will be taught to learn from their mistakes in a positive atmosphere, they relax and are more likely to produce good work. Be a good teacher for yourself and those around you. Maturity is being able to learn from the mistakes you make.

How we learn from mistakes is a trait we learned in childhood. What happened when you made a mistake as a child? When you spilled something at the dinner table or you did poorly on a test? Were you berated and yelled at for the mistake or were you encouraged to learn something from it? One of the most critical lessons a parent can teach a child is how to learn from mistakes. Too often as parents we are hypercritical of ourselves when we fail, which then transfers to how we treat our children when they fail at something. To help our children feel good about themselves, we must help them be competent. Of course competent people make mistakes; the difference is that they have the ability to learn from them and move on to other things rather than beating themselves up for it.

For example, think about the four-year-old child who spills orange juice at breakfast. Many parents, who are in a hurry to get off to work, get stressed by the delay in schedule and take their frustration out by yelling at the child. The child feels incompetent and the next time he tries to pour juice he'll feel anxious and tense—making him more likely to spill it again. Parents need to focus their energy on helping their children learn from the mistakes they make. So instead of yelling at the child for the spilled orange juice, I recommend that you teach him how to clean up the mess and then take him over to the sink and have him pour ten glasses of orange juice. In that way, he's gone from making a mistake to learning two skills: cleaning up a mess and pouring juice. He's gone from feeling clumsy and stupid to feeling competent. To raise healthy children, and be healthy adults, it is critical to teach them how to learn from the mistakes they make and to give them a framework for problem solving.

The fear of failure may be preventing you from trying. When you do fail, you may do everything you can to not think about it and thus end up repeating the same mistakes. Success involves many failures and lessons along the way. Think about some of the major mistakes you have made in your life. How did you respond to those failures?

- Did you learn from them?
- Did you berate yourself over and over?
- Did you blame someone else for it?
- Did you do everything you could to forget about it?
- Did you repeat the failure?
- Did you get through it and learn along the way?
- Did you stay away from similar situations in the future?
- Did you allow the mistake to stimulate you to look deeper inside yourself to become a better person?

8. USE POSITIVE EMOTIONS, ESPECIALLY LAUGHTER

There is a growing body of scientific literature suggesting that positive emotions, especially laughter, counteracts stress and is involved in resilience. According to Professor Lee Berk of the University of California–Irvine, "If we took what we know about the medical benefits of laughter and bottled it up, it would require FDA approval." Laughter can lower blood pressure, trigger a flood of endorphins—the brain chemicals that bring on euphoria and decrease pain—and enhance our immune systems. Gamma-interferon, a disease-fighting protein, rises with laughter. So do B cells, which produce disease-destroying antibodies, and T cells, which orchestrate our body's immune response. Laughter lowers the flow of dangerous stress hormones that suppress the immune system, raise blood pressure, and increase the number of platelets, which cause clots and potentially fatal coronary artery blockages. The average child laughs hundreds of times a day. The average adult laughs only a dozen times a day. If only we could collect those lost laughs and use them to our advantage. One person was able to do this quite effectively.

In Norman Cousins's classic book, *Anatomy of an Illness,* he describes how he used laughter to treat a debilitating immune disorder that attacked his body called ankylosing spondylitis. The illness caused him pain, fatigue, and a great deal of anxiety. He believed that he became sick because he was overtired from travel and work, and his body was in a state of adrenal exhaustion. He went from doctor to doctor, took medicine after medicine, and was not getting better. One specialist estimated his chances of recovery at one in five hundred. In partnership with his physician, he gradually stopped all of his medications, added large doses of intravenous vitamin C, and began a program of laughter. Allen Funt, famed producer of the television series *Candid Camera,* sent him films of the TV series along with a projector for his laughter therapy. He also watched Marx Brothers and Laurel and Hardy films. He discovered that ten minutes of a genuine belly laugh had a pain relieving effect and would give him restful sleep for two hours. He laughed and laughed. After a period of time, his illness started to improve and eventually went away.

Put laughter in your life every day. Watch comedies (this could be a helpful form of TV), go to comedy clubs, read joke books (my favorite is the *Far Side* by Gary Larson), and swap jokes with your friends. President Lincoln suffered from serious periods of depression. He used laughter and telling jokes as one form of medicine. Here are three of my favorite humorous Lincoln sayings.

- Common-looking people are the best in the world: that is the reason the Lord makes so many of them.
- If I were two-faced, would I be wearing this one?
- It is said an Eastern monarch once charged his wise men to invent him a sentence to be ever in view, and which should be true and appropriate in all times and situations. They presented him the words: "And this, too, shall pass away."

9. RELY ON A MORAL COMPASS

Another characteristic of resilience is relying on a strong moral compass and a solid core belief system. Having a commitment to deeply religious or spiritual beliefs and practices seems to have a protective effect on physical and emotional well-being and helps people cope with stress and illness. A recent survey of the available scientific literature involving 126,000 people in forty-two independent studies indicated that spiritual practice or religious participation was highly correlated with a longer life and survival once an illness was present. Additionally, strong religious beliefs have been correlated with a decreased incidence of depression in numerous studies, ranging from students to grief stricken adults to elderly who were medically ill. In a similar way, teenagers who attended church services had lower suicide rates than those who didn't. The specific religious affiliation did not seem to matter in the studies.

Obviously, people who have a strong moral compass are not limited to those with religious beliefs. It is likely that morality is intrinsic to human nature. Greek philosopher Epictetus, living in the first century A.D., wrote: "Every one of us has come into this world with innate conceptions as to good and bad, noble and shameful, fitting and inappropriate." Moral sense is necessary in a high-functioning society. In looking at the brain, it becomes obvious that morality is brain based. When the prefrontal cortex is damaged, some people acquire sociopathic tendencies.

Caring for others is putting one's moral compass into action. Altruism is a powerful enhancer of resilience. During World War II, people who cared for others after bombing attacks suffered less depression and anxiety than would be expected. Those who suffered with symptoms before the bombs had a significant decrease in symptoms afterward if they were helping others. Many people find meaning in tragedy and use their suffering to help others. When that happens, resilience is enhanced.

10. NURTURE SOCIAL SUPPORT

Relationships are critical to how we deal with stress and trauma. In his wonderful book *Love and Survival,* cardiologist Dean Ornish detailed the many benefits from having close relationships. Dr. Ornish cited numerous studies indicating that those who feel close, connected, loved, and supported have a lower incidence of depression, anxiety, suicide, heart disease, infections, hypertension, and cancer. Connection enhances brain function and aides resilience.

I was a military psychiatrist for seven years. One of the most striking findings I discovered was that the incidence of suicides and suicide attempts among military service personnel and their dependents peaked in the months of January and July. In a civilian population, suicide is highest in April. What was responsible for the discrepancy between the civilian and military population? January and July are the months of military moves. When people move they become disconnected from their social support network and are at greater risk for depression and suicide. They are less resilient. I frequently treated military wives who became depressed for six months after a move. Their depression seemed to lift after they developed a new social network—friends, church participation, social groups. The women who did not become depressed were much more skilled in getting involved and developing social support right away.

Enhancing emotional bonds can help increase resilience and heal anxiety and depression. In one large study in which patients were treated for major depression, the National Institutes of Health compared three approaches: antidepressant medication, cognitive therapy (the automatic negative thoughts therapy discussed earlier), and interpersonal therapy or teaching people how to get along better with those they loved. Researchers were surprised to find that the treatments were equally effective in treating depression. Not surprising was the fact that combining all three treatments had an even more powerful effect.

How you get along with other people can either help or hurt your brain! Our day-to-day interactions with others enhance the brain or tear down how it works. Being more connected to the people in your life helps you strengthen your brain. Love is as powerful as drugs and usually a lot more fun. The improvements gained through interpersonal therapy appear to go all the way to the brain. In two brain imaging studies, interpersonal therapy showed significant enhancement of brain function.

Use these ten ways to boost your resilience to the tough times we all must weather.

| 15 |

Brain Trust

ENHANCE YOUR SOCIAL NETWORKS

None of us is as smart as all of us.
—KEN BLANCHARD, author and management expert

Success in almost any adventure in life—at home, work, in our hobbies and churches—is enhanced when we build a brain trust of personal relationships and social networks. Unlike polar bears, humans belong to a relational species. We end up enlisting and using the brains of thousands of people, maybe more, during a lifetime. Acquiring and implementing the behaviors that encourage your social communities to thrive is essential for a magnificent mind. Relating effectively to other people is ultimately a brain-based skill. When your brain is healthy you can perceive others more accurately, have good control over your emotions, and act in a healthy way that brings people toward you. Your brain allows you to read social cues, listen, respond appropriately, deal with conflict, act inclusively, and be attentive in the moment of interactions. A brain with short circuits often interrupts effective relationships. As you care for your brain, your relationships improve.

The brain health of the people you interact with also matters to individual happiness and success. Brains nurture, influence, stimulate, irritate, calm, and incite each other. Being raised by a parent with a difficult brain, having a spouse or boss with brain problems, even dealing with a friend, teacher, or a judge who needs brain help can cause immeasurable stress to those in their immediate sphere. Understanding the dynamics of brain health in relationships will give you an advantage that few other people have.

The first practical step in enhancing relationships is to make brain health an important aspect of your family, friendships, and work. With proper education, brain health can become a common goal. When groups of people come together, here are some simple strategies.

- Make ordering food at restaurants a collaborative effort, focusing on brain-healthy options, such as salmon, salads, and vegetables.
- Spend time together taking walks and playing word games rather than getting drinks at a bar, eating chili cheese fries at the burger place, or playing violent video games.
- Supply healthy foods at meetings and parties, not just pastries, muffins, sodas, candy, or alcohol.
- Get the candy off the desks at work.
- Exercise together at work by taking group walks during lunch.
- Make sure others wear their seat belts when traveling together.
- Avoid too much alcohol or too much caffeine.

As brain health enters the consciousness of relationships, it becomes easier to interact, because the group brain is working better.

What Brain Skills Do You Need to Be a People Person?

Professor Howard Markman, Ph.D., director of the Center for Marital and Family Studies at the University of Denver, can predict with 90 percent accuracy who will get divorced and who will stay married after watching only a fifteen-minute conversation between couples in which they are instructed to discuss an issue where they disagree. More important, he found that he could reduce divorce by one third in the couples to whom he taught several critical skills. If the argument between the couple involved a significant amount of blaming, belittling, escalation, invalidation, or withdrawal, their future was not likely to be happy. On the other hand, if the couple communicated respect, shared purpose, and stopped escalation in a respectful way, the future would look much more positive. The great news is that these skills can be taught, and they are enhanced by a healthy brain that can remember them.

In this chapter I will discuss eight clinically proven steps to increase your people skills in any situation. These techniques come from research in the field of interpersonal therapy. Enhancing interpersonal skills has proven effective in decreasing stress and promoting business effectiveness, and it has antidepressant qualities. In several studies this technique has been shown to be as effective as antidepressant medication in treating serious mood disorders. I coined the acronym RELATING to help you remember the steps.

R for responsibility
E for empathy
L for listening
A for assertiveness
T for time
I for inquiry
N for noticing what you like more than what you don't
G for connecting with great groups

R IS FOR RESPONSIBILITY

"It is my job to make this relationship better."

"I have power to improve how we communicate and act toward each other."

"I have influence in my relationships that I exert in a positive way."

"I am responsible for my behavior in our interactions."

People who feel a sense of empowerment and personal responsibility do better in relationships. Those who constantly blame others set up a lifetime of problems.

The first and most devastating hallmark of self-defeating behavior in relationships is blaming other people for how your life is turning out. Whenever you blame someone else, you become a victim of their moods and behavior and you cannot change anything. You are powerless. Typically, you'll hear yourself say things like "It wasn't my fault that you took things the wrong way" or "That wouldn't have happened if you had listened to me" or "It's your fault that we are having trouble."

The bottom-line statement goes something like this: "If only you had done something differently, then I wouldn't be in the predicament I am in. It's your fault, and I am not responsible."

Blaming others for relationship troubles or making excuses when things don't go as you would like is the first step in a dangerous downhill slide. The slide goes something like this:

Blames others
"It's your fault."

|

|

Sees life as beyond personal control
"My life would be better if you hadn't done . . ."

|

|

Feels like a victim of circumstances
"If only you would be different, then . . ."

|

|

Gives up trying
"It is never going to work. Why try?"

Blaming others serves the purpose of temporarily ridding ourselves of feelings of guilt or responsibility. However, it also reinforces the idea that your life is out of control, that others can determine how things are going to go for you. This causes much inner turmoil, leading to anxiety and feelings of helplessness.

Sarah came to see me for marital stress. She had been in psychotherapy with another psychiatrist for over three years but seemed to be getting nowhere. She complained that her husband was an alcoholic who mistreated her. She was often tearful, depressed, and had problems concentrating. In our initial interview it was clear that she took no responsibility for how her life was turning out. She blamed her first husband for getting her pregnant at age nineteen. She then felt "forced" to marry him but complained that he was unmotivated so she divorced him. Then in succession she impulsively married two different men who were alcoholics and physically abusive toward her. Tearfully, she expressed her feelings of being continually victimized by men, including her current husband.

At the end of the session I asked her what she had done to contribute to the problems she had. Her mouth dropped open. Her other psychiatrist had been a good paid listener, but he never challenged her notion of helplessness. At the beginning of the next session she told me that she almost hadn't come back to see me. She said, "You think it's all my fault, don't you?" I replied, "I don't think it's all your fault, but I think you've contributed to your troubles more than you give yourself credit for, and if it's true that you've contributed to your problems then you can do things to change them. As long as you stay an innocent victim of others there's nothing you can do to help yourself."

In several sessions she got the message of personal responsibility and made a dramatic turnaround. As a child she grew up in a severely abusive alcoholic home where she really was a victim of her circumstances; unfortunately for her, she maintained that role in her adult relationships and work. Her unconscious continuation of her abusive childhood was ruining her ability to have control in her life.

Invariably, in classes where I teach this concept I'll have a person tell me that her problem is not blaming others but blaming herself for the difficulties in her life. One woman who had been sexually abused by her father said that for many years she had blamed herself for the abuse and was now learning not to blame herself. I told her that these two concepts—blaming others versus blaming yourself—are not mutually exclusive. She was certainly not responsible for her father's abuse, and there are things that have happened to you that aren't your fault. It is possible to go overboard blaming yourself for troubles and getting stuck in such a mire of guilt that you become powerless to change your life. A good "personal responsibility" statement goes something like this: "Bad things have happened in my life, some of which I had something to do with and some not. Either way, I need to learn from these experiences and be responsible to find ways to overcome the difficulties and bad feelings that resulted."

Taking responsibility in relationships means continually asking yourself what you can do to make the relationship better. When my patients thoughtfully evaluate and change their own behavior their relationships often dramatically improve. The wisdom for so many years in the mental health field was that we have no control over the behavior of others. The saying goes, "We are just responsible for ourselves." My experience tells me that it is not completely true. We have a lot of influence on how others behave. I often ask my patients what they do to make their relationships better. They usually can come up with a number of positive behaviors. Then I ask them what they do to make the relationships worse. Initially, they hesitate, not wanting to face their negative behaviors, but after a bit of time they start to own up to the myriad behaviors we need to work on. Here is an example.

Eight-year-old Carlos came to my office to address behavioral problems, especially those he was experiencing at home. He started by telling me how much he hated his younger sister. "She irritates me all the time," he said. "I have no choice but to yell at her and hit her."

When he said he had no choice, my eyebrows reflexively raised.

Seeing my reaction, he justified his behavior further. "I had no choice. She irritates me all the time."

"What do you do to irritate her?" I asked softly.

"Nothing." Then he paused and repeated, "Absolutely nothing."

I sat quietly.

"Well," he paused and then showed a wry smile, "I take some of her things sometimes."

"Anything else?"

Carlos had the look of thinking hard. "I yell at her, tell her she cannot play with me, and ignore her when she talks to me."

"Okay," I said. "You do irritate her. I sort of suspected it. But what do you do that makes her happy?"

He then listed several things he did that helped them get along better, including playing with her, helping her with her kindergarten homework, saying thank you, smiling at her. He had a lot more power than he believed. Tapping in to Carlos's power to make his relationship with his sister better, as well as knowing his ability to make things worse, helped change his victim mentality and ultimately his behavior. What can you do today to make your relationships better? You win more in relationships when you stay away from blaming the other person and asking yourself what you can do better.

E IS FOR EMPATHY

> *If, as a result of reading this book, you get only one thing—an increased tendency to think always in terms of the other person's point of view, and see things from his angle as well as your own—if you get only that one thing from this book, it may easily prove to be one of the milestones of your career.*
>
> —DALE CARNEGIE, *How to Win Friends and Influence People*

While writing this book I was on vacation with my family in Hawaii. I was reading a book on the pull-out sofa bed with our four-year-old, Chloe. Her mother walked into the room and accidentally bumped into the corner of the television armoire. Watching what happened, Chloe immediately said, "Ouch" as if she felt the pain herself. Touched by her caring, Tana gave Chloe a hug and told her she was okay. That simple interaction stayed with me all during the trip. It was the essence of empathy, the human ability to feel what others feel. I wondered if my patients with autism, who are so poor at reading social interactions, would have understood the importance of the event. Chloe's mirror neurons were at work.

In an exciting piece of research serendipity, Italian neuroscientists Giacomo Rizzolatti, Leonardo Fogassi, and Vittorio Gallese placed recording electrodes into the inferior frontal cortex of the macaque monkey. As the researchers were working to carefully map neurons to the monkey's actions, Fogassi was standing next to a bowl of fruit. When he reached for a banana some of the monkey's neurons reacted. Even though the monkey hadn't reached, his neurons associated with reaching fired away. These weren't the neurons that reflect thinking about someone else reaching; they were neurons that supposedly fire only when the subject reaches. The "mirror neurons," as Rizzolatti labeled them, were first identified as a relatively primitive system in monkeys. It was then discovered that such systems in humans were sophisticated and "allow us to grasp the minds of others not through traditional conceptual reasoning, but through direct simulation—by feeling, not by thinking."

Back to autism: in a fascinating article published in *Nature Neuroscience,* researchers indeed found mirror neuron deficits in these children. To examine mirror neuron abnormalities in autism, high-functioning children with autism and matched controls underwent a functional brain study, called fMRI, while imitating and observing emotional expressions. Although both groups performed the tasks equally well, children with autism showed no mirror neuron activity in the inferior frontal gyrus. Notably, activity in this area was inversely related to symptom severity in the social domain, suggesting that a dysfunctional mirror neuron system may underlie the social deficits observed in autism.

The mirror neuron system seems to be foundational to empathy. When it is healthy, we can experience the feelings of others. When the system works too hard, we can be too sensitive. When it does not work hard enough we can likely hurt others without its bothering us. A healthy system, like so many parts of the brain, helps us best.

Empathy helps us navigate the social environment and answer such questions as Is this person going to feed me? Love me? Attack me? Faint? Run away? Cry? The more accurately you can predict the actions and needs of others, the better off you are. The ability to "tune in" and empathize with others is a prerequisite for understanding, attachment, bonding, and love—all of which are important for our survival.

In several studies about why executives fail, "insensitivity to others," or a lack of empathy, was cited more than any other flaw as a reason for derailment. Statements like the following were typically used about those who did not succeed:

> "He never negotiated; there was no room for any views contrary to his."
> "He could follow a bull through a china shop and still break the china."
> "He made others feel stupid."
> "She was always talking down to her employees."
> "Whenever something went right, he took all the credit. Whenever things fell through, heads would roll."
> "It was her way or no way. If you disagreed with her, you were out."

Lack of empathy can cause failure in almost any endeavor. A lack of interpersonal skills not only causes others to avoid you, but it can make them "mad as hell" and feel active ill will toward you too. Co-workers may look the other way if you are making serious mistakes, lovers may start finding fault in any area they can to retaliate for their hurt, and acquaintances may start making excuses to decrease the time they spend with you. Lacking empathy also has a serious isolating effect that not only causes loneliness but also decreases the "reality" feedback from others and cuts you off from co-workers' or friends' creativity and knowledge. One example from my practice is of a supervisor who came back to his office after being chewed out by the owner of a company. He snapped at his assistant for not having a report ready. She had just returned from taking her child to the emergency room because he cut his head open falling against the corner of a table at day care. She started to cry and ran into the bathroom. The supervisor and assistant didn't speak to each other for a week and she finally quit a job she needed. If, instead of thinking only of their own trying days, each had taken a minute to think about what was going on with the other (empathy), this fight could have been avoided.

How is your empathy? Can you feel what others feel? Do you sabotage your relationships by being insensitive? Do you take the behavior of others too personally? Or when someone dumps on you, do you wonder what might be going on with him that caused him to act that way? Of course, you can carry that last question to an extreme and attribute any negative criticism directed your way as someone else's problem. Balance is the key. When negative stuff comes your way, you always need to ask yourself two questions. First, did I do anything to bring this on myself? Second, what is going on with him to cause him to act that way? Those two questions will help you to be more sensitive to other people and increase your chances for success.

Developing empathy involves a number of important skills, including mirroring, being able to get outside of yourself, and treating others in a way you'd like to be treated. The following three exercises were designed to help you increase your empathic skills—your ability to get outside of yourself and understand the needs of others.

MIRRORING

Your ability to understand and communicate with others will be enhanced by learning what psychiatrists call the mirroring technique. You can use this technique in any interpersonal situation to increase rapport with those around you. When you mirror someone, you assume or imitate his body language—posture, eye contact, and facial expression—and you use the same words and phrases in conversation that the other person uses. For example, if someone is leaning forward in his chair, looking intensely at you, without making a big point of it, do the same. If you note that he uses the same phrase several times, such as "I believe we have a winner here," pick it up and make it part of your vocabulary for that conversation. This is not mimicry, which implies ridicule; rather, this technique helps set up an unconscious identification with you in the mind of the other person.

THE GOLDEN RULE EXERCISE

Another exercise that will help you get outside of yourself and into the feelings of others is what I call the Golden Rule Exercise. In one interaction per day, treat someone else as you would like to be treated in that situation. For example, if your spouse has a headache when you feel amorous, instead of feeling rejected make a conscious effort to understand and say something like "It must be awful to have a headache before going to bed. Can I get anything for you?" This line will get you more in the way of passion than the accusation "You always have a headache!"

THE GET-OUTSIDE-OF-YOURSELF EXERCISE

The next couple of times you get into a disagreement with someone, take her side of the argument. At least verbally, begin to agree with her point of view. Argue for it, understand it, see where she's coming from. Although this can be a difficult exercise, it will pay royally if you use it to learn to understand others better. To do this exercise effectively, you must first listen to the opposing point of view without interrupting. Really listening is difficult, but if you concentrate on repeating back what you hear, you'll be almost there. *Note:* What you'll also notice when you do this exercise is that a difficult person will become less difficult. By agreeing with them you'll take the wind out of their sails and deflate their anger. I have seen this technique work wonders.

L IS FOR LISTENING

Poor communication is at the core of many relationship problems. Jumping to conclusions, mind reading, and always having to be right are only a few traits that doom communication. When people do not connect with each other in a meaningful way, their own minds take over the "relationship" and many imaginary problems arise. This occurs at home, with friends, and at work.

Donna was frequently angry at her husband. During the day, she'd imagine their evening together in which they spent time talking and being attentive to each other's needs. When her husband came home tired and preoccupied about a hard day at work, she felt disappointed and reacted angrily toward him. Her husband felt bewildered. He was unaware of his wife's thoughts during the day and didn't know he was disappointing her. After six couples sessions, the wife learned how to express her needs up front and she found a very receptive man.

Too often in relationships we have expectations and hopes that we never clearly communicate to our partners or colleagues. We assume they should know what we need and become disappointed when they don't accurately read our minds. Clear communication is essential if relationships are to be mutually satisfying.

Here are ten ways that communication is sabotaged in relationships.

1. Poor attitude. This is where you expect the conversation to go nowhere and subsequently you don't even try to direct it in a positive way. Negative assumptions about the other person feeds into this poor attitude. You don't trust the other person and you remain stiff and guarded when you are together.

2. Unclear expectations and needs. Do you expect people to guess what you want or need? It is great when others can anticipate our needs, but most people are so busy that it's hard for them to see the needs of other people. That does not make them good or bad; it simply means it's important to speak up about what you need.

3. No reinforcing body language. Body language is so important because it sends both conscious and unconscious messages. When you fail to make eye contact or acknowledge the other person with facial or body

gestures, he or she begins to feel lost, alone, and unenthusiastic about continuing the conversation. Eye contact and physical acknowledgment are essential to good communication.

4. Competing with distractions. Distractions frequently doom communication. It's not a good idea, for example, for my daughter to talk to me about something important during the fourth quarter of a Lakers basketball play-off game. Decrease distractions to have clear communication.

5. Never asking for feedback on what you're saying. You might assume that you are sending clear messages to the other person when, in fact, what they understand is completely different from what you meant. Feedback is essential to clear communication.

6. Kitchen sinking. This occurs in arguments when people feel backed into a corner and bring up unrelated issues from the past in order to protect themselves or intensify the disagreement. Stay on track until an issue is fully discussed.

7. Mind reading. This is where you arbitrarily predict what another person is thinking and then react on that "imagined" information. Mind reading is often a projection of what you think. Even after couples have been married for thirty years it's impossible for them to always be right about what is going on in the other person's head. Checking things out is essential to good communication.

8. Having to be right. This destroys effective communication. When a person has to be right in a conversation there is no communication, only a debate.

9. Sparring. Using putdowns, sarcasm, or discounting the other's ideas erodes meaningful dialogue and sets up distance in relationships.

10. Lack of monitoring and follow-up. Often it takes repeated efforts to get what you need. It's very important not to give up. When you give up asking for what you need, you often silently resent the other person, which subverts the whole relationship. Persistence is very important to getting what you want.

Clear communication is a key to success in almost any area of life. Too often in personal or business relationships we have hopes and expectations that we never clearly communicate to others. As a consultant to organizations and businesses, I've found that the underlying problem in employer-employee disputes was often a lack of clear communication. In many cases, when the communication problems were improved other problems were also quickly resolved.

For example, Billie Jo was an administrative assistant who was frequently angry at her boss. He would give her general guidelines for projects and then become irritated with her when it wasn't done to his satisfaction. Because of his gruff manner, she was too afraid to ask him specific questions about the work. She began to really hate her job. She developed frequent headaches and neck tension and was constantly looking for another job. A friend pushed her to tell her boss about her frustrations. The friend said, "If you're going to quit anyway, you have little to lose." To her surprise, the boss was receptive to her direct approach and encouraged her to ask more questions about the projects he assigned.

Here are six keys to effective communication in relationships.

1. Have a good attitude and assume the other person wants the relationship to work as much as you do. Too often people become caught up in their own anger and disappointment and they unknowingly set things up to turn out poorly. Having a good attitude can set the mood for a positive outcome. I call this having "positive basic assumptions" about the relationship.

2. State what you need clearly and in a positive way. Most people are too wrapped up in themselves to think about what's going on with you. In most situations being direct is the best approach. But how you ask is important. You can demand and be met with hostility, you can ask in a meek manner and no one will take you seriously, or you can be firm yet kind in the way you ask and get what you need. How you approach someone has a lot to do with your success rate.

3. Decrease distractions and make sure you have the other person's attention. Find a time when the person is not busy or in a hurry to go somewhere.

4. Ask for feedback to ensure the other person correctly understands you. Clear communication is a two-way street and it's important to know if you got your message across. A simple "Tell me what you understood I said" is often all that is needed.

5. Be a good listener. Before you respond to what people say, repeat back what you think they've said to ensure that you've correctly heard them. Statements such as "I hear you saying . . ." or "You mean to

say . . ." are the gold standard of good communication. This allows you to check out what you hear before you respond.

6. Monitor and follow up on your communication. Often it takes repeated efforts to get what you need. It's very important not to give up.

ACTIVE LISTENING

The "I hear you saying . . . ," or active listening, technique is taught by therapists to increase communication. It forces you to really hear and understand what the other person is saying. This technique involves repeating back what you have understood the other person to say. In this way, you check out with the sender whether the message you received is the one you were intended to get. Communication often breaks down because of distortions between intention and understanding, especially in emotionally charged encounters. Simply saying, "I hear you saying . . . Is that what you meant?" can help avoid misunderstandings. This technique is particularly helpful when you suspect a breakdown in communication.

Different phrases to use with this technique include the following.

"I heard you say . . . Am I right?"
"Did you mean to say . . . ?"
"I'm not sure I understand what you said. Did you say . . . ?"
"Did I understand you correctly? Are you saying that . . . ?"
"Let me see if I understand what you're saying to me. You said . . . ?"

Here are the advantages to active listening.

1. You receive more accurate messages.
2. Misunderstandings are cleared up immediately.
3. You are forced to give your full attention to the other person.
4. Both parties are now responsible for accurate communication.
5. The sender is likely to be more careful with what he says.
6. It increases your ability to really hear the other person and thus learn from him.
7. It stops you from thinking about what you're going to say next so that you can really hear what the other person is saying.
8. It increases communication.
9. It tends to cool down conflicts.

Begin practicing this technique on at least two people every day for a week. See if it doesn't increase your communication abilities and thus your ability to learn from others.

A IS FOR ASSERTIVENESS

It's very important to say what you mean. Assertiveness and communication go hand in hand. Assertiveness means you express your thoughts and feelings in a firm yet reasonable way, not allowing others to emotionally run over you and not saying yes when it's not what you mean. Do not equate assertiveness with becoming mean or aggressive. Here are five rules to help you assert yourself in a healthy manner.

1. Do not give in to the anger of others just because it makes you uncomfortable. Anxious people do this a lot. We're just so anxious that we just agree. But by just agreeing, we're actually teaching that other person to be mean to us. We're teaching the other person that it's okay to manipulate us with anger. It doesn't mean you have to be angry back, but don't agree just because you're feeling anxious. When you are feeling anxious about another person's anger, it is a good time to do the deep breathing techniques I taught you earlier. Take three deep, slow breaths and really think about what your opinion is; state it clearly without much emotion.

2. Do not allow the opinion of others to control how you feel. Your opinion, within reason, needs to be the one that counts for you. What do you think about that situation? People with anxiety tend to flip-flop on their position. Work on knowing what you think and believe.

3. Say what you mean and stick up for what you believe is right. People respect you more. People like you more if you are a real person who says exactly what's on your mind.

4. Maintain self-control. Being angry, mean, or aggressive is not being assertive. Be assertive in a calm and clear way.

5. Be kind, if possible. But above all be firm in your stance. We teach other people how to treat us. When we give in to their temper tantrums we actually teach them that that is a way to control us. When we assert ourselves in a firm yet kind way others have more respect for us and they treat us accordingly. Now, if you've allowed others to emo-

tionally run over you for a long time, they're going to be a little resistant to change. If you stick to your guns, you help them learn a new way of relating to you, and the relationship will be better. Ultimately, you will respect yourself more.

T IS FOR TIME

Relationships require actual time. With our lives already constrained by two-parent working households, traffic-intensive commutes, e-mail, the Internet, television, video games, and other distractions, the time we have available for the people in our lives is seriously diminished. But making time for the people who are important to you will make a huge difference in your relationships. When I teach our parenting course, I emphasize time. In the course I say relationships really require two things, time and a willingness to listen. Time is critically important to relationships. It doesn't have to be a lot of time, but it needs to be focused on the relationship.

There's an exercise in my parenting course I call Special Time. It involves spending twenty minutes a day doing something with your child that he or she wants to do. Twenty minutes is not much time, but this exercise makes a huge difference in the quality of relationships. During this time, I have one rule: no commands, no questions, and no directions. It's not a time to try to resolve issues; it is just a time to be together and do something your partner wants to do, whether it's playing a game or taking a walk. The difference it made in parent-child relationships was much more dramatic than anything else I did for them, including medicine. Look for ways to spend time on the relationships that are important to you. Think of the time as an investment in the health of the relationship.

You also need to be present when you are spending time with others at work or at home. Too often, there are so many distractions. In the powerful book *Influencer: The Power to Change Anything,* the authors tell a story about a large regional health care organization that went from terrible customer satisfaction to becoming one of the region's class organizations. In studying the employees who ranked great versus those who were poor, there were only five simple differences. The effective employees smiled, made eye contact, identified themselves by name, let people know what they were doing and why, and ended every interaction by asking, "Is there anything else you need?" These things were easy to do. They indicated that the service providers were present and focused on the interaction at hand.

I IS FOR INQUIRY

Earlier in the book we discussed killing the ANTs, or automatic negative thoughts, that invade your mind. When you're suffering in a relationship it's very important to inquire into the thoughts that make you suffer. For example, if you are fighting with your husband and you hear yourself thinking, "He never listens to me," write that down. Then ask yourself if it is true. The little lies we tell ourselves about other people often put unnecessary wedges between us and them. Relationships require accurate thinking in order to thrive. Whenever you feel sad, mad, or nervous in relationships, check out your thoughts. If there are ANTs or lies, stomp them out.

N IS FOR NOTICING WHAT YOU LIKE MORE THAN WHAT YOU DON'T

One of the secrets to having great relationships is noticing what you like more than what you don't. When you do this you are shaping the other person's behavior. Noticing what you like encourages more of the behavior you like to happen. I learned this concept for the first time when my son was seven years old and we were living in Hawaii. I was in my child psychiatry fellowship-training program.

One day I wanted special time with my son, Antony. I took him to a place called Sea Life Park, which is like SeaWorld. And we had a great day together. We went to the killer whale show, the dolphin show, and saw sea lion antics on-stage. Toward the end of the day my son sort of grabbed my shirt and said, "Daddy, take me to see Fat Freddie." I said, "Who's Fat Freddie?" "It's the penguin, Dad," he said. I looked on the show schedule and there was one more Fat Freddie show. Fat Freddie was an emperor penguin who performed in the large stadium at Sea Life Park. When we got to our seats the stadium was filled.

Freddie was amazing. To start the show he climbed a ladder to a high diving board. He went to the end of the board, bounced up and down, then jumped into the water. When he got out of the water, on command he bowed with his nose, counted with his flippers, and jumped through a hoop of fire. I thought to myself, "How cool is this?" And my son was clapping. He was very happy that we were at the show. Toward the end of the show, the trainer asked Freddie to retrieve something. Freddie went and got it and brought it to the trainer. In my mind, when I saw this action, I thought, "Damn, I ask this kid to get me something and he wants to have a discussion for twenty minutes and then he doesn't do it." I knew my son was smarter than the penguin. I used to find myself frequently frustrated and angry at my son.

After the show I went up to the trainer and asked her how she got Fat Freddie to do all the things he did. The trainer understood what I was asking her, because she looked at my son and then she looked at me and said, "Unlike parents, whenever Freddie does anything like what I want him to do, I notice him. I give him a hug and I give him a fish." The light went on in my head that whenever my son did what I wanted him to do I paid no attention to him because I'm a busy guy. But when he didn't do what I wanted him to do, I gave him a ton of attention because I didn't want to raise bad kids. I was inadvertently teaching him to be a little monster in order to get my attention. So now I actually collect penguins to remind myself to notice what I like about others more than what I do not like. I have more than two thousand penguins.

What do you think Fat Freddie would have done if he were having a bad day and didn't do what the trainer asked him to do? What if the trainer started screaming at him, "You stupid penguin. I can't believe I ever met a penguin as stupid as you. We ought to ship you off to the Antarctic and get a replacement." Depending on his temperament, if he understood her, he would have either bitten her or gone off to a corner and cried.

What do you do when the important people in your life do not do what you want them to do? Do you criticize them and make them feel miserable? Or do you just pause and notice what you like more than what you don't like? This is a critical point. It is an important secret to changing behavior. Focus on the behaviors that you like, eight, ten, twenty times more than the behaviors you don't. This doesn't mean you're not assertive when you need to be. But it means in your mind you're figuring out how to shape the situation in a positive way.

G IS FOR CONNECTING WITH GREAT GROUPS

Continually working to build your support groups buffers you against many of the stresses you are likely to face. Within those groups, who you spend time with matters. When you are with positive, supportive, and loving people, you will feel happier, more content, and you'll likely live longer. In a study at Case Western Reserve in Cleveland, Ohio, ten thousand men were asked, "Does your wife show you her love?" The detailed health histories of the men followed for over ten years who answered yes showed fewer ulcers and less chest pain and lived longer than whose who answered no.

When you spend time with negative or hostile people, you tend to feel tense, anxious, upset, and sick, and you increase your stress hormones. Increases in the stress hormone cortisol can disrupt neurons in the hippocampus, one of the main memory centers in the brain. Through the years people have told me that living with a person who suffered from schizophrenia, bipolar disorder, depression, panic disorder, ADD, or borderline personality disorder has had a negative impact on their physical and emotional health. The chronic stress for family members associated with these illnesses when they are untreated or undertreated can be devastating. Mothers of untreated ADHD children, for example, have a higher incidence of depression themselves and often complain that they are physically sick more often and cognitively less sharp than before they had the child.

Look at your own situation. Are you surrounded by people who believe in you and who give you positive messages? People who encourage you to feel good about yourself? Or do you spend time with people who are constantly putting you down and downplaying your ideas? Who are the five people you spend the most time with? Are they positive or negative? Rate how you feel about each of the relationships on a scale of 1 to 10, with 1 being a very negative relationship and 10 being an uplifting and supportive relationship. Use this information to evaluate your relationships to see which you need to work on and which ones you may want to consider ending. As Oprah Winfrey says, "Surround yourself with only those people who are going to lift you higher." I would add that this is a sure way to build a trusted support network.

These eight keys will improve your relationships and help you build social networks. Being responsible, empathic, listening, assertive, spending time, inquiring into negative thoughts, noticing what you like more than what you don't, and striving to spend time with positive people will all help you achieve your maximum potential.

| 16 |

Be a Maverick Thinker

———

STOP ANXIETY FROM ALLOWING OTHERS TO RUN YOUR LIFE

I once dated a guy who was a Heisman trophy candidate and he told me they don't try to tackle you unless you are running with the ball.

—A note from a grateful patient

It was 6:30 A.M. in the busy emergency room at the Walter Reed Army Medical Center in Washington, D.C. I was just putting on my white lab coat as I walked through the doors to the unit. It was my third day as an intern and the emergency room would be my home for the next month. From down the hall I heard a woman screaming. Curious, I went to see what was going on.

Beth, a forty-year-old woman, was lying on a gurney with a swollen right leg. She was in obvious pain and screamed whenever anyone touched her leg. Bruce White, a brand-new psychiatry intern like myself, and Wendy Bernstein, the internal medicine chief resident, were trying to start an IV in Beth's foot. The patient was anxious, scared, uncooperative, and hyperventilating. She had a blood clot in her calf that caused tremendous swelling in her lower leg. The IV was necessary before we could send Beth to radiology where a scan could be done to see exactly where the clot was so the surgeons could operate to remove it. With each stick of the IV needle to her swollen foot

Beth's screams became louder. Wendy was anxious and frustrated; sweat started to appear on her face.

She snapped at the patient, "Calm down!"

Beth looked scared and confused. There was a lot of tension in the room.

Wendy paged the surgeon on call. It took him several minutes to get back to her. She paced. When the phone rang, Wendy quickly answered it. "I need you to come to the ER right away. I need you to do a 'cut down' on a patient's foot. It looks like she has a blood clot in her leg and we need to start an IV before sending her to x-ray. Her foot is swollen, and she's being difficult!"

Wendy listened for a few moments and then said, "What do you mean you can't come for an hour! This has got to be done right away. I'll do it myself." She cursed as she slammed down the phone.

Hearing this, Beth looked even more panicked.

Being a brand-new intern in the hospital, I didn't want to say anything. But I hated to see Beth in pain. I had heard of Wendy's reputation for harassing interns. It was going to be an interesting day, I thought.

"Wendy, can I try to start the IV?" I softly said.

She glared at me, and with a tone that was both sarcastic and condescending, she said, "Your name is Amen, right? I've been starting IVs for five years. What makes you think you're so special? But if you want to try and look stupid, hotshot, go for it." She rudely tossed the IV set at me and left the room. I motioned to Bruce to shut the door.

The first thing I did was to walk around the gurney to Beth's head and establish eye contact with her. I gave her a gentle smile. Wendy had been yelling at her from the other side of her feet.

"Hi, Beth, I'm Dr. Daniel Amen. I need you to slow down your breathing. When you breathe too quickly all of the blood vessels clamp down, making it impossible for us to find a vein. Breathe with me." I slowed my own breathing down, thinking that Wendy was going to kill me when I finished.

"Do you mind if I help you relax?" I asked. "I know some tricks."

"Okay," Beth said nervously.

"Look at that spot on the ceiling." I pointed to a spot on the ceiling tiles overhead. "I want you to focus on it and ignore everything else in the room . . . I'm going to count to ten, and as I do let your eyes feel very heavy. Only focus on the spot and the sound of my voice. One . . . two . . . three . . . let your eyes feel very heavy . . . four . . . five . . . let your eyes feel heavier still . . . six . . . seven . . . eight . . . your eyes are feeling very heavy and want to close . . . nine . . . ten . . . let your eyes close and keep them closed.

"Very good," I said as Beth closed her eyes. "I want you to breathe very slowly, very deeply, and pay attention only to the sound of my voice. Let your whole body relax from the top of your head all the way down to the bottom of your feet. Let your whole body feel warm, heavy, and very relaxed. Now I want you to forget about the hospital and imagine yourself in a beautiful park. The most beautiful park you can think of. See the park, the grass, the hillside, a gentle flowing brook, beautiful trees. Hear the sounds in the park, the brook flowing, the birds singing, a light breeze rustling the leaves in the trees. Smell and taste the freshness in the air. And feel the feelings in the park—a light breeze on your skin, the warmth of the sun."

All of the tension in the room had calmed down. Wendy popped her head in the room, but Bruce put his finger over his lips for her to be quiet and motioned for her to leave. She rolled her eyes and quietly shut the door.

"Now I want you to imagine a beautiful pool in the middle of the park," I continued. "It is filled with a special, warm healing water. In your mind, sit on the edge of the pool and dangle your feet in it. Feel the warm water surround your feet. You are doing really great."

Beth had quickly gone into a deep trance.

I continued. "Now I know this might sound strange, but many people can actually make blood vessels pop up if they direct their attention to them. With your feet in the pool, allow the blood vessels in your feet to pop up so that I can put an IV in it, so that you can get the help you need, still allowing your mind to stay in the park and feel very relaxed . . ."

In medical school I took a month elective in hypnosis. I had watched a film of an Indian psychiatrist put a patient in a hypnotic trance and had her pop up a vein in her hand. Then she stuck a needle in the vein, removed it, and was bleeding out of both sides of the puncture wounds. Then, with suggestion, she stopped the bleeding on one side of the vein and then the other side. It was one of the most amazing feats of self-control I had seen. Thinking of Beth's situation reminded me of the film. In truth, I had no expectation that Beth would actually be able to pop the vein up in her foot.

To my great surprise, at that moment a vein clearly appeared on her swollen foot. I gently slipped the needle into the vein and attached it to the bag of IV fluid.

Bruce's eyes widened. He couldn't believe what he saw, even though he just saw it.

"Beth," I softly said, "you can stay in this deep relaxed state as long as you need. You can go back to the park anytime you want."

Bruce and I wheeled Beth to radiology. When I returned to the unit an hour later, Wendy gave me a hostile look.

"So we have a maverick and miracle worker among us," she said. "Remember what happened to Jesus. I believe he was crucified. You might not want to make me look bad . . . you never know what might happen."

"I'm sorry to interfere," I said. "When people are scared they breathe too fast and their blood vessels tend to constrict. I just asked her to slow down her breathing. It was a simple trick I learned in medical school. The hypnosis was to get her very relaxed. I've heard about people who could dilate veins under hypnosis. I thought it was worth a try."

"You just got lucky," Wendy retorted. She wasn't giving an inch.

A female nurse overheard our conversation and said, "You can do hypnosis? Could you hypnotize me to get rid of these?" She pointed to the cigarettes in her pocket.

An overweight male nurse chimed in, "Could you hypnotize me to lose weight?"

Another female nurse said with excitement, "In nursing school I read about a study where hypnosis was used to enlarge breast size. And it really worked! Can you help me with these?" She pointed to her smallish breasts.

Wendy looked disgusted. Totally embarrassed, I said, "I don't know. I have a lot to do right now. I'll see you all later."

Maverick Thinking

The etymology of the word "maverick" is from the Texas lawyer Samuel Maverick, who refused to brand his cattle. It has come to represent people who think for themselves. From the time I was young my father called me a maverick. It was not a compliment. I never went along with his ideas just to make peace. My older brother, Jimmy, was much more diplomatic with him, although he pounded me regularly when we were young. When I had my own thoughts or ideas I had to express them; it caused a fair amount of tension between my dad and me.

When I was eighteen years old in July 1972, I had to sign up for the military draft. I drew the lottery number 19, out of 365, which meant that it was highly likely I would be drafted. I talked to a military recruiter about my options. At the time, I was interested in becoming a veterinarian and I learned that the army had a program that would train me to become a veterinarian's assistant. That sounded interesting. That night I told my father what I had learned. In his usual way, he told me I couldn't join the army. There was a war going on! When I pushed the conversation, that I was likely to be drafted anyway and this job sounded interesting, plus I could go to Europe rather than Vietnam, he said, "Good, I will drive you to the bus station." I was sad that I couldn't please him, but there was no way he was making my decisions. Joining the military, and getting some extra time to grow up before college and having time away from a powerful father, was one of the best decisions of my life.

My father taught me that authority figures, even very successful ones, were not always right. Years later, the maverick tendency has been one of the cornerstones of my own personal success. I was able to make decisions independently, even when others did not agree with me. The work we do at the Amen Clinics has been called maverick by many of our colleagues. We do brain imaging work in psychiatry, believing we need more information than the standard symptom clusters most psychiatrists use to make diagnoses. We use nutritional supplements when we believe they may work instead of or in addition to medication. We believe in educating our patients and the general public about brain health, and publish high school and college courses to encourage it. None of this is standard fare for psychiatric clinics. But this is precisely why so many people have come to see us. Our patients want a different approach to the standard fifteen-minute psychiatric appointments to get their medications refilled.

In their book *Mavericks at Work: Why the Most Original Minds in Business Win*, Bill Taylor and Polly LaBarre explain why innovators and upstarts are inventing the future of business. They say, "If you want to know the future, invent it . . . Unconventional ideas and groundbreaking strategies will become the business plan for the twenty-first century and a better way to lead, compete and succeed." In the right context, being a maverick is a critical trait of many successful people.

Going along just to get along, especially when things are not right, is harmful and often demoralizing. There is no question that on the surface it would have been easier for me to go along with my father when he wanted me to agree with him or with my chief resident, Wendy, but over time I would have lost my soul. I wouldn't have known where they ended and I began. Going along with others to quell your own internal anxiety or fear of rejection sets you up for frustration, abuse, heartbreak, and a lack of original thought. In this chapter, I will discuss four traits of maverick thinkers and some fascinating brain imaging research about what inhibits people from thinking more independently or creatively. Let me be clear: being a maverick does not mean being negative, oppositional, or argumentative. Being contrary just for the sake of being different is a two-year-old's trait and a sign of an immature, rigid brain.

What Is Maverick Thinking?

Maverick thinking involves four traits.

1. Independent thinking
2. Not accepting the norm just because it is the norm
3. Creativity or thinking in a way that is different from others'
4. A passionate belief that you can make a difference

Mavericks think for themselves. They are fiercely independent and believe in their own abilities. They are good at listening to others, gathering needed data, and doing their homework, but they synthesize information in their own unique way. Some independent thinkers may come from having had encouraging early environments. Others may come from people who were actively discouraged, people whose maverick tendencies emerged as a reaction to the overcontrol of their parents, teachers, or coaches.

Tony Dungy, coach of the 2007 Super Bowl champion Indianapolis Colts, describes maverick thinking in his book *Quiet Strength.* A deeply religious man who was encouraged by his father, Coach Dungy did not believe in yelling, cursing, or belittling players. He tells them at the beginning of a season that he will never talk louder than his usual voice and if he is really upset he, in fact, is likely to talk softer. He has been criticized for not having displayed more emotion, like other coaches, but that is not his style. He has obviously been effective coaching his way.

Independent thinkers tend not to follow rules just because someone else thinks they should. They do not go along with the group norm just because there is a norm. Unlike sociopaths who break rules just because they can, mavericks evaluate the rules to see if they make sense. If the rules are working, they use them to their advantage; if not, they look for better rules. Mavericks are smart and they are moral. They do not break rules that could cost them their livelihoods or damage the welfare of their families, unless there are really good reasons to do so.

In their best-selling business book *First, Break All the Rules: What the World's Greatest Managers Do Differently,* Gallup Organization consultants Marcus Buckingham and Curt Coffman challenge the thinking of many standard management techniques. They argue that commonly held notions about management (e.g., people are capable of almost anything and a manager's role is diminishing in today's economy) are wrong. "Great managers," they write, "are revolutionaries . . . They break the rules and make ones that work." The authors have culled their observations from more than eighty thousand interviews conducted by Gallup during the past twenty-five years. Great managers, they argue, do not just go with the flow.

Rudolf Flesch, author of *Why Johnny Can't Read,* once wrote that "creative thinking may mean simply the realization that there's no particular virtue in doing things the way they always have been done." Once you realize this concept, you are on your way to being a part of the maverick club. Being creative is having the ability to look at common things in an uncommon way, to take a different approach. Unfortunately, many people have come to erroneously equate creativity with madness, citing van Gogh, Hemingway, and others as examples. Current medical research, however, teaches us that the healthier our brains, the more creative we are likely to be. Psychiatrist Daniel Offer, M.D., studied several hundred teenagers to see what characterizes "normal" adolescence. He described three distinct patterns of psychological growth: turbulent, sporadic, and continuous. The turbulent group was in trouble most of the time during adolescence, the sporadic group had periodic issues, and the continuous group had very few problems. Dr. Offer then gave the inkblot test to the young people in his study and found that those with the healthiest growth pattern (i.e., the continuous growth group) gave the most creative and unusual responses to the cards. Creativity correlated with health. Creative people explore all of the options available to them, conventional and unconventional, and they try new ideas, even when they're not sure if they will work out.

The last hallmark of a maverick is the sense that your life matters, that you can make a difference and have a positive impact. Having passion and purpose drives the maverick's motives to create something useful or to buck the system to make life more effective, more wonderful, more meaningful. As discussed in chapter 9, there are passion circuits in the brain that involve the nucleus accumbens and basal ganglia. These brain areas respond to the neurotransmitter dopamine, which is involved with drive, motivation, and salience. The power of being part of a group and being accepted by others is so strong, as we will see below, that in order to do something different, or outside the group, it must be intrinsically rewarding in and of itself or have deep personal meaning to you.

Within two years of starting our brain imaging work, I created a firestorm of criticism among my colleagues. "Psychiatrists don't do this" was something I heard a lot. Being naturally anxious, I hated the criticism. It caused sleepless nights and a general underlying uneasiness. For over a year I stopped talking about the work at the Amen Clinics. I was trying to figure out how to handle the conflict. Then late one night in April 1995 I received a phone call from my sister-in-law, Sherrie, who was in tears. She told me that Andrew, my nine-year-old nephew and godson, had attacked a little girl on the baseball field that day for no particular reason. The attack was unprovoked and out of the blue. Sherrie told me that for the last year Andrew's behavior had been getting increasingly worse. His personality had changed from a sweet, happy child to someone who was angry and depressed, who had serious suicidal and homicidal thoughts. In his room she found two drawings, one of him hanging from a tree, another one in which he was shooting other children. I told Sherrie to bring Andrew to see me the next day. His parents drove to my clinic, which was eight hours away.

As I sat with Andrew and his parents I knew something was wrong. I had never seen him look so angry or so sad. He had no explanations for his behavior other than "I am just mad all the time." He said no one was hurting or teasing him. He had no idea why he felt the way he did. There was no family history of serious psychiatric illnesses or head injuries. And he had a wonderful family. Unlike most clinical situations, I knew this family. Andrew's parents were loving, caring, and concerned. What was the matter?

The vast majority of my colleagues would have placed Andrew on some sort of medication and had him see a counselor for psychotherapy. Having performed more than a thousand SPECT studies by that time, I first wanted a picture of Andrew's brain. But with my colleagues' hostility over my imaging work fresh in my mind, I questioned myself. Maybe this was really due to a family problem that I just didn't know about. Maybe this was a psychological problem. (As an aside, if you have good psychoanalytic training you can find dirt in anybody's family.) I thought, "Maybe Andrew is acting out because his older brother is a 'perfect' child who does well in school and is very athletic. Maybe Andrew has these thoughts and behaviors to ward off feelings of insecurity related to being the second son in a Lebanese family. Maybe Andrew wants to feel powerful and these behaviors are associated with issues of control." Then logic took over my brain. Nine-year-old children do not attack other children for no reason. They do not normally think about suicide or homicide. I needed to scan his brain. If it appeared normal, then I could look further into the underlying emotional problems that might be present.

I went with Andrew to the imaging center and held his hand while he had the study performed. As his brain appeared on the computer screen I thought a mistake had been done in performing the procedure. Andrew had *no* left temporal lobe (see Image 16.1). Upon quick examination of the complete study, I realized the quality of the scan was fine. He was indeed missing the function of his left temporal lobe. Did he have a cyst, a tumor, a prior stroke? A part of me felt scared for him as I was looking at the monitor. Another part of me felt relieved that we had some explanation for his aggressive behavior. My research and the research of others had implicated the left temporal lobe in aggression. The next day Andrew had a magnetic resonance imaging scan, which showed a cyst (a fluid-filled sac) about the size of a golf ball occupying the space where his left temporal lobe should have been. I knew the cyst had to be removed. Getting someone to take this seriously, however, proved frustrating.

That day I called Andrew's pediatrician in Orange, California, and told him of both the clinical situation and brain findings. I told him to find the best person possible to take this thing out of his head. He contacted three pediatric neurologists. All of them said that Andrew's negative behavior was probably not in any way related to the cyst in his brain and they would not recommend operating on him until he had "real symptoms." When the pediatrician told me this information, I became furious. *Real symptoms!* I had a child with homicidal and suicidal thoughts who lost control over his behavior and attacked people. I contacted a pediatric neurologist in San Francisco

Image 16.1: Andrew's Missing
Left Temporal Lobe
(3-D underside surface view)

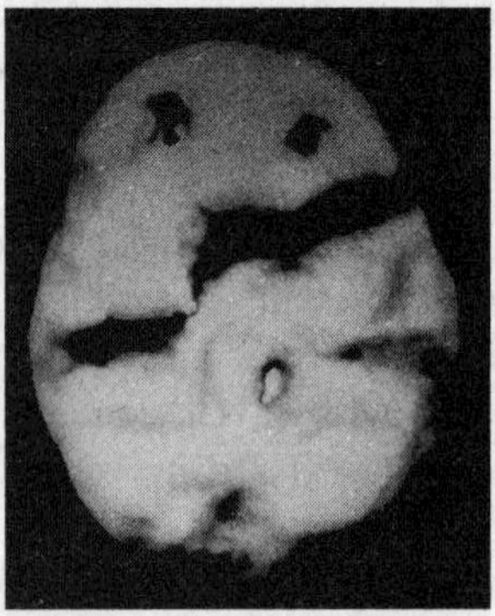

Missing left temporal lobe

who told me the same thing. I then called a friend of mine at Harvard Medical School, also a pediatric neurologist, who told me yet again the same thing. She even used the words *real symptoms*. When I pressed her, she attempted to clarify her reasoning. "When I say 'real symptoms,' I mean problems like seizures or speech problems." I was angry and appalled! Could the medical profession really not connect the brain to behavior? But I wasn't going to wait until this child killed himself or someone else. I called the pediatric neurosurgeon Jorge Lazarette, M.D., at UCLA and told him about Andrew. He told me that he had operated on three other children with left temporal lobe cysts who were all aggressive. He wondered if it was related. Thankfully, after evaluating Andrew he agreed to take it out.

When Andrew woke up from the surgery he smiled at his mother. It was the first time in a year that he had smiled. Upon awaking from the surgery his aggressive thoughts were gone and his temperament changed back to the sweet child he always wanted to be. Andrew was lucky. He had someone who loved him paying attention to his brain when his behavior was off. With this very personal experience resonating in the memory and emotional centers of my brain, I decided that I had to share this work with a larger audience, no matter how much criticism came my way. Sometimes I still cry when I think about or tell this story. I think of all the children, teenagers, and adults who do terrible things that we just label as bad, evil, or less than human, even though we have never looked at their brains. We just condemn them. It is so much easier to judge people if you never look at how their brains struggle. Andrew is now age twenty-one; he's employed and a wonderful young man. That personal experience gave me the motivation and courage to deal with my critics and do the work I have loved for so long.

Why Is Maverick Thinking So Rare?

One of the biggest obstacles to maverick thinking is the powerful desire to be accepted by our peer group. The need to belong, to be part of a group of family, friends, and colleagues, is hardwired in our brain. When we venture out on our own, when we think independently for ourselves, we risk rejection or ridicule from the group we love.

In a fascinating study from Emory University, researchers uncovered a key to how social cooperation is processed in the brain. Cooperation works on the same centers as cocaine does. When we cooperate with others the pleasure circuits light up, even when it costs us money. It feels good to get along. Cooperation reinforces itself. Literally, it feels bad to buck the group. James Rilling,

Ph.D., Gregory Berns, M.D., Ph.D., and colleagues scanned the brains of thirty-six women while they played the Prisoner's Dilemma game. This game explores cooperation based on the principle of reciprocal altruism.

A little detail about the game will help you better understand the study. Prisoner's Dilemma is a non-zero-sum game. A zero-sum game is simply a win-lose game such as tic-tac-toe, poker, or chess. For every winner, there's a loser. If I win, you lose. Non-zero-sum games allow for cooperation. There are moves that benefit both players. In the Prisoner's Dilemma, you and Albert (the game got its name from Princeton mathematician Albert Tucker) are picked up by the police for a suspected crime and interrogated in separate cells without a chance to communicate with each other. For the purpose of this game, it makes no difference whether or not you or Albert is guilty. You are both given the following pieces of information.

- If you both confess, you will both get four years in prison.
- If neither of you confesses, the police will pin part of the crime on you, and you'll both get two years.
- If one of you confesses but the other doesn't, the confessor will make a deal with the police and will go free while the other one goes to jail for five years.

The best strategy appears simple. No matter what Albert does, you are better off confessing: you either go free or get four years. But Albert knows this too, so you'd both end up getting four years. If you both "cooperate" (refuse to confess), you would both be better off, getting only two years. The game is much more complicated than it first appears. If you play repeatedly, the goal is to figure out Albert's strategy and use it to minimize your own total jail time. Albert will be doing the same thing. The object of the game is not to hurt Albert but rather to limit your own time of incarceration, either by exploiting Albert's kindness or through cooperation.

Back to the study results. The most common outcome in games played by the women was mutual cooperation, even though players were maximally rewarded for defecting when the other player cooperated. During the mutually cooperative social interactions on scans, activation was noted in the brain's pleasure centers, such as the nucleus accumbens and caudate nucleus. "Our study shows, for the first time, that social cooperation is intrinsically rewarding to the human brain, even in the face of pressures to the contrary," said Dr. Berns, author of *Satisfaction: Sensation Seeking, Novelty, and the Science of Finding True Fulfillment.* "It suggests that the altruistic drive to cooperate is biologically embedded—either genetically programmed or acquired through socialization during childhood and adolescence."

"Reciprocal altruism activates a reward circuit, and this activation may often be sufficiently reinforcing to override subsequent temptations to accept but not reciprocate altruism. This may be what motivates us to persist with cooperative social interactions and reap the benefits of sustained mutual cooperation," said Dr. Rilling.

On the surface, the researchers argue that cooperation and altruism is a good thing, an adaptive social skill. I agree that it certainly can be. But it can also be a terrible thing and cause you to lose yourself if you cooperate so much that you have no idea what your own thoughts are. Cooperation, according to this study, works in the same areas of the brain implicated in addictions. It is so important for some of us to be cooperative that we allow our husbands or wives to control us, belittle us, sometimes abuse us; we allow our children to get away with bad behavior, because we want them to like us; we stay in jobs that are not a good fit for us, because we "just want to get along"; we ignore underperforming employees because we do not want to confront them. When cooperation gets out of hand, it is similar to an addiction. It generates anxiety and such thoughts as "Please love me, no matter what"; "Don't be mad at me"; "I'll do anything to get you back"; and "I'll do anything to get along."

The anxiety becomes too intense to deal with the problems, so you go along to get along. The anxiety can prevent you from speaking your mind or even thinking your own thoughts. It is part of the reason that rigid religions and cults flourish.

In another fascinating study, Dr. Rilling and colleagues explored the impact of the neurotransmitter serotonin on cooperation. As mentioned earlier, serotonin is involved with mood control and cognitive flexibility. It helps you shift attention easily, be more flexible, and let go of hurts. Again, using the Prisoner's Dilemma game, healthy participants were randomly assigned to two groups. One group was given a drink that contained tryptophan, the amino acid precursor molecule for serotonin, while the other group's drink did not contain any tryptophan. The group whose drink contained no tryptophan had significantly lower levels of cooperation when playing the game, even in light of their previously cooperative behavior. The researchers concluded that serotonin is important to social interactions. "These results suggest that serotonin plays a significant role in the acquisition of socially cooperative behavior."

Psychiatrists who prescribe selective serotonin reuptake inhibitors, which increase serotonin availability in the brain, often see an increase in cooperation and a decrease in contrary or socially negative behavior. I wonder, however, if medications like Lexapro, Zoloft, and Prozac do not also decrease independent thought and creativity. It seems to me that we need a balance between enough serotonin so that we feel good and can be flexible and cooperative, without going overboard and losing our identity to the will of the group. You need some angst to know when things are not right. That is what I experienced when I saw the chief resident abusing Beth in the story at the beginning of this chapter. If I had been on Prozac, I very well may have thought to myself, "That is an interesting interaction. I hope they work it out. Where's breakfast?"

How You Lose Your Maverick Voice

Overcontrol, dependence, anxiety, and stress also inhibit independent thinking. Parents, teachers, or managers who overcontrol or demand "blind" compliance often work against themselves. Whenever you demand sameness or blind compliance, you lock the independent minds away and do not hear what they are thinking. You limit your own growth. When other people demand that you think the way they do, your mind no longer has to work, and if you are lazy you simply comply. Or you may get mad and start pushing against them, actively sabotage them, or walk away. The Gallup Organization estimated that "actively disengaged" workers are costing U.S. businesses three hundred billion dollars a year in productivity losses. According to their research, 17 percent or 22.5 million employees are actively disengaged. Gallup defined "actively disengaged" as employees who are not just unhappy in their work but who are sabotaging their businesses. Each one of these angry and alienated workers is costing their employers roughly thirteen thousand dollars in yearly productivity losses on average. There is more bad news. A majority of workers (54 percent) falls into the "not engaged" category. Not engaged workers are defined as "checked out," putting time but not energy or passion into their work. Look around your own workplace. According to this research, every other person you see is on autopilot. Only 29 percent of workers are estimated by Gallup to be truly "engaged"—employees who "work with passion and who feel a profound connection to their company." With so many people checked out, you dramatically decrease the amount of independent thinkers helping to bring your business to the next level.

Overcontrol, dependence, and anxiety is a common dynamic ruining our families and inhibiting the individual member's independent thinking and creativity. Adam and Lindsay were in their late twenties when they came to see me. Their relationship was ending. They had been together for twelve years when their marriage fell apart. They met in high school. Lindsay grew up in a severely abusive alcoholic home. She clung to Adam to get away from her nonstop stressful family. Adam's family was much more stable, although he struggled for independence from his parents. Lindsay's relationship with Adam was so important to her that she would do anything to keep it, even let him think for her. Adam, by nature, had a controlling personality. He was a cingulate kid, oppositional and stubborn. He always wanted his way. He wanted Lindsay to agree with him on every issue. Early in the relationship she agreed with him about everything so that he would stay with her. As Lindsay moved into her midtwenties, she became weary of the control and started to disagree with Adam. She was going through her own adolescent rebellious stage, just ten years later than most people and with her husband, not her parents. Adam feared losing the reins of the relationship and became even more controlling, keeping her up frequently until three or four in the morning, trying to get her to see his point of view. Over time, Lindsay grew up and had her own thoughts. She was done with Adam's one-sided behavior and left him. He was devastated. He didn't understand why things changed. Adam's family had warned him this would happen, telling him to lighten up on Lindsay and act more like a partner than a controlling father. He didn't listen. For Lindsay's part, she had basically taught Adam it was okay to treat her in a negative way, by staying with him and never speaking up for herself, until behaviors were entrenched. Through therapy they understood their tendencies and were able to reconcile by building a more reciprocal relationship and better communication skills.

Strategies to Find Your Maverick Voice

Finding your maverick voice is not easy. It requires some discontentment with the status quo and then the bravery to do something about it in an effective way. Here are five ideas to help you find your voice.

First, keep your brain healthy. Effective behavior, assertiveness, clear communication, passion, and creative thinking are all brain functions. A healthy brain leads the way to a productive life.

Second, work to be happy, but also value the tough times. Mavericks are about change, and change requires some impetus, often pain, to go forward. Few epiphanies occur during the good times. It is often turbulence that drives new ideas and gives people the emotional drive to put the energy into change, something in your life that disturbs you enough that you consciously work to change it, as in Lindsay's case above. For example, a job crisis may precipitate assertiveness at work; marital affairs often lead to counseling, where partners find their voice (I have seen this happen many times); and a health crisis may lead to a complete evaluation of priorities. Welcome the uncomfortable moments in your life and stop trying to immediately medicate them with alcohol, shopping trips, video games, or pornography. The tough times may be the seeds of your maverick voice.

Third, have hope. If you have lost your voice, know that it is possible to find it. You are not a grasshopper. If you place a grasshopper in a jar with a lid, you can learn a powerful lesson. A grasshopper in this kind of captivity behaves as many people do throughout their lives. At first, the imprisoned grasshopper tries desperately to escape from the jar, using its powerful hind legs to launch its body up against the lid. It tries and tries, and then it tries again. Initially, it is very persistent. It may try to get out of its trap for several hours. When it finally stops, however, its trying days are over. It will never again try to escape from the jar by jumping. You can take the lid off the jar and have a pet grasshopper for life. Once it believes that it cannot change its situation, that's it. It stops trying. It is easy to see the parallel between grasshoppers and people who lose their voice. Once people believe they are defeated, that they cannot do things to change their situation, they stop trying and give up, never to try again. Even if the lid is removed from their traps, it doesn't occur to them to leave; even if success or happiness is within their grasp, they are unable to reach out and grab it. You are not a grasshopper. Look for areas of your life where you have lost your voice and ask yourself what you need to do to get it back. When you change the inside, often the outside is not far behind. Your brain, as we have seen, makes happen what it sees.

Fourth, practice independence and personal responsibility. When you disagree with someone, tell him, but do it in a smart way, being firm and polite. Take a chance to see if you can get a dopamine boost by being independent. Find and practice expressing your own thoughts. As you speak your mind, do it effectively. Mavericks are effective communicators. I often say to my patients, "There are ways to say things and there are ways to say things."

Jenny came to see me feeling powerless in her relationship with her air force colonel husband. Even though she would scream at him, she had lost her voice. I asked her to describe her concerns.

"He never listens to me," she complained.

"What do you mean?" I said.

"He comes home and hides behind the newspaper. He doesn't talk to me."

"How do you try to communicate with him?" I asked.

With emotion she said, "I get in his face and yell at him that I want a divorce and wish I never married him."

Surprised by her comments, I chuckled.

She gave me a hostile look. "You think that is funny?"

"No," I said, "just not very effective. How would you feel if someone talked like that to you? I would be scared."

At first Jenny was defensive, telling me about all the ways he had hurt her over the years, but over time she learned better communication skills. Several weeks after I started to see her she went home determined to be more effective in communicating with her husband. He was sitting in his chair reading the paper when she started. "I missed you today. When would you have time tonight to talk with me?" Surprised, her husband looked up from his paper and said, "Anytime you want, sweetheart. Am I in trouble?" In that moment, Jenny realized how much her own behavior had contributed to the demise of the relationship, and if that was true, she could help make it better. She had more voice than she gave herself credit for. It is very hard for others to hear you when you yell.

Fifth, strive to hone your creative skills. See options and alternatives. Mavericks see a need that is not being addressed, then think of a novel way to deal with it. They think outside the box of standard answers. But how do you get outside the box? How do you think creatively? According to Robert Franken in his book *Human Motivation,* creativity is defined as the tendency to generate or recognize ideas, alternatives, or possibilities that may be useful in solving problems, communicating with others, and entertaining ourselves and others. Creativity is seeing common things in an uncommon way. Among other things, you need to be able to generate new possibilities or new alternatives. Realize that there are many ways to solve problems, and when you open your mind, new solutions may come. Tests of creativity measure not only the number of alternatives that people can generate but the uniqueness of those alternatives. The ability to generate alternatives or to see things uniquely does not occur by chance; it is linked to other, more fundamental qualities of thinking, such as flexibility, tolerance of ambiguity or unpredictability, and the enjoyment of things not previously known, an innate curiosity.

In his book *Flow: The Psychology of Optimal Experience,* Mihaly Csikszentmihalyi, one of the world's leading researchers on positive psychology, outlined his theory that people are most happy and creative when they are in a state of *flow*—a state of concentration or complete absorption with the activity at hand and the situation. This dovetails nicely with Eckhart Tolle's healing work discussed in *The Power of Now*. The idea of flow is identical to the feeling of being "in the zone" or "in the groove." The flow state is an optimal state of *intrinsic motivation,* whereby the person is fully immersed in what he or she is doing. The moment matters. He is not in the past with regret or the future with fear. He is in the now. This is a sensation everyone has at times, characterized by a feeling of great freedom, enjoyment, fulfillment, and skill. Temporal concerns (time, food, ego/self, etc.) are typically ignored. In an interview with *Wired* magazine, Csikszentmihalyi described flow as "being completely involved in an activity for its own sake. The ego falls away. Time flies. Every action, movement and thought follows inevitably from the previous one, like playing jazz. Your whole being is involved, and you're using your skills to the utmost." To achieve a flow state, a balance must be struck between the challenge of the task and the skill of the performer. If the task is too easy or too difficult, flow cannot occur. The flow state also implies a kind of *focused attention,* and indeed, it has been noted that mindfulness meditation, yoga, and martial arts seem to improve a person's capacity for flow. Among other benefits, all of these activities train and improve attention. In short, flow could be described as a state in which attention, motivation, and the situation meet, resulting in a kind of productive harmony or feedback.

Here's an example of creative problem solving and maverick thinking. David and Celia met online. They had many things in common. They were both in the teaching profession, loved to grow spiritually, had similar habits, and were attracted to each other. They fell in love. Celia was at the tail end of a difficult divorce. Even though she cared deeply for David, her heightened anxiety and persistent stress caused deep ambivalence in her new relationship and she decided to take a break after six months. Initially, the break was very hard for David. He missed Celia and felt they were a good match. David's family gave him a lot of grief. If Celia went away, he should let her go and move on. There were plenty of fish in the sea. She was not good enough for him. Celia continued to keep in contact with David and considered coming back. Her prior husband, like her father, was a very controlling man, and anything that resembled control sent Celia running. David was patient and wanted to find a way to keep Celia in his life, even if they did not end up as partners. One afternoon, as they discussed their relationship over lunch, as Celia continued to express her ambivalence, David pulled out five cards and gave them to her one at a time. He said they had many options; there was no pressure.

He gave her the first card. On the outside it had a picture of a couple in a loving embrace. On the inside, in David's handwriting it read, "Option number one: We are exclusive partners who live together. If you must, you can force me into it."

He could see the card made Celia nervous, so he handed her the second card. It had a picture of a couple walking together. It read, "Option number two: We are partners who live separately, who see each other several times a week (this is my first choice)."

Celia smiled. He handed her the third card. It had a picture of a dog and a cat cuddled up next to each other. It read, "Option number three: We are friends with benefits, who see each other on a somewhat regular basis but who also date others, sort of a break, with moments of closeness and passion."

Celia laughed and gave him a naughty look. He then handed her the fourth card. It had a picture of friends talking at the beach. It read, "Option number four: We are just friends and break any romantic ties for the foreseeable future."

Celia looked sad. He handed her the last card. It was a sympathy card. It read, "I am sorry for your loss. Option number five: We are ex-lovers, ex-friends, ships that docked for a while together, break up completely, and go out of each other's lives forever."

Touched, Celia said, "No way."

Within a week, they were back together, and a year later they were married. If David had taken the path of ultimatum—"Either you're my girlfriend or not"—he would have lost his best friend and future wife. There are many ways to solve problems. To be a maverick you must take a different approach from the standard one, even if it means doing what is difficult.

| 17 |

Create Lasting Trust

———

SEND THE SIGNALS THAT BUILD INTEGRITY

Honesty is the first chapter in the book of wisdom.

—THOMAS JEFFERSON

No man has a good enough memory to make a successful liar.

—ABRAHAM LINCOLN

Micca worked very hard. She often put in sixty- to eighty-hour work-weeks as the clinic manager at a new health care start-up company, and on the surface she appeared to be a team player. Over time, however, her frequent conflicts with the employees she supervised caused concern among the owners. When they called in an outside consultant it was discovered that she was, in fact, not following the company's policies and procedures and she lied about her compliance. With her history of hard work, the owners gave her another chance. But in their minds she had become associated with being unreliable and less than honest. All of her behaviors were filtered through these negative assumptions, and the smallest things, including how she ordered office supplies, came into question. It was not a good situation and the constant stress led to Micca taking time off from the company owing to depression and anxiety.

I saw Micca when she first went out on stress leave. She had virtually no insight into her own contribution to the problems she faced. She believed she was a victim of unfair management practices. Her brain scan indicated very low prefrontal cortex activity. The prefrontal cortex, the brain's supervisor, is also involved in our sense of self and affects our ability to read our own behavior. Having low prefrontal cortex activity was consistent with her conflict-seeking nature, her impulsive inability to follow directions from the owners, and her lying, despite working long hours and truly wanting to be successful at her job. Through therapy, supplements, and medication I was able to balance her prefrontal cortex, and when she returned to work her behavior was much more consistent. Four years later she remains with the company and has been promoted twice. Over time, with consistent behavior, the trust with the company owners was restored. Balancing her brain changed her life.

Ultimately, trust and integrity are brain functions. These critical characteristics of success stem from honesty and consistent behavior, which are also brain functions. How you behave day to day makes a lasting impression or legacy in the brains of other people. If you behave in a consistent, honest, predictable way, people will tend to trust you. When you behave erratically or you lie, people tend not to trust you, and their brains remember you as untrustworthy. The brain actually develops nerve cell networks tagged with the names of the people in your life who become connected with descriptors such as honest, lying, lifesaving, trustworthy, hardworking, lazy, dependable, unreliable, and so on. To be successful in any area of life, we need other people, and it is best when they have us labeled in their brains as trustworthy and dependable.

How the Brain Builds Trust

Developing trust involves the brains of both the sender and the receiver. Sending consistent, honest, reliable messages is the first part of the equation of trust. As important is the ability to receive messages in a consistent, honest, and reliable way, without filters that distort incoming information. To send and receive trustworthy signals that build integrity, a person's brain needs to work right. Let's revisit five of the six brain systems we have previously discussed and see how they can impact trustworthy and dependable behavior. For the sender and receiver to transmit and receive trustworthy messages that breed integrity each of these systems need to be healthy. A problem in any one of them can short-circuit trust. Let's look at each of these systems in more detail to see how they build and erode trust.

PREFRONTAL CORTEX—CEO

I think of the prefrontal cortex (PFC) as the major system that breeds trust, honesty, and integrity. When the PFC works right, people tend to be thoughtful, truthful, and goal oriented. They can effectively supervise their words and deeds. They are able to think before they say things and tend to do things that effect their goals in a positive way. A healthy PFC helps inhibit behavior and first impulses. All of us, at one point or another, have hurtful thoughts cross our mind about our partner (e.g., "He looks like he is gaining a little weight" or "She has a few more wrinkles") that are not helpful to just blurt out. Inhibiting these thoughts so they don't just escape your mouth helps the relationship stay on an even track. People with a healthy PFC also tend to learn from their mistakes and follow through on commitments. They are generally able to express their feelings and have good communication. And they tend to dislike conflict, tension, and turmoil. Healthy PFC activity is associated with consistent, thoughtful behavior.

When there are problems in the PFC people tend to be impulsive, often causing serious erosion of trust in relationships. They tend to live in the moment and have trouble delaying gratification. This "I want it now" mind-set is a dangerous breeding ground for affairs, lying, and stealing. They also have trouble listening and tend to be easily distracted, so there is often miscommunication. In addition, many people with PFC problems have an unconscious tendency to be conflict seeking or to look for problems when none exist. I call this tendency the game of "let's have a problem." This behavior pushes people away and leaves them off balance in a relationship they cannot trust. PFC problems cause inconsistent, unreliable, and often dishonest behavior that breeds mistrust.

ANTERIOR CINGULATE GYRUS—GEAR SHIFTER

The anterior cingulate gyrus (ACG) is the brain's gear shifter. It is involved with shifting attention from task to task or idea to idea. It helps people be flexible, so they can go with the flow, and it is also involved in cooperation and helps people get outside of themselves. In addition, it is the part of the brain that helps with error detection. For example, if you walk in a room and something is out of place, this is the part of the brain that notifies you about it.

People with high activity in the ACG, usually owing to lower levels of the neurotransmitter serotonin, have a high sense of fairness and right and wrong. They can be very loyal and want to do things perfectly. They do not tend to lie but can be fairly rigid in their beliefs. Over time, however, too much activity in this system can erode trust because it can cause people to get stuck on negative thoughts, behaviors, and old hurts. If you hurt them, they may never forget it and punish you for years with their grudge holding. They may nag their partners about events from the past, and they may get stuck in their own position and become rigid, oppositional, or argumentative. In addition, they may become micromanagers at home or work, which pushes others away. They often get easily upset when things do not go their way, so on the surface they appear selfish. Sometimes they are viewed by their spouses or employees as controlling, because things have to be their way.

DEEP LIMBIC SYSTEM—MOOD AND BONDING

The deep limbic system (DLS) sets a person's emotional tone. When the DLS is less active, there is generally a positive, more hopeful state of mind. When it is heated up, or overactive, negativity and depression can take over. Because of this emotional shading, the DLS provides the filter through which you interpret the events of the day; it tags or colors events, depending on the emotional state of mind. Trust is intimately involved in how we interpret what happens to us. All events have multiple possible interpretations. For example, if your spouse has an affair, you can totally blame her for the indiscretion and file for divorce, or you can ask yourself if your behavior contributed to the problem and seek solutions. How your limbic brain works will help determine how you interpret what happens to you. If it is set to negative, you will have a hard time trusting anyone. If it is set to positive you may trust people you shouldn't. As in all brain systems, balance is needed.

BASAL GANGLIA—ANXIETY AND MOTIVATION

When the basal ganglia (BG) system functions properly people tend to be calm, relaxed, and more trusting. They tend to predict the best and, in general, see a positive future. Trust is easier for them. They are able to deal with conflict in an effective way, which breeds trust and honesty. They can speak the truth. Overactivity in the BG results in a tendency toward anxiety, fear, insecurity, and placating others. They tend to focus on the negative and what can go wrong in a situation. They filter information through fear and they are less likely to give others the benefit of the doubt. Most of their memories are filled with anxiety or fear. They tend to wear out people by the constant fear they project. People with high BG activity have trouble trusting but can also appear clingy and insecure. When the BG work too hard, people tend to struggle with conflict avoidant behavior. Anything that reminds them of a worry (such as confronting an employee who is not doing a good job) produces anxiety, and high BG people tend to avoid it because it makes them feel uncomfortable.

TEMPORAL LOBES—PERCEPTION AND MEMORY

The temporal lobes (TLs) are involved with language (hearing and reading), reading social cues, getting memories into long-term storage, mood stability, and temper control. Problems in the temporal lobes can lead to miscommunication, misreading social cues, memory lapses, moodiness, and temper issues—all traits that erode trust. The TLs encode new information and facilitate memory. It is one of the areas first damaged by Alzheimer's disease. Paranoia and suspiciousness are common in Alzheimer's disease and other TL disorders because people do not process information fully.

Strong emotions facilitate memory. One of the biggest trust builders is the ability to navigate emotionally hard times successfully. Going through an illness, financial hardship, or work stress effectively allows another person to know you will be there for him or her during the tough times, and positive experience builds long-term trust circuits in the brain. On the other hand, negative intense emotional experiences, such as growing up in an abusive home or being robbed or raped, often changes the function in the TLs and significantly erodes a person's ability to trust. Trust is based on accurate perception, and if the TLs do not perceive incoming information properly or if memory is distorted, trust is likely to be lacking.

Symphony of Mistrust

Problems in any one area of the brain can challenge trust, but when there are multiple troubled areas trust becomes even harder. For example, it is not uncommon for patients to see me who have problems in two, three, four, or even five systems. They may be impulsive and unpredictable (low PFC activity), hold on to hurts from the past (high ACG activity), depressed and negative (high DLS activity), anxious and insecure (high BG activity) and do not perceive or remember information accurately (low TL activity). Treating each of these systems is important to getting people well and boosting their ability to trust (see chapter 4 for a summary of problems and treatments for each of these systems).

Oxytocin and the Chemistry of Trust

Interestingly, certain chemicals, found everywhere in the brain, are also involved with trust, especially the bonding hormone oxytocin. In a landmark study by Michael Kosfeld and colleagues from Switzerland, intranasal oxytocin was found to increase trust. Men who inhaled a nasal spray spiked with oxytocin gave more money to partners in a risky investment game than did men who sniffed a spray containing a placebo. Previous studies of animals had suggested that oxytocin in the brain encourages long-term mating in pairs of adults and nurturing behaviors by mothers toward their offspring. Oxytocin fosters the trust needed for friendship, love, families, economic transactions, and political networks. According to the study's authors, "Oxytocin specifically affects an individual's willingness to accept social risks arising through interpersonal interactions."

The scientists studied oxytocin's influence on male college students playing an investment game. Each of fifty-eight men was paid a sum of money to participate in the experiment. The volunteers were paired up, and one man in each pair was randomly assigned to play the role of an investor and the other to play the role of a trustee. Each participant received tokens, valued with real money and redeemable at the end of the experiment. The investor in each pair decided how many tokens to cede to the trustee. Both participants, sitting face to face, knew that the experimenters would quadruple that investment. The trustee then determined whether to keep the entire enhanced pot or to give some portion of the proceeds, whatever amount seemed fair, to the investor. Among the investors who had inhaled oxytocin, about half gave all their tokens to trustees and most of the rest contributed a majority of their tokens. In contrast, only one fifth of investors who had inhaled a placebo spray forked over all their tokens and another one third parted with a majority of their tokens. The oxytocin influence is "a remarkable finding," says neuroscientist Antonio Damasio of the University of Iowa College of Medicine in Iowa City in an editorial published with the research report. Damasio had previously argued that the hormone acts somewhat as a love potion. "It adds trust to the mix, for there is no love without trust," he says.

Why Lie Detectors Do Not Work for the People Who Need Them Most

One of the reasons that traditional lie detectors do not work is that there is a certain percentage of the population that does not react emotionally when they lie, cheat, or steal. In a very real sense they are cold-blooded.

They actually have less blood flow to the most thoughtful part of their brain, the PFC.

Lie detectors typically work by professionals observing how a person's physiology responds to lying. Most people exhibit physical symptoms when they lie. Their bodies respond to the stress they feel when they think they will be found out. Immediately, their hearts beat faster as adrenaline bathes their system, their breathing becomes more shallow in response to feelings of panic, their hands become colder as blood flow becomes constricted, and their hands sweat and their muscles become tense. Examiners can see this pattern on the lie detector equipment and the liar is caught. This technology works nicely for most people. Most of us have brains that want to tell the truth, want to be trusted, and we feel guilty when we lie or when we think we will be caught. Our bodies respond to our thoughts and feelings. There is even new brain imaging lie detector equipment and companies springing up, such as No Lie MRI, to swear in court whether or not you are telling the truth. Not only does your body react to lies, your brain does as well. Whenever most people lie, their brain becomes overall much more active than when telling the truth. It really does take more out of you to lie than to tell the truth.

But the problem with lie detectors, including the latest brain imaging additions, is that there is a certain percentage of people who do not respond in the typical way to lying. Their brains and bodies do not respond with anxiety to the lies they tell. It is just routine for them. These people often have antisocial personality disorder, which is characterized by a long-standing pattern of disregard for the rights of others. They frequently break rules, inhabit prisons, and have constant relationship and work problems. They often get into fights. With little or no empathy, they may steal, destroy property, or manipulate or deceive others for their own selfish ends. They tend to be impulsive and lack forethought. Psychologist Adrienne Raine from the University of Southern California found that compared with a group of healthy men, the magnetic resonance imaging scans of the men with antisocial personality disorder showed decreased PFC volume. They are likely dealing with less access to the part of the brain that controls conscience, free will, right and wrong, and good and evil. A fascinating additional finding of Dr. Raine's work was that people with antisocial personality disorder also had slower heart rates than the control group and decreased sweat gland activity. Lower heart rates and sweat gland activity are often associated with low anxiety states (your hands sweat and your heart races when you are anxious). Could this mean that people with this type of temperament do not have enough internal anxiety? Could the PFC be involved with appropriate anxiety? Intriguing questions. For example, most people feel anxious before they do something bad or risky. If I needed money and got the thought in my head to rob the local grocery store, my next thoughts would be filled with anxiety:

"It is wrong," "I am better than that action," "I don't want to get caught," "I don't like institutional food," and "I could lose my medical license" are just a few of the thoughts that might run through my head. The anxiety would prevent me from acting out on the bad thoughts. But what if, as Dr. Raine's study suggests, I do not have enough anxiety and I get an evil thought in my head such as "Go rob the store"? With poor PFC activity, I am likely to rob the store without considering all of the consequences to my behavior. There is an interesting treatment implication from this work. Typically, psychiatrists try to help lessen a person's anxiety. Maybe we have it backward for people with antisocial personality disorder—perhaps we should try to increase their anxiety. Perhaps that's what spiritual leaders had in mind when they talk about hell, fire, and damnation. There is a certain percentage of us who need to be scared into behaving right, who need more anxiety, who need to know that there will be hell to pay for bad behavior.

So Whom Should You Trust?

The best predictor of behavior is behavior. How people have been acting is a likely indicator of how they will act, unless they do something meaningful to change. That is why once people see you as dishonest, disingenuous, unreliable, or lacking integrity, their brain is wired to keep that label for you until it learns otherwise. Our brains remember emotionally laden material, and when we see someone important as untrustworthy, it is often a very emotional event. When President George H. W. Bush reversed his campaign promise of no new taxes—"Read my lips, no new taxes"—many Americans felt betrayed, which was instrumental in costing him reelection.

Over time, once the brain develops a reason to trust someone, new information can replace old ideas, as in the case of Micca, who was discussed at the beginning of the chapter. Adolescents are a great example of how the brain can learn to trust again. Many teens struggle with consistent behavior, and lose their parents' trust. But over time, as their behavior becomes more consistent, usually when their PFC becomes more fully developed in their midtwenties, parents become more trusting. Over the years I have seen hundreds of teenagers struggling for independence. They want their parents to trust them, yet they consistently exhibit untrustworthy behavior. As we discuss their plight, I encourage them to articulate their goals, such as to be trusted and have more independence, and then act accordingly, despite the temptations of parties, easily available drugs, and friends who might lead them astray. Often the counseling is effective, especially when I can balance their brains. Sometimes it just takes time. Of course, it is possible to repair a bad reputation. Consider Muhammad Ali, who was hated by many in the 1960s for his refusal to sign up for the draft. In 1996 he was one of the most beloved sports figures in the world and carried the Olympic torch during the opening ceremonies of the games in Atlanta.

Let's look deeper into applying this principle to your life. When interviewing people for a job position in your company, it is critical to know about their past jobs. Remember, the best predictor of current behavior is past behavior. You want to know what they excelled at, what, if anything, went wrong, and what other people thought of them. Many people have blinders to their own weaknesses, so talking with others can provide essential information. Background checks are a key component of good business. For example, if someone has had multiple jobs in a short period of time, likely they will only be with you for a short while. Sometimes our own excitement or needs cause us to override our PFC and make hasty decisions about who to invite into our businesses.

Impulsive decisions can also adversely affect our personal lives. Taking time to get to know someone and meeting her family and friends before we hop into bed with her is essential to protecting your heart, health, and wealth. Unfortunately, our society's obsession with instant gratification causes many people to rush intimacy before really knowing the other person whose body and brain they are getting into. Besides the obvious health issues, when you make love to someone, the chemical oxytocin surges through our brains (500 percent in men after an orgasm), causing us to be more trusting, perhaps undeservedly so. I caution my patients to be careful and go slowly. Getting someone into your head may be a lot easier than getting him or her out.

Live for the Long Haul, Not Just the Moment

Think about your long-term goals. It is easy to cheat in the moment, whether it is cheating on your spouse, your boss, or your taxes. But think about how your behavior fits with your goals over time. What kind of character do you desire? Matching your behavior to your goals is a PFC function.

I once had lunch with a close friend who was having marital problems. I knew Chuck had ADD and was struggling at home in his relationships with his wife and children. As usual, Chuck was telling me about the turmoil. His wife was struggling with one of their daughters who was being defiant. Then all of a sudden his affect changed, his eyes brightened, and his tone became more excited and hushed. He told me about a woman he had recently met on an airplane. She was pretty, smart, interesting, and seemed to really like him a lot. She had even come to his office for a visit. As he started to go on, I interrupted him.

"Chuck, do you like attorneys?"

"What do you mean?" he said looking surprised.

"Play it out," I said. "You are having marital problems. You meet this attractive woman who seems interested in you. She has been to your office. The next step, if it has not happened already, is for you to have sex with her. Then your wife will probably find out. You have ADD so you are not good at hiding things. She has a hot cingulate so she will never forgive you. She will file for divorce, you will spend a lot of money and time with attorneys, and hate yourself for putting your family through all this stuff, and then a year from now you will lose half of your net worth and you will be visiting your children on the weekends."

"Wow," Chuck said, looking deflated. "I never thought about it like that."

"That is what your prefrontal cortex does for you," I said. "It plays things out."

Chuck later told me that he never called the woman back.

A lack of honesty and integrity breeds mistrust and has destroyed people's success through the ages. One of the most precious things each of us has is our word. When we say something is true and we have integrity, people believe us. Without integrity, people always look at us and wonder.

Integrity is being who you say you are. We are faced with the choices of integrity every day. Sometimes we choose for it; sometimes not. When we circumvent our commitments, we cheat not only ourselves but also those who depend on us. When we live up to our commitments, the bonds of trust are strengthened. Integrity, goal setting, consistent effort, and navigating change are ultimately all brain functions.

When More Help Is Needed

Even after applying all of the brain-healthy and natural strategies in this book, some people will want or need to seek professional help. Some people will need psychotherapy, some will need medication, and others will need more directed guidance with supplements or other alternative treatments. This appendix will help you decide if and when you should seek professional help. In lecturing around the world, I am frequently asked the following questions: When is it time to see a professional about my brain? What should I do when a loved one is in denial about needing help? How do I go about finding a competent professional? Here are some thoughts for you to consider.

When Is It Time to See a Professional About My Brain?

This question is relatively easy to answer. People should seek professional help for themselves or a family member when their behaviors, feelings, thoughts, or memory (all brain functions) interfere with their ability to reach their potential in their relationships, work, or school. If you are experiencing persistent relationship struggles (parent-child, sibling, friends, romantic), it's time to get help. If you have ongoing school or work problems related to your memory, moods, actions, or thoughts, it is time to get professional help. If your impulsive behavior, poor choices, or anxiety are causing consistent monetary problems, it's time to get help. Many people think they cannot afford to get professional help. I think it is usually much more costly to live with brain problems than it is to get appropriate help.

Pride and denial can get in the way of seeking proper help. People want to be strong and rely on themselves, but I am constantly reminded of the strength it takes to make the decision to get help. Also, getting help should be looked at as a way to get your brain operating at its full capacity.

What Should I Do When a Loved One Is in Denial About Needing Help?

Unfortunately, the stigma associated with a "psychiatric illness" prevents many people from getting help. People do not want to be seen as crazy, stupid, or defective and do not seek help until they (or their loved one) can no longer tolerate the pain (at work, in their relationships, or within themselves). Most people do not see psychiatric problems as brain problems but rather as weak character problems. Men are especially affected by denial.

Here are several suggestions to help people who are unaware or willing to get the help they need. Try the straightforward approach first (but with a new brain twist). Clearly tell the person what behaviors concern you, and explain to him that the problems may be due to underlying brain patterns that can be easily tuned up. Tell him help may be available—help not to cure a defect but rather help to optimize how his brain functions. Tell him you know he is trying to do his best, but his behavior, thoughts, or feelings may be getting in the way of his success (at work, in relationships, or within themselves). Emphasize better function, not defect.

Give him information. Books, videos, and articles on the subjects you are concerned about can be of tremendous help. Many people come to see us because they read a book or article or saw a video. Good information can be very persuasive, especially if it is presented in a positive, life-enhancing way.

When a person remains resistant to help, even after you have been straightforward and given him good information, plant seeds. Plant ideas about getting help and then water them regularly. Drop an idea, article, or other information about the topic from time to time. If you talk too much about getting help, he might become resentful and won't get help to spite you, especially if he's the overfocused type. Be careful not to go overboard.

Protect your relationship with the other person. People are more receptive to people they trust than they are to people who nag and belittle them. Work on gaining the person's trust over the long run. It will make him more receptive to your suggestions. Do not make getting help the only thing that you talk about. Make sure you are interested in his whole life, not just his potential medical appointments.

Give him new hope. Many people with these problems have tried to get help and it did not work or it even made them worse. Educate your loved one on new brain technology that helps professionals be more focused and more effective in treatment efforts.

There comes a time when you have to say enough is enough. If, over time, the other person refuses to get help, and his behavior has a negative impact on your life, you may have to separate yourself. Staying in a toxic relationship is harmful to your health, and it often enables the other person to remain sick as well. Actually, I have seen that the threat or act of leaving motivates people to change, whether it is about drinking, drug use, or treating ADD. Threatening to leave is not the first approach I would take, but after time it may be the best approach. Realize you cannot force a person into treatment unless he is dangerous to himself or others or is unable to care for himself. You can only do what you can do. Fortunately, there is a lot more we can do today than even ten years ago.

How Do I Go About Finding a Competent Professional?

At the Amen Clinics we get many calls, faxes, and e-mails a week from people all over the world looking for competent professionals in their area who think in similar ways to the principles outlined in this book. Because this approach is on the edge of what is new in brain science, other professionals who know and practice this information may be hard to find. However, finding the right professional for evaluation and treatment is critical to the healing process. The right professional can have a very positive impact on your life. The wrong professional can make things worse.

There are a number of steps to take in finding the best person to assist you. We maintain a list of people I have trained and we are collegial with on our website at www.amenclinic.com. Get the best person you can find. Saving money up front may cost you in the long run. The right help is not only cost effective but saves unnecessary pain and suffering, so don't rely on a person simply because they are on your managed care plan. That person may or may not be a good fit for you. Search for the best. If he or she is on your insurance plan, great, but don't let that be the primary criterion. Once you get the names of competent professionals, check their credentials. Very few patients ever check a professional's background. Board certification is a positive credential. To become board certified, physicians must pass additional written and verbal tests. They have had to discipline themselves to gain the skill and knowledge that was acceptable to their colleagues. Don't give too much weight to the medical school or graduate school the professional attended. I have worked with some doctors who went to Yale and Harvard who did not have a clue on how to appropriately treat patients, while other doctors from less prestigious schools were outstanding, forward thinking, and caring. Set up an interview with the professional to see whether or not you want to work with him or her. Generally you have to pay for their time, but it is worth spending the money to get to know the people you will rely on for help.

Many professionals write articles or books or speak at meetings or local groups. Read the work of or hear the professional speak if possible. By doing so you may be able to get a feel for the kind of person they are and their ability to help you. Look for a person who is open-minded, up-to-date, and willing to try new things. Look for a person who treats you with respect, who listens to your questions and responds to your needs. Look for a relationship that is collaborative and respectful. I know it is hard to find a professional who meets all of these criteria who also has the right training in brain physiology, but these people can be found. Be persistent. The caregiver is essential to healing.

Why SPECT?

WHAT BRAIN SPECT IMAGING CAN TELL CLINICIANS AND PATIENTS

If we agree that mental disorders and difficult behaviors may be related to functional problems in the brain, then a logical next step is to consider physically evaluating the brain itself when faced with people who struggle with complex problems or who are unresponsive to our best diagnostic and treatment efforts. Why are psychiatrists the only physicians who rarely look at the organ they treat?[1]

It is time to change. Amen Clinics, Inc. (ACI) has provided leadership and understanding on the clinical use of brain imaging in psychiatry. Over the past eighteen years, ACI has built the world's largest database of brain scans related to emotional, learning, and behavioral problems. The study we do is called brain SPECT imaging. *SPECT* stands for "single photon emission computed tomography." It is a nuclear medicine procedure widely used in medicine to study heart, liver, thyroid, bone, and brain problems. Brain SPECT imaging is a proven safe, reliable measure of cerebral blood flow. Because brain activity is directly related to blood flow, SPECT effectively shows us the patterns of activity in the brain.[2] SPECT allows physicians to look deep inside the brain to observe three things: areas of the brain that work well, areas of the brain that work too hard, and areas of the brain that do not work hard enough. ACI has performed over fifty thousand scans on patients from age ten months to 101 years and has scanned many normal, "healthy brain" individuals as well.

The procedure guidelines of the Society of Nuclear Medicine lists the

| APPENDIX

evaluation of suspected brain trauma, evaluation of patients with suspected
dementia, presurgical location of seizures, and the detection and evaluation
of cerebral vascular disease as common indications for brain SPECT.[3] The
guidelines also say that many additional indications appear promising. At
ACI, because of our experience, we have added the indications of evaluating
violence, substance abuse, the subtypes of ADD, anxiety and depression,
complex or resistant psychiatric problems, and general health screening for
brain SPECT.

An important question for today's mental health clinicians is "When and
why would I order a SPECT study for my patients or get one for myself or
loved one?" My purpose in this appendix is to answer this question and to
point out some of the benefits and caveats for using this powerful tool.

Benefits of SPECT Brain Imaging

A SPECT scan can provide distinct benefits to clinicians and to the patient
and the patient's family. There are also some things that should *not* be expected from a SPECT scan.

BENEFITS FOR PHYSICIANS AND CLINICIANS

1. A SPECT scan can show:

    a. Areas of the brain implicated in specific problems, such as the
       prefrontal cortex with executive function and the medial tempo-
       ral lobes with long-term memory storage

    b. Unexpected findings that may be contributing to the presenting
       problem(s), such as toxicity, potential areas of seizure activity, or
       past brain trauma

    c. Potential seizure activity, in many cases more accurately seen by
       SPECT than standard electroencephalograms (EEGs), especially
       in the areas of the medial temporal lobe. There are over forty-one
       studies with more than thirteen hundred patients on SPECT and
       epilepsy (see www.amenclinic.com for references).

    d. Targeted areas for treatment, such as overactive basal ganglia or an-
       terior cingulate gyrus (seen on anxiety and obsessive-compulsive
       spectrum disorders) or an underactive temporal lobe (seen in
       seizure disorders and trauma)

    e. Specific effects of medication on the brain to help guide us in adjusting dosages or augmenting treatment. Often patients report that selective serotonin reuptake inhibitors (SSRIs) are helpful but also cause decreased motivation or memory problems, seen as decreased prefrontal or temporal lobe activity on SPECT.

   f. Changes in brain function with treatment, improved or worsened. You can review many before-and-after scans at www.amenclinic .com.

2. The image occurs at the time of injection and outside the imaging camera, which gives SPECT several significant advantages. Most notably, we are able to sedate people after they have been injected so that they can lie still for the scan, often difficult for hyperactive or autistic children or demented adults (motion artifact ruins the scan in all of these imaging techniques).

3. A SPECT scan can provide explanations for refractory symptoms and help clinicians ask better and more targeted questions (e.g., about toxic exposure, brain injuries, anoxia, inflammation, or infections that patients may have denied or forgotten).

4. A SPECT scan can help us avoid prescribing treatments that make the problem worse, such as unnecessarily stimulating an already overactive brain or calming an underactive one.

5. A SPECT scan can help evaluate risk for dementia. The brain starts to change long before people show symptoms. There is usually a loss of 30 percent of hippocampal tissue before symptoms occur. Using autopsy data in fifty-four patients, Bonte reported that brain SPECT had a positive predictive value for Alzheimer's disease of 92 percent.[4]

6. A SPECT scan can also help differentiate among types of dementia. Early in the disease, Alzheimer's disease, frontal temporal lobe dementia, Lewy body dementia, and multi-infarct dementia each have their own patterns. There are over eighty-three studies with more than forty-five hundred patients on this subject (see www.amenclinic.com for references).

7. A SPECT scan helps clinicians understand the rationale for using certain medications (such as anticonvulsants to stabilize temporal lobe function or calm focal areas of marked hyperactivity; stimulants to enhance decreased prefrontal perfusion; or SSRIs to calm basal ganglia and anterior cingulate hyperactivity).

8. A SPECT scan can identify specific areas of the brain affected by trauma; better target treatment; and help deal with insurance, legal, and rehabilitation issues. There are over seventy-two studies with more than seventeen hundred patients on brain trauma (see www.amenclinic.com for references).

9. A SPECT scan can often identify factors contributing to relapse in people recovering from substance abuse, eating disorders, or sexual addictions. For example, the patient may have suffered an injury to the prefrontal cortex or temporal lobes or have overactivity in the anterior cingulate gyrus, basal ganglia, limbic system, or prefrontal cortex, each of which could indicate comorbid disorders requiring treatment.

10. A SPECT scan can often identify a specific cause that contributes to recovering alcoholics', drug addicts', sexual addicts', or eating-disordered people's relapse behavior. For example, the patient may have suffered an injury in the prefrontal cortex or temporal lobes or have overactivity in the anterior cingulate gyrus, basal ganglia, limbic system, or prefrontal cortex, each of which could contribute to the relapsing behaviors.

11. A SPECT scan is also useful to determine if further adjustment of medication is needed. Scans of patients on medication will reveal areas of the brain still overactive or underactive.

BENEFITS FOR PATIENTS AND THEIR FAMILIES

1. A SPECT scan helps develop a deeper understanding of the problem, resulting in reduced shame, guilt, stigma, and self-loathing. This can promote self-forgiveness, often the first step in healing. Patients can see that their problems are, at least in part, medical and physical.

2. A SPECT scan allows patients to see a physical representation of their problems that is accurate and reliable and helps to increase compliance. Pictures are powerful and can influence a patient's willingness and ability to accept and adhere to the treatment program. She can then better understand that not taking medication for anxiety, depression, rage, ADD, and so on is similar to not wearing corrective prescription glasses.

3. A SPECT scan helps families understand when permanent brain damage from an injury will not get better, so they can better accept the condition and provide accordingly.

4. A SPECT scan shows substance abusers the damage they have done to their own brain, thus helping to decrease denial, provide motivation for treatment, and support perseverance in sobriety.

5. A SPECT scan shows patients how treatments have impacted (improved or worsened) brain function.

6. A SPECT scan helps motivate abusive spouses to follow medication protocols by showing that there is a physical abnormality contributing to their problems.

7. A SPECT scan is useful for cancer patients suffering with a "chemotherapy toxic brain." It gives them insight into their cognitive struggles and also helps their doctors see the neurophysiologic and emotional effects of having cancer and its treatment.

8. A SPECT scan can help take modern psychopharmacology from mystery and unknown consequences to reality and more predictable outcomes.

9. A SPECT scan allows patients to understand why specific treatments are indicated, which medications are likely to be most helpful, and what other interventions may be indicated.

What a SPECT Scan Cannot Provide

Despite the many benefits that might be derived from a SPECT scan, there are clearly some things that it cannot provide.

1. SPECT scans cannot give a diagnosis in the absence of clinical information.
2. SPECT scans cannot give the date of a head injury, infection, or toxic exposure.
3. SPECT scans cannot assess or evaluate IQ.
4. SPECT scans cannot assess or evaluate the guilt, innocence, motivation, or sanity of a criminal defendant.
5. SPECT scans cannot guarantee a perfect diagnosis, or a cure.

How SPECT Scans Differ from Magnetic
Resonance Imaging Scans

A SPECT scan is similar to a magnetic resonance imaging (MRI) scan in that both can show three-dimensional images and "slices" of the brain. However, whereas MRI shows the *physical anatomy* of the brain, SPECT shows brain *functional activity*. That is, SPECT yields images showing where the brain is functioning well, where it is working too hard, and where it is not working hard enough. A newer version of MRI, functional MRI or "fMRI," is also capable of showing brain activity and is used extensively in scientific research on brain function. An fMRI shows instantaneous neural activity so you can see, for example, how the brain responds to a specific stimulus event. With SPECT we see brain activity averaged over a few minutes so it is better at showing the brain doing everyday activities such as concentrating, meditating, reading, and so on. Positron emission tomography, another nuclear imaging technique, is very similar to SPECT but is much more costly.

Ensuring High-Quality SPECT Images

Although a SPECT scan is simple from the patient's perspective, it takes considerable skill and experience to dependably generate accurate brain SPECT images suitable for psychiatric applications. Equally important is the need for total consistency in imaging techniques among patients so that results are quantifiable, repeatable, and consistent. The following factors need to be considered in SPECT scans..

VARIABILITY OF TECHNIQUE ISSUES

Processing protocols need to be standardized and optimized. Motion can ruin a scan, so it is important that there be *no motion* on the scan. The physician needs to know how to identify and deal with image artifacts and other sophisticated technical issues.

VARIABILITY OF CAMERAS

Multiheaded cameras are clearly superior as they can scan much faster. It takes an hour to do a scan with a single-headed camera, thirty minutes on a dual-headed camera, and fifteen minutes on a triple-headed camera.

EXPERIENCE OF READERS

At the Amen Clinics, we have developed a standardized reading technique for which we have documented high interrater and intrarater reliability.

IMAGE DISPLAY

Scans must be clear, understandable, easily illustrative of brain function, and available to the patient on a timely basis. We believe our three-dimensional rendering software makes the scans easy for professionals, patients, and families to understand.

DRUGS

Scans can be affected by a number of substances that need to be controlled for, such as medications, street drugs, and caffeine.

All of the above issues have been addressed at the Amen Clinics by carefully standardized procedures for all our SPECT scans.

Common Concerns

Concern: Low resolution—it is commonly said that a SPECT scan is a "poor man's PET study."

Response: With multiheaded cameras, SPECT scans have the same resolution as PET scans with considerably lower cost, better insurance coverage, greater availability, and fewer image artifacts.[5] Also, it is an easier procedure to do. SPECT provides more than adequate resolution for our applications.

Concern: Radiation exposure, especially in children

Response: The average radiation exposure for one SPECT scan is 0.7 rem (similar to a nuclear bone scan or computerized axial tomography scan) and is a safe procedure, according to the guidelines established by the American Academy of Neurology.[6] These other procedures are routinely ordered for many common medical conditions (e.g., bone fractures or head trauma), further suggesting that the levels of radiation exposure are generally acceptable in medical practice. Ineffective treatment of psychiatric illness has many more risks than the low levels of radiation associated with a SPECT scan.

Concern: What is considered normal?

Response: In the SPECT literature over the past twenty years, there have been more than forty-three studies looking at "normal" issues in over 2,450 patients, including 150 children from birth on (see www.amenclinic.com for references). These do not include the thousands of control subjects used in studies of specific neurological and psychiatric conditions. Chiron and colleagues reported that at birth, cortical regional cerebral blood flow (rCBF) was lower than those for adults.[7] After birth, it increased by five or six years of age to values 50–85 percent higher than those for adults, thereafter decreasing to reach adult levels between fifteen and nineteen years. At the age of three, however, children had the same relative blood flow patterns as adults. Other common findings in normal studies suggest that women have generally higher perfusion than men and that age, drug abuse, and smoking have a negative effect on rCBF.

Concern: Some physicians say, "I don't need a scan for diagnosis; I can tell clinically."

Response: Often, well-trained physicians can make clinical determinations. But a SPECT scan is ordered when the physician is confused, the patient hasn't responded to the doctor's best treatment, or the patient's situation is otherwise complicated.

Concern: Lack of reproducibility

Response: An article by Villanueva-Meyer and colleagues elegantly answers this question, showing that there is less than 3 percent variability in SPECT scans over time for the same activity.[8] Our own clinical experience, scanning people sequentially, and sometimes twelve years apart, finds that SPECT patterns remain the same unless you do something to change the brain. A SPECT scan is a reproducible and reliable method for sequential evaluation.

Conclusion

At the Amen Clinics we feel that our experience with more than thirty-five thousand brain SPECT scans over sixteen years guides us in being the best in the world for brain SPECT imaging.

COMMON QUESTIONS ABOUT BRAIN SPECT IMAGING

Here are several common questions and answers about brain SPECT imaging.

Will the SPECT study give me an accurate diagnosis? No. A SPECT study by itself will not give a diagnosis. SPECT studies help the clinician understand more about the specific function of your brain. Each person's brain is unique, requiring unique responses to medicine or therapy. Diagnoses about specific conditions are made through a combination of clinical history, personal interview, information from families, diagnostic checklists, SPECT studies, and other neuropsychological tests. No study is "a doctor in a box" that can give accurate diagnoses on individual patients.

Why are SPECT studies ordered? Some of the common reasons include:
1. Evaluating memory problems, dementia, and distinguishing among different types of dementia and pseudodementia (depression that looks like dementia)
2. Evaluating seizure activity
3. Evaluating blood vessel diseases, such as stroke
4. Evaluating the effects of mild, moderate, and severe head trauma
5. Suspicion of underlying organic brain condition, such as seizure activity contributing to behavioral disturbance, prenatal trauma, or exposure to toxins
6. Evaluating atypical or unresponsive aggressive behavior
7. Determining extent of brain impairment caused by drug or alcohol abuse
8. Typing anxiety, depression, and ADDs when clinical presentation is not clear
9. Evaluating people who are atypical or resistant to treatment
10. General health screening

Do I need to be off medication before the study? This question must be answered individually between you and your doctor. In general, it is better to be off medications until they are out of your system, but this is not always practical or advisable. If the study is done while on medication, let the technician know so that when the physician reads the study he will include that information in the interpretation of the scan. In general, we recommend patients try to be off stimulants at least four days before the first scan and remain off them until after the second scan, if one is ordered. It is generally not practical to stop taking medications such as Prozac because they last in the body for four to six weeks. Check with your doctor for specific recommendations.

What should I do the day of the scan? On the day of the scan decrease or elim-inate your caffeine intake and try to not take cold medication or aspirin (if you do, please write it down on the intake form). Eat as you normally would.

Are there any side effects or risks to the study? The study does not involve a dye and people do not have allergic reactions to the study. The possibility exists, although in a very small percentage of patients, of a mild rash, facial redness and edema, fever, and a transient increase in blood pressure. The amount of radiation exposure from one brain SPECT study is approximately the same as one abdominal x-ray.

How is the SPECT procedure done? The patient is placed in a quiet room and a small intravenous (IV) line is started. The patient remains quiet for ap-proximately ten minutes with his or her eyes open to allow their mental state to equilibrate to the environment. The imaging agent is then injected through the IV. After another short period of time, the patient lies on a table and the SPECT camera rotates around his or her head (the patient does not go into a tube). The time on the table is approximately fifteen minutes. If a concentration study is ordered, the patient returns on another day.

Are there alternatives to having a SPECT study? In our opinion, SPECT is the most clinically useful study of brain function. There are other studies, such as EEGs, PET studies, and MRIs. PET studies and fMRI are considerably more costly and they are performed mostly in research setting. EEGs, in our opinion, do not provide enough information about the deep structures of the brain to be as helpful as SPECT studies.

Does insurance cover the cost of SPECT studies? Reimbursement by insurance companies varies according to your plan. It is often a good idea to check with the insurance company ahead of time to see if it is a covered benefit.

Is the use of brain SPECT imaging accepted in the medical community? Brain SPECT studies are widely recognized as an effective tool for evaluating brain function in seizures, strokes, dementia, and head trauma. There are literally hundreds of research articles on these topics. In our clinic, based on our ex-perience for over a decade, we have developed this technology further to evaluate aggression and nonresponsive psychiatric conditions. Unfortu-nately, many physicians do not fully understand the application of SPECT imaging and may tell you that the technology is experimental, but over two thousand physicians and mental health professionals in the United States have referred patients to us for scans.

1. B. L. Holman and M. D. Devous, "Functional brain SPECT: The emergence of a powerful clinical method," *Journal of Nuclear Medicine* 33 (1992): 1888–1904.

2. D. Amen, S. Bracha, J. C. Wu, "Functioning neuroimaging in clinical practice," *The Comprehensive Textbook of Psychiatry,* ed. Kaplan and Sadock, 373–385 (Philadelphia: Lippincott Williams & Wilkins, 2000).

3. M. S. George, *Neuroactivation and Neuroimaging with SPECT* (New York: Springer-Verlag, 1991).

4. F. J. Bonte, M. F. Weiner, E. H. Bigio, et al., "Brain blood flow in the dementias: SPECT with histopathologic correlation in 54 patients," *Radiology* 202 (1997): 793–797.

5. D. Amen, C. Blake, J. C. Wu, "The clinical use of brain SPECT imaging in neuropsychiatry," *Alasbimn Journal* 5(19) (2003): http://www2.alasbimnjournal.cl/alasbimn/CDA/sec_b/0,1206,SCID%253D3212,00.html.

6. Report of the Therapeutics and Technology Assessment Subcommittee of the American Academy of Neurology: Assessment of brain SPECT 46 (1996): 278–285.

7. C. Chiron, C. Raynaud, B. Maziere, et al., "Changes in regional cerebral blood flow during brain maturation in children and adolescents," *Journal of Nuclear Medicine* 3(5) (1992): 696–703.

8. J. Villanueva-Meyer, I. Mena, B. Miller, et al., "Cerebral blood flow during a mental activation task: Responses in normal subjects and in early Alzheimer disease patients," *Alasbimn Journal* 1(3) (1999): http://www.alasbimnjournal.cl/revistas/3/villanuevaa.htm.

GLOSSARY

Acetylcholine—A neurotransmitter involved with memory formation, mostly excitatory, that has been implicated in problems with muscles, Alzheimer's disease, and learning problems

Amygdala—Part of the limbic or emotional system of the brain that is found on the front, inside aspect of the temporal lobes; involved with tagging emotional valences to experiences or events

Anterior cingulate gyrus—The brain's gear shifter, which runs lengthwise through the frontal lobes; helps with cognitive flexibility

Antioxidants—Help prevent damage from free radical formation

Axon—Usually a long process that projects from the cell body to connect with other cells

Basal ganglia—Large structures deep in the brain involved with motor movements, anxiety, and pleasure

Central nervous system—Composed of the spinal cord and parts of the brain, brain stem, thalamus, basal ganglia, cerebellum, and cerebral cortex

Deep limbic system—Deep structures in the brain that influence emotional responsiveness

Dendrites—Structures that branch out from the cell body and serve as the main receivers of signals from other nerve cells; they function as the "antennae" of the neuron

Dopamine—A neurotransmitter involved with attention, motor movements, and motivation that has been implicated in problems with Parkinson's disease, attention deficit disorder, addictions, depression, and schizophrenia

fMRI—A brain scan that uses powerful magnets to look at brain blood flow and activity patterns

Free radicals—Oxygen combined with other molecules to generate highly toxic substances that must be neutralized by antioxidants or they cause damage to cells

Gamma-aminobutyric acid—An inhibitory neurotransmitter involved with calming brain function that has been implicated in problems with seizures, bipolar disorder, anxiety, and pain

Glutamate—Excitatory (stimulating) neurotransmitter

Hippocampus—Part of the inside of the temporal lobes that facilitates memory function

Magnetic resonance imaging—A brain scan that uses powerful magnets to look at the physical structure of organs

Myelin—The whitish protein covering of neurons

Myelination—The act of laying myelin onto neurons

Nerve growth factors—One of several growth factors in the brain that promote the regeneration of nerve cells after injury

Neurogenesis—The growth of new neurons

Neuron—Nerve cell

Neurotransmitter—A chemical that is released from one neuron at the presynaptic nerve terminal (the end of an axon) across the synapse where it may be accepted by the next neuron (on the dendrites) at specialized sites called receptors. There are many different neurotransmitters, such as acetylcholine, serotonin, dopamine, and norepinephrine.

Norepinephrine—A neurotransmitter involved with mood, concentration, and motivation and thought to be associated with problems of attention, depression, and anxiety

Occipital lobes—Visual cortex in the back of the brain

Oxytocin—A hormone involved with bonding

Parietal lobes—Top, back part of the brain involved with sensory processing, visual processing, seeing movement, and direction sense

Positron emission tomography—A brain scan that uses isotopes to look at glucose metabolism and activity patterns in the brain

Prefrontal cortex—Front third of the brain, responsible for executive functions such as forethought and judgment

Serotonin—A neurotransmitter involved with mood, flexibility, and shifting attention that is often involved with problems of depression, obsessive-compulsive disorder, eating disorders, sleep disturbances, and pain

Single photon emission computed tomography—A brain scan that uses isotopes to look at blood flow and activity patterns in the brain

Synapses—Junctions formed between nerve cells where the presynaptic terminal of an axon comes into "contact" with the dendrite's postsynaptic membrane of another neuron. There are two types of synapses, electrical and chemical.

Synaptic plasticity—The ability of synapses to change to more efficiently signal other neurons

Temporal lobes—Large structures involved in memory, auditory processing, mood stability, and temper control that are located underneath the temples and behind the eyes

REFERENCES AND FURTHER READING

CHAPTER 1

Amen, D. G. 2005. *Making a Good Brain Great.* New York: Harmony Books.

Amen, D. G., C. Hanks, J. R. Prunella, et al. 2007. An analysis of regional cerebral blood flow in impulsive murderers using single photon emission computed tomography. *Journal of Neuropsychiatry and Clinical Neuroscience* 19(3): 304–309.

Gilbert, S. 2005. Married with problems? Therapy may not help. *New York Times.* April 19. http://www.nytimes.com/2005/04/19/health/psychology/19coup.html?_r=1&oref=slogin.

Recidivism Rates

U.S. Department of Justice. http://www.ojp.usdoj.gov/bjs/crimoff.htm#recidivism.

CHAPTER 2

Adams, J., C. M. Adler, K. Jarvis, et al. 2007. Evidence of anterior temporal atrophy in college-level soccer players. *Clinical Journal of Sport Medicine* 17(4): 304–306.

Feldman, H. A., I. Goldstein, D. G. Hatzichristou, et al. 1994. Impotence and its medical and psychological correlates: Results of the Massachusetts Male Aging Study. *Journal of Urology* 151: 54–61.

Firlik, K. *Another Day in the Frontal Lobe: A Brain Surgeon Exposes Life on the Inside.* New York: Random House.

CHAPTER 3

Amen, D. G., and J. Payne. *Making a Good Brain Great High School Course*, 2005. http://amenclinics.com/store/index.php?main_page=product_info&cPath=6&products_id=39.

Anderson, C. A., and K. E. Dill. 2000. Video games and aggressive thoughts, feelings, and behavior in the laboratory and in life. *Journal of Personality and Social Psychology* 78(4): 772–790.

Bartholow, B. D., M. A. Sestir, and E. B. Davis. 2005. Correlates and consequences of exposure to video game violence: hostile personality, empathy, and aggressive behavior. *Personality and Social Psychology Bulletin* 2005 Nov 31(11): 1573–1586.

Christakis, D. A., F. J. Zimmerman, D. L. DiGiuseppe, et al. 2004. Early television exposure and subsequent attentional problems in children. *Pediatrics* 113(4): 708–713.

Ding, J., M. L. Eigenbrodt, T. H. Mosley, Jr., et al. 2003. Alcohol intake and cerebral abnormalities on magnetic resonance imaging in a community-based population of middle-aged adults: The Atherosclerosis Risk in Communities (ARIC) study. *Stroke* 35(1): 16–21.

Hancox, R. J., B. J. Milne, and R. Poulton. 2004. Association between child and adolescent television viewing and adult health: A longitudinal birth cohort study. *Lancet* 364(9430): 257–262.

Lindstrom, H. A., T. Fritsch, G. Petot, et al. 2005. The relationships between television viewing in midlife and the development of Alzheimer's disease in a case-control study. *Brain and Cognition* 58(2): 157–65.

McCann, D., A. Barrett, A. Cooper, et al. 2007. Food additives and hyperactive behaviour in 3-year-old and 8/9-year-old children in the community: a randomised, double-blinded, placebo-controlled trial. *Lancet* 370(9598): 1560–1567.

Park, R. M., P. A. Schulte, J. D. Bowman, et al. 2005. Potential occupational risks for neurodegenerative diseases. *American Journal of Industrial Medicine* 48(1): 63–77.

Shoja, M. M., R. S. Tubbs, A. Malekian, et al. 2007. Video game epilepsy in the twentieth century: A review. *Child's Nervous System* 23(3): 265–267.

Trenité, D. G. 2006. Photosensitivity, visually sensitive seizures and epilepsies. *Epilepsy Research* 70(Suppl. 1): S269–S279.

Wilson, G. D. http://www.cnn.com/2005/WORLD/europe/04/22/text.iq/.

Zimmerman, F. J., D. A. Christakis, and A. N. Meltzoff. 2007. Associations between media viewing and language development in children under age 2 years. *Journal of Pediatrics* 151(4): 364–368.

CHAPTER 4

Amen, D. G. 2000. *Change Your Brain, Change Your Life*. 2000. New York: Three Rivers Press.

Kessler, R. C., P. A. Berglund, O. Demler, et al. 2005. Lifetime prevalence and age-of-onset distributions of DSM-IV disorders in the National Comorbidity Survey Replication (NCS-R). *Archives of General Psychiatry* 62(6): 593–602.

CHAPTER 5

Multiple Vitamins

Fairfield, K. M., and R. H. Fletcher. 2002. Vitamins for chronic disease prevention in adults: Scientific review. *Journal of the American Medical Association* 287(23): 3116–3126.

Fletcher, R. H., and K. M. Fairfield. 2002. Vitamins for chronic disease prevention in adults: Clinical applications. *Journal of the American Medical Association* 287(23): 3127–3129.

Omega-3 Fatty Acids / Fish Oil

Appel, L. J., E. R. Miller III, A. J. Seidler, et al. 1993. Does supplementation of diet with "fish oil" reduce blood pressure? A meta-analysis of controlled clinical trials. *Archives of Internal Medicine* 153(12): 1429–1438.

Dietary supplementation with n-3 polyunsaturated fatty acids and vitamin E after myocardial infarction: Results of the GISSI-Prevenzione trial. 1999. Gruppo Italiano per lo Studio della Sopravvivenza nell'Infarto miocardico. *Lancet* 354(9177): 447–455.

Gapinski, J. P., J. V. VanRuiswyk, G. R. Heudebert, et al. 1993. Preventing restenosis with fish oils following coronary angioplasty: A meta-analysis. *Archives of Internal Medicine* 153(13): 1595–1601.

Hirashima, F., A. M. Parow, A. L. Stoll, et al. 2004. Omega-3 fatty acid treatment and T(2) whole brain relaxation times in bipolar disorder. *American Journal of Psychiatry* 161(10): 1922–1924.

Stoll, A. L., K. E. Damico, B. P. Daly, et al. 2001. Methodological considerations in clinical studies of omega-3 fatty acids in major depression and bipolar disorder. *World Review of Nutrition and Dietetics* 88: 58–67.

Stoll, A. L., C. A. Locke, L. B. Marangell, et al. 1999. Omega-3 fatty acids and bipolar disorder: A review. *Prostaglandins, Leukotrienes and Essential Fatty Acids* 60(5–6): 329–337.

Stoll, A. L., W. E. Severus, M. P. Freeman, et al. 1999. Omega-3 fatty acids in bipolar disorder: A preliminary double-blind, placebo-controlled trial. *Archives of General Psychiatry* 56(5): 407–112.

CHAPTER 6

ADD

Amen, D. G. 2001. Healing ADD: *The Breakthrough Program That Allows You to See and Heal the 6 Types of ADD*. New York: Putnam.

Benton, D., and G. Roberts. 1988. Effect of vitamin and mineral supplementation on intelligence of a sample of schoolchildren. *Lancet* 1(8578): 140–143.

Fletcher, R. H., and K. M. Fairfield. 2002. Vitamins for chronic disease prevention in adults: Clinical applications. *Journal of the American Medical Association* 287(23): 3127–3129.

McCann, D., A. Barrett, A. Cooper, et al. 2007. Food additives and hyperactive behaviour in 3-year-old and 8/9-year-old children in the community: A randomised, double-blinded, placebo-controlled trial. *Lancet* 370(9598): 1560–1567.

Pelsser, L. M., K. Frankena, J. Toorman, et al. A randomised controlled trial into the effects of food on ADHD. *European Child & Adolescent Psychiatry.*

Omega-3 Fatty Acids / Fish Oil

Colter, A. L., C. Cutler, and K. A. Meckling. 2008. Fatty acid status and behavioural symptoms of attention deficit hyperactivity disorder in adolescents: a case-control study. *Nutrition Journal* 7: 8.

Johnson, M., S. Ostlund, G. Fransson, et al. Omega-3/Omega-6 fatty acids for attention deficit hyperactivity disorder: A randomized placebo-controlled trial in children and adolescents. *Journal of Attention Disorders.*

Richardson, A. J., and P. Montgomery. 2005. The Oxford-Durham study: A randomized, controlled trial of dietary supplementation with fatty acids in children with developmental coordination disorder. *Pediatrics* 115(5): 1360–1366.

Sinn, N., and J. Bryan. 2007. Effect of supplementation with polyunsaturated fatty acids and micronutrients on learning and behavior problems associated with child ADHD. *Journal of Developmental and Behavioral Pediatrics* 28(2): 82–91.

Sinn, N., J. Bryan, and C. Wilson. Cognitive effects of polyunsaturated fatty acids in children with attention deficit hyperactivity disorder symptoms: A randomised controlled trial. *Prostaglandins, Leukotrienes and Essential Fatty Acids* 75(4–5): 311–326.

Sorgi, P. J., E. M. Hallowell, H. L. Hutchins, et al. 2007. Effects of an open-label pilot study with high-dose EPA/DHA concentrates on plasma phospholipids and behavior in children with attention deficit hyperactivity disorder. *Nutrition Journal* 6(1): 16.

Acetyl-L-Carnitine

Arnold, L. E., A. Amato, H. Bozzolo, et al. Acetyl-L-carnitine (ALC) in attention-deficit / hyperactivity disorder: A multi-site, placebo-controlled pilot trial. *Journal of Child and Adolescent Psychopharmacology* 17(6): 791–802.

Bianchetti, A., R. Rozzini, and M. Trabucchi. 1992. Effects of acetyl-L-carnitine in Alzheimer's disease patients unresponsive to acetylcholinesterase inhibitors. *Current Medical Research and Opinion* 19(4): 350–353.

Bowman, B. 1992. Acetyl-carnitine and Alzheimer's disease. *Nutrition Reviews* 50: 142–144.

Carta, A., M. Calvani, and D. Bravi. 1993. Acetyl-L-carnitine and Alzheimer's disease. Pharmacologic considerations beyond the cholinergic sphere. *Annals of the New York Academy of Science* 695: 324–326.

Moyano, D., M. A. Vilaseca, R. Artuch, et al. 1998. Plasma amino acids in anorexia nervosa. *European Journal of Clinical Nutrition* 52(9): 684–689.

Ott, B. R., and N. J. Owens. 1998. Complementary and alternative medicines for Alzheimer's disease. *Journal of Geriatric Psychiatry and Neurology* 11: 163–173.

Pettegrew, J. W., J. Levine, and R. J. McClure. 2000. Acetyl-L-carnitine physical-chemical, metabolic, and therapeutic properties: Relevance for its mode of action in Alzheimer's disease and geriatric depression. *Molecular Psychiatry* 5: 616–632.

Plioplys, A. V., and S. Plioplys. 1997. Amantadine and L-carnitine treatment of chronic fatigue syndrome. *Neuropsychobiology* 35(1): 16–23.

Postiglione, A., A. Soricelli, U. Cicerano, et al. 1991. Effect of acute administration of L-acetyl-carnitine on cerebral blood flow in patients with chronic cerebral infarct. *Pharmacological Research* 23(3): 241–246.

Rossini, M., O. Di Munno, G. Valentini, et al. 2007. Double-blind, multicenter trial comparing acetyl-L-carnitine with placebo in the treatment of fibromyalgia patients. *Clinical and Experimental Rheumatology* 25(2): 182–188.

Tempesta, E., L. Casella, C. Pirrongelli, et al. L-acetylcarnitine in depressed elderly subjects. A cross-over study vs. placebo. *Drugs Under Experimental & Clinical Research* 13(7): 417–423.

Thal, L. J., A. Carta, W. R. Clarke, et al. 1996. A 1-year multicenter placebo-controlled study of acetyl-L-carnitine in patients with Alzheimer's disease. *Neurology* 47: 705–711.

Tomassini, V., C. Pozzilli, E. Onesti, et al. 2004. Comparison of the effects of acetyl-L-carnitine and amantadine for the treatment of fatigue in multiple sclerosis: results of a pilot, randomised, double-blind, crossover trial. *Journal of the Neurological Sciences* 218(1–2): 103–108.

Torrioli, M. G., S. Vernacotola, L. Peruzzi, et al. A double-blind, parallel, multicenter comparison of L-acetylcarnitine with placebo on the attention deficit hyperactivity disorder in fragile X syndrome boys. *American Journal of Medical Genetics Part A* 146(7): 803–812.

Van Wouwe, J. P. 1995. Carnitine deficiency during valproic-acid treatment. *International Journal for Vitamin and Nutrition Research* 65: 211–214.

Werbach, M. R. 2000. Nutritional strategies for treating chronic fatigue syndrome. *Alternative Medicine Review* 5(2): 93–108.

Zanardi, R., and E. Smeraldi. 2006. A double-blind, randomised, controlled clinical trial of acetyl-L-carnitine vs. amisulpride in the treatment of dysthymia. *European Neuropsychopharmacology* 16(4): 281–287.

DL-Phenylalanine

Baker, G. B., R. A. Bornstein, A. C. Rouget, et al. 1991. Phenylethylaminergic mechanisms in attention-deficit disorder. *Biological Psychiatry* 29(1): 15–22.

Beckmann, H., D. Athen, M. Olteanu, et al. 1979. DL-phenylalanine versus imipramine: a double-blind controlled study. *Archiv für Psychiatrie und Nervenkrankheiten* 227(1): 49–58.

Beckmann, H., M. A. Strauss, and E. Ludolph. 1977. DL-phenylalanine in depressed patients: An open study. *Journal of Neural Transmission* 41(2–3): 123–134.

Fugh-Berman, A., and J. M. Cott. 1999. Dietary supplements and natural products as psychotherapeutic agents. *Psychosomatic Medicine* 61: 712–728.

Meyers, S. 2000. Use of neurotransmitter precursors for treatment of depression. *Alternative Medicine Review* 5(1): 64–71.

Russell, A. L., and M. F. McCarty. 2000. DL-phenylalanine markedly potentiates opiate analgesia—an example of nutrient pharmaceutical up-regulation of the endogenous analgesia system. *Medical Hypotheses* 55(4): 283–288.

Sabelli, H. C., J. Fawcett, F. Gusovsky, et al. 1986. Clinical studies on the phenylethylamine hypothesis of affective disorder: urine and blood phenylacetic acid and phenylalanine dietary supplements. *Journal of Clinical Psychiatry* 47: 66–70.

Walsh, N. E., S. Ramamurthy, L. Schoenfeld, et al. 1986. Analgesic effectiveness of DL-phenylalanine in chronic pain patients. *Archives of Physical Medicine and Rehabilitation* 67(7): 436–439.

Wood, D. R., F. W. Reimherr, and P. H. Wender. 1985. Treatment of attention deficit disorder with DL-phenylalanine. *Psychiatry Research* 16(1): 21–26.

GABA

Abdou, A. M., S. Higashiguchi, K. Horie, et al. 2006. Relaxation and immunity enhancement effects of gamma-aminobutyric acid (GABA) administration in humans. *Biofactors* 26(3): 201–208.

Deng, S., B. J. West, A. K. Palu, et al. 2007. Noni as an anxiolytic and sedative: a mechanism involving its gamma-aminobutyric acidergic effects. *Phytomedicine* 14(7–8): 517–522.

Gottesmann, C. 2003. GABA mechanisms and sleep. *Neuroscience* 111: 231–239.

Nemeroff, C. B. 2003. The role of GABA in the pathophysiology and treatment of anxiety disorders. *Psychopharmacological Bulletin* 37: 133–146.

Treiman, D. M. 2001. GABAergic mechanisms in epilepsy. *Epilepsia* 42: 8–12.

Grape Seed Extract / Pine Bark / Pycnogenol

Chovanová, Z., J. Muchová, M. Sivonová, et al. Effect of polyphenolic extract, Pycnogenol, on the level of 8-oxoguanine in children suffering from attention deficit/hyperactivity disorder. *Free Radical Research* 40(9): 1003–1010.

Dvořáková, M., D. Jezová, P. Blazícek, et al. 2007. Urinary catecholamines in children with attention deficit hyperactivity disorder (ADHD): Modulation by a polyphenolic extract from pine bark (pycnogenol). *Nutritional Neuroscience* 10(3–4): 151–157.

Dvořáková, M., M. Sivonová, J. Trebatická, et al. 2006. The effect of polyphenolic extract from pine bark, Pycnogenol on the level of glutathione in children suffering from attention deficit hyperactivity disorder (ADHD). *Redox Report* 11(4): 163–172.

Rohdewald, P. 2002. A review of the French maritime pine bark extract (Pycnogenol), an herbal medication with a diverse clinical pharmacology. *International Journal of Clinical Pharmacology and Therapeutics* 40(4): 158–168.

Tenenbaum, S., J. C. Paull, E. P. Sparrow, et al. 2002. An experimental comparison of Pycnogenol and methylphenidate in adults with Attention-Deficit/Hyperactivity Disorder (ADHD). *Journal of Attention Disorders* 6(2): 49–60.

Trebatická, J., S. Kopasová, Z. Hradecná, et al. 2006. Treatment of ADHD with French maritime pine bark extract, Pycnogenol. *European Child & Adolescent Psychiatry* 15(6): 329–335.

L-Tyrosine

Chiaroni, P., J. M. Azorin, P. Bovier, et al. 1990. A multivariate analysis of red blood cell membrane transports and plasma levels of L-tyrosine and L-tryptophan in depressed patients before treatment and after clinical improvement. *Neuropsychobiology* 23(1): 1–7.

Deijen, J. B., and J. F. Orlebeke. 1994. Effect of tyrosine on cognitive function and blood pressure under stress. *Brain Research Bulletin* 33(3): 319–323.

Gelenberg, A. J., J. D. Wojcik, W. E. Falk, et al. 1990. Tyrosine for depression: a double-blind trial. *Journal of Affective Disorders* 19: 125–132.

Kelly, G. S. 1999. Nutritional and botanical interventions to assist with the adaptation to stress. *Alternative Medicine Review* 4(4): 249–265.

Meyers, S. 2000. Use of neurotransmitter precursors for treatment of depression. *Alternative Medicine Review* 5(1): 64–71.

Neri, D. F., D. Wiegmann, R. R. Stanny, et al. 1995. The effects of tyrosine on cognitive performance during extended wakefulness. *Aviation, Space, and Environmental Medicine* 66(4): 313–319.

Thomas, J. R., P. A. Lockwood, A. Singh, et al. 1999. Tyrosine improves working memory in a multitasking environment. *Pharmacology Biochemical Behavior* 64(3): 495–500.

Wagenmakers, A. J. 1999. Amino acid supplements to improve athletic performance. *Current Opinion in Clinical Nutrition and Metabolic Care* 2(6): 539–544.

SAMe

Baldessarini, R. J. 1987. Neuropharmacology of S-adenosyl-L-methionine. *American Journal of Medicine* 83(5A): 95–103.

Bell, K. M., et al. 1994. S-adenosylmethionine blood levels in major depression: changes with drug treatment. *Acta Neurologica Scandinavica Supplement* 154: 15–18.

Berlanga, C., H. A. Ortega-Soto, M. Ontiveros, et al. Efficacy of S-adeno-L-methionine in speeding the onset of action of imipramine. *Psychiatry Research* 44(3): 257–262.

Bottiglieri, T., P. Godfrey, T. Flynn, et al. 1990. Cerebrospinal fluid S-adenosylmethionine in depression and dementia: Effects of treatment with parental and oral-adenosylmethionine. *Journal of Neurology, Neurosurgery & Psychiatry* 53: 1096–1098.

Bottiglieri, T., K. Hyland, E. H. Reynolds. 1994. The clinical potential of ademetionine (S-adenosylmethionine) in neurological disorders. *Drugs* 48(2): 137–152.

Bradley, J. D., D. Flusser, B. P. Katz, et al. 1994. A randomized, double blind, placebo controlled trial of intravenous loading with S-adenosylmethionine (SAM) followed by oral SAM therapy in patients with knee osteoarthritis. *Journal of Rheumatology* 21(5): 905–911.

Bressa, G. M. 1994. S-adenosylmethionine (SAMe) as antidepressant: meta-analysis of clinical studies. *Acta Neurologica Scandinavica Supplement* 154: 7–14.

Carney, M. W., B. K. Toone, and E. H. Reynolds. 1987. S-adenosylmethionine and affective disorder. *American Journal of Medicine* 83(5A): 104–106.

di Pavoda, C. 1987. S-adenosylmethionine in the treatment of osteoarthritis. Review of clinical studies. *American Journal of Medicine* 83(suppl. 5A): 60–65.

Fava, M., A. Giannelli, V. Rapisarda, et al. 1995. Rapidity of onset of the antidepressant effect of parenteral S-adenosyl-L-methionine. *Psychiatry Research* 56(3): 295–297.

Fava, M., J. F. Rosenbaum, R. MacLaughlin, et al. 1990. Neuroendocrine effects of S-adenosyl-L-methionine, a novel putative antidepressant. *Journal of Psychiatric Research* 24(2): 177–184.

Fetrow, C. W., and J. R. Avila. 2001. Efficacy of the dietary supplement S-adenosyl-L-methionine. *Annals of Pharmacotherapy* 35(11): 1414–1425.

Fugh-Berman, A., and J. M. Cott. 1999. Dietary supplements and natural products as psychotherapeutic agents. *Psychosomatic Medicine* 61: 712–728.

Gaby, A. R. 1999. Natural treatments for osteoarthritis. *Alternative Medicine Review* 4(5): 330–341.

Gatto, G., D. Caleri, S. Michelacci, et al. 1986. Analgesizing effect of a methyl donor (S-adenosylmethionine) in migraine: An open clinical trial. *International Journal of Clinical Pharmacology Research* 6: 15–17.

Glorioso, S., S. Todesco, A. Mazzi, et al. 1985. Double-blind multicentre study of the activity of S-adenosylmethionine in hip and knee osteoarthritis. *International Journal of Clinical Pharmacology Research* 5: 39–49.

Jacobsen, S., B. Danneskiold-Samsoe, R. B. Andersen. 1991. Oral S-adenosyl-methionine in primary fibromyalgia. Double-blind clinical evaluation. *Scandinavian Journal of Rheumatology* 20: 294–302.

Konig, B. 1987. A long-term (two years) clinical trial with S-adenosylmethionine for the treatment of osteoarthritis. *American Journal of Medicine* 83(5A): 89–94.

Leventhal, L. J. 1999. Management of fibromyalgia. *Annals of Internal Medicine* 131: 850–858.

Maccagno, A., E. E. di Giorio, O. L. Caston, et al. 1987. Double-blind controlled clinical trial of oral S-adenosylmethionine versus piroxicam in knee osteoarthritis. *American Journal of Medicine* 83(Suppl. 5A): 72–77.

Müller-Fassbender, H. 1987. Double-blind clinical trial of s-adenosylmethionine versus ibuprofen in the treatment of osteoarthritis. *American Journal of Medicine* 83(Suppl. 5A): 81–83.

SAMe for depression. 1999. *Medical Letter* 41(1065): 107–108.

Shekim, W. O., F. Antun, G. L. Hanna, et al. 1990. S-adenosyl-L-methionine (SAMe) in adults with ADHD: preliminary results from an open trial. *Psychopharmacological Bulletin* 26(2): 249–253.

Tavoni, A., C. Vitali, S. Bombardieri, et al. 1987. Evaluation of S-adenosyl-methionine in primary fibromyalgia. A double-blind crossover study. *American Journal of Medicine* 83(5A): 107–110.

Vetter, G. 1987. Double-blind comparative clinical trial with S-adenosyl-methionine and indomethacin in the treatment of osteoarthritis. *American Journal of Medicine* 83(Suppl. 5A): 78–80.

St. John's Wort

Anghelescu, I. G., R. Kohnen, A. Szegedi, et al. 2006. Comparison of Hypericum extract WS 5570 and paroxetine in ongoing treatment after recovery from an episode of moderate to severe depression: Results from a randomized multi-center study. *Pharmacopsychiatry* 39(6): 213–219.

Behnke, K., G. S. Jensen, H. J. Graubaum, et al. 2002. Hypericum perforatum versus fluoxetine in the treatment of mild to moderate depression. *Advances in Therapy* 19(1): 43–52.

Bjerkenstedt, L., G. V. Edman, R. G. Alken, et al. 2005. Hypericum extract LI 160 and fluoxetine in mild to moderate depression: A randomized, placebo-controlled multicenter study in outpatients. *European Archives of Psychiatry and Clinical Neuroscience* 255(1): 40–47.

Brenner, R., V. Azbel, S. Madhusoodanan, et al. 2000. Comparison of an extract of hypericum (LI 160) and sertraline in the treatment of depression: A double-blind, randomized pilot study. *Clinical Therapeutics* 22(4): 411–419.

Farabaugh, A., D. Mischoulon, M. Fava, et al. 2005. The relationship between early changes in the HAMD-17 anxiety/somatization factor items and treatment outcome among depressed outpatients. *International Clinical Psychopharmacology* 20(2): 87–91.

Fava, M., J. Alpert, A. A. Nierenberg, et al. 2005. A double-blind, randomized trial of St John's wort, fluoxetine, and placebo in major depressive disorder. *Journal of Clinical Psychopharmacology* 25(5): 441–447.

Findling, R., N. K. McNamara, M. A. O'Riordan, et al. 2003. An open-label pilot study of St. John's wort in juvenile depression. *Journal of the American Academy of Child & Adolescent Psychiatry* 42(8): 908–914.

Gastpar, M., A. Singer, and K. Zeller. 2005. Efficacy and tolerability of hypericum extract STW3 in long-term treatment with a once-daily dosage in comparison with sertraline. *Pharmacopsychiatry* 38(2): 78–86.

Gastpar, M., A. Singer, and K. Zeller. 2006. Comparative efficacy and safety of a once-daily dosage of hypericum extract STW3-VI and citalopram in patients with moderate depression: A double-blind, randomized, multicenter, placebo-controlled study. *Pharmacopsychiatry* 39(2): 66–75.

Hypericum Depression Trial Study Group. 2002. Effects of *Hypericum perforatum* (St John's wort) in major depressive disorder: A randomized controlled trial. *Journal of the American Medical Association* 287(14): 1807–1814.

Kalb, R., R. D. Trautmann-Sponsel, and M. Kieser. 2001. Efficacy and tolerability of hypericum extract WS 5572 versus placebo in mildly to moderately depressed patients. A randomized double-blind multicenter clinical trial. *Pharmacopsychiatry* 34(3): 96–103.

Kasper, S., I. Anghelescu, A. Szegedi, et al. 2006. Superior efficacy of St John's wort extract WS 5570 compared to placebo in patients with major depression: A randomized, double-blind, placebo-controlled, multi-center trial. *BMC Medicine* 4:14.

Kasper, S., I. Anghelescu, A. Szegedi, et al. 2007. Placebo controlled continuation treatment with Hypericum extract WS 5570 after recovery from a mild or moderate depressive episode. *Wiener Medizinische Wochenschrift* 157(13–14): 362–366.

Kasper, S., and A. Dienel. 2002. Cluster analysis of symptoms during antidepressant treatment with Hypericum extract in mildly to moderately depressed out-patients: A meta-analysis of data from three randomized, placebo-controlled trials. *Psychopharmacology* 164(3): 301–308.

Kasper, S., A. Dienel, and M. Kieser. 2004. Continuation and long-term maintenance treatment with Hypericum extract WS 5570 after successful acute treatment of mild to moderate depression—rationale and study design. *International Journal of Methods in Psychiatric Research* 13(3): 176–183.

Kieser, M., and A. Szegedi. 2005. Predicting stable treatment response in patients with major depression treated with hypericum extract WS 5570/5572. *Pharmacopsychiatry* 38(5): 194–200.

Kobak, K., L. Taylor, G. Warner, et al. 2005. St. John's wort versus placebo in social phobia: Results from a placebo-controlled pilot study. *Journal of Clinical Psychopharmacology* 25(1): 51–58.

Kobak, K., L. Taylor, A. Bystritsky, et al. 2005. St. John's wort versus placebo in obsessive-compulsive disorder: results from a double-blind study. *International Clinical Psychopharmacology* 20(6): 299–304.

Laakmann, G., et al. 1998. St. John's wort in mild to moderate depression: The relevance of hyperforin for the clinical efficacy. *Pharmacopsychiatry* 31(Suppl. 1): 54–59.

Lecrubier, Y., G. Clerc, R. Didi, et al. 2002. Efficacy of St. John's wort extract WS 5570 in major depression: A double-blind, placebo-controlled trial. *American Journal of Psychiatry* 159(8): 1361–1366.

Linde, K., M. Berner, M. Egger, et al. 2005. St John's wort for depression: meta-analysis of randomized controlled trials. *British Journal of Psychiatry* 186: 99–107.

Linde, K., G. Ramirez, C. Mulrow, et al. 1996. St John's wort for depression—an overview and meta-analysis of randomized clinical trials. *British Medical Journal* 313(7052): 253–258.

Moreno, R. A., C. Teng, K. Almeida, et al. 2006. Hypericum perforatum versus fluoxetine in the treatment of mild to moderate depression: A randomized double-blind trial in a Brazilian sample. *Revista Brasileiva Psiquiatria* 28(1): 29–32.

Müller, T., M. Mannel, H. Murck, et al. 2004. Treatment of somatoform disorders with St. John's wort: A randomized, double-blind and placebo-controlled trial. *Psychosomatic Medicine* 66(4): 538–547.

Murck, H., M. Fava, J. Alpert, et al. 2005. Hypericum extract in patients with MDD and reversed vegetative signs: reanalysis from data of a double-blind, randomized trial of hypericum extract, fluoxetine, and placebo. *International Journal of Neuropsychopharmacology* 8(2): 215–221.

Philipp, M., R. Kohnen, and K. Hiller. 1999. Hypericum extract versus imipramine or placebo in patients with moderate depression: Randomized multicenter study of treatment for eight weeks. *British Medical Journal* 319(7224): 1534–1539.

Randov, C., J. Mehlsen, C. Thomsen, et al. 2006. The efficacy of St. John's Wort in patients with minor depressive symptoms or dysthymia—a double-blind placebo-controlled study. *Phytomedicine* 13(4): 215–221.

Scrader, E. 2000. Equivalence of St John's wort extract (Ze 117) and fluoxetine: A randomized, controlled study in mild-moderate depression. *International Journal of Clinical Psychopharmacology* 15(2): 61–68.

Shelton, R. C., M. Keller, A. Gelenberg, et al. 2001. Effectiveness of St. John's wort in major depression: A randomized controlled trial. *Journal of the American Medical Association* 285(15): 1978–1986.

Simeon, J., M. Nixon, R. Milin, et al. 2005. Open-label pilot study of St. John's wort in adolescent depression. *Journal of Child & Adolescent Psychopharmacology* 15(2): 293–301.

Szegedi, A., R. Kohnen, A. Dienel, et al. 2005. Acute treatment of moderate to severe depression with hypericum extract WS 5570 (St John's wort): Randomized controlled double blind non-inferiority trial versus paroxetine. *British Medical Journal* 330(7490): 503.

Taylor, L., and K. Kobak. 2000. An open-label trial of St. John's Wort (Hypericum perforatum) in obsessive-compulsive disorder. *Journal of Clinical Psychiatry* 61(8): 575–578.

Uebelhack, R., J. Gruenwald, H. Graubaum, et al. 2004. Efficacy and tolerability of Hypericum extract STW 3-VI in patients with moderate depression: A double-blind, randomized, placebo-controlled clinical trial. *Advances in Therapy* 21(4): 265–275.

van Gurp, G., G. Meterissian, L. Haiek, et al. 2002. St John's wort or sertraline? Randomized controlled trial in primary care. *Canadian Family Physician* 48: 905–912.

Vitiello, B., R. Shader, C. Parker, et al. 2005. Hyperforin plasma level as a marker of treatment adherence in the National Institute of Health Hypericum Depression Trial. *Journal of Clinical Psychopharmacology* 25(3): 243–249.

Volz, H., H. Murck, S. Kasper, et al. 2002. St John's wort extract (LI 160) in somatoform disorders: Results of a placebo-controlled trial. *Psychopharmacology* 164(3): 294–300.

Vorbach, E., K. Arnoldt, and W. Hubner. 1997. Efficacy and tolerability of St. John's wort extract LI 160 versus imipramine in patients with severe depressive episodes according to ICD-10. *Pharmacopsychiatry* 30(Suppl. 2): 81–85.

Woelk, H. 2000. Comparison of St John's wort and imipramine for treating depression: randomized controlled trial. *British Medical Journal* 321(7260): 536–539.

Theanine

Bryan, J. 2008. Psychological effects of dietary components of tea: caffeine and L-theanine. *Nutrition Review* 66(2): 82–90.

Dimpfel, W., A. Kler, E. Kriesl, et al. 2007. Source density analysis of the human EEG after ingestion of a drink containing decaffeinated extract of green tea enriched with L-theanine and theogallin. *Nutritional Neuroscience* 10(3–4): 169–180.

Gomez-Ramirez, M., B. A. Higgins, J. A. Rycroft, et al. 2007. The deployment of intersensory selective attention: A high-density electrical mapping study of the effects of theanine. *Clinical Neuropharmacology* 30(1): 25–38.

Haskell, C. F., D. O. Kennedy, A. L. Milne, et al. 2008. The effects of L-theanine, caffeine and their combination on cognition and mood. *Biological Psychology* 77(2): 113–122.

Kimura, K., M. Ozeki, L. R. Juneja, et al. 2007. L-Theanine reduces psychological and physiological stress responses. *Biological Psychology* 74(1): 39–45.

Lu, K., M. A. Gray, C. Oliver, et al. 2004. The acute effects of L-theanine in comparison with alprazolam on anticipatory anxiety in humans. *Human Psychopharmacology* 19(7): 457–465.

Nobre, A. C., A. Rao, and G. N. Owen. 2008. L-theanine, a natural constituent in tea, and its effect on mental state. *Asia Pacific Journal of Clinical Nutrition* 17(Suppl. 1): 167–168.

Rogers, P. J., J. E. Smith, S. V. Heatherley, et al. 2008. Time for tea: Mood, blood pressure and cognitive performance effects of caffeine and theanine administered alone and together. *Psychopharmacology* 195(4): 569–577.

Zinc

Akhondzadeh, S., M. R. Mohammadi, and M. Khademi. 2004. Zinc sulfate as an adjunct to methylphenidate for the treatment of attention deficit hyperactivity disorder in children: A double blind and randomized trial. *BMC Psychiatry* 4: 9.

Arnold, L. E., H. Bozzolo, J. Hollway, et al. 2005. Serum zinc correlates with parent- and teacher-rated inattention in children with attention-deficit/hyperactivity disorder. *Journal of Child & Adolescent Psychopharmacology* 15(4): 628–636.

Arnold, L. E., and R. A. DiSilvestro. 2005. Zinc in attention-deficit/hyperactivity disorder. *Journal of Child & Adolescent Psychopharmacology* 15(4): 619–627.

Bekaroğlu, M., Y. Aslan, Y. Gedik, et al. 1996. Relationships between serum free fatty acids and zinc, and attention deficit hyperactivity disorder: A research note. *Journal of Child Psychology and Psychiatry* 37(2): 225–227.

Bilici, M., F. Yildirim, S. Kandil, et al. 2004. Double-blind, placebo-controlled study of zinc sulfate in the treatment of attention deficit hyperactivity disorder. *Progress in Neuropsychopharmacology & Biological Psychiatry* 28(1): 181–190.

Yorbik, O., M. F. Ozdag, A. Olgun, et al. 2008. Potential effects of zinc on information processing in boys with attention deficit hyperactivity disorder. *Progress in Neuropsychopharmacology & Biological Psychiatry* 32(3): 662–667.

CHAPTER 7

Amen, D. G., and L. C. Routh. 2003. *Healing Anxiety and Depression*. New York: Putnam.

Antidepressant Effects of Exercise

Babyak, M., J. A. Blumenthal, S. Herman, et al. 2000. Exercise treatment for major depression: Maintenance of therapeutic benefit at 10 months. *Psychosomatic Medicine* 62(5): 633–638.

Blumenthal, J. A., M. A. Babyak, P. M. Doraiswamy, et al. 2007. Exercise and pharmacotherapy in the treatment of major depressive disorder. *Psychosomatic Medicine* 69(7): 587–596.

Blumenthal, J. A., M. A. Babyak, K. A. Moore, et al. 1999. Effects of exercise training on older patients with major depression. *Archives of Internal Medicine* 159(19): 2349–2356.

Brenes, G. A., J. D. Williamson, S. P. Messier, et al. 2007. Treatment of minor depression in older adults: A pilot study comparing sertraline and exercise. *Aging and Mental Health* 11(1): 61–68.

Kessler, R. C., P. A. Berglund, O. Demler, et al. 2005. Lifetime prevalence and age-of-onset distributions of DSM-IV disorders in the National Comorbidity Survey Replication (NCS-R). *Archives of General Psychiatry* 62(6): 593–602.

GABA

Abdou, A. M., S. Higashiguchi, K. Horie, et al. 2006. Relaxation and immunity enhancement effects of gamma-aminobutyric acid (GABA) administration in humans. *Biofactors* 26(3): 201–208.

Cocito, L., A. Bianchetti, L. Bossi, et al. 1994. GABA 30 and phosphatidylserine in human photosensitivity: A pilot study. *Epilepsy Research* 17: 49–53.

Green, M. L., R. G. Green, and W. Santoro. 1988. Daily relaxation modifies serum and salivary immunoglobulins and psychophysiologic symptom severity. *Biofeedback & Self Regulation* 13: 187–199.

Kendell, S. F., J. H. Krystal, and G. Sanacora. 2005. GABA and glutamate systems as therapeutic targets in depression and mood disorders. *Expert Opinion on Therapeutic Targets* 9: 153–168.

Loeb, C., E. Benassi, G. P. Bo, et al. 1987. Preliminary evaluation of the effect of GABA and phosphatidylserine in epileptic patients. *Epilepsy Research* 1: 209–212.

Streeter, C. C., J. E. Jensen, R. M. Perlmutter, et al. 2007. Yoga asana sessions increase brain GABA levels: A pilot study. *Journal of Alternative and Complementary Medicine* 13: 419–426.

Hyperbaric Oxygen Treatment

Harch, P. HOTFAST: Hyperbaric Oxygen Therapy for Acute Stroke, *HBOT Online,* March 11, 2003, http://www.hbot.com/Hotfast.html.

Hopkins, R. O., L. K. Weaver, K. J. Valentine, et al. 2007. Apolipoprotein E genotype and response of carbon monoxide poisoning to hyperbaric oxygen treatment. *American Journal of Respiratory and Critical Care Medicine* 176(10): 1001–1006.

Lo, C. P., S. Y. Chen, M. C. Chou, 2007. Diffusion-tensor MR imaging for evaluation of the efficacy of hyperbaric oxygen therapy in patients with delayed neuropsychiatric syndrome caused by carbon monoxide inhalation. *European Journal of Neurology* 14(7): 777–782.

Inositol

Barak, Y., J. Levine, A. Glasman, et al. 1996. Inositol treatment of Alzheimer's disease: a double-blind, cross-over placebo controlled trial. *Progress in Neuropsychopharmacology and Biological Psychiatry* 20(4): 729–735.

Benjamin, J., J. Levine, M. Fux, et al. 1995. Double-blind, placebo-controlled, crossover trial of inositol treatment for panic disorder. *American Journal of Psychiatry* 152(7): 1084–1086.

Carey, P. D., J. Warwick, B. H. Harvey, et al. 2004. Single photon emission computed tomography (SPECT) in obsessive-compulsive disorder before and after treatment with inositol. *Metabolic Brain Disease* 19(1–2): 125–134.

Chengappa, K. N., J. Levine, S. Gershon, et al. 2000. Inositol as an add-on treatment for bipolar depression. *Bipolar Disorders* 2(1): 47–55.

Fux, M., J. Benjamin, and R. H. Belmaker. 1999. Inositol versus placebo augmentation of serotonin reuptake inhibitors in the treatment of obsessive-compulsive disorder: A double-blind cross-over study. *International Journal of Neuropsychopharmacology* 2(3): 193–195.

Fux, M., J. Levine, A. Aviv, et al. 1996. Inositol treatment of obsessive-compulsive disorder. *American Journal of Psychiatry* 153(9): 1219–1221.

Gelber, D., J. Levine, and R. H. Belmaker. 2001. Effect of inositol on bulimia nervosa and binge eating. *International Journal of Eating Disorders* 29(3): 345–348.

Levine, J. 1997. Controlled trials of inositol in psychiatry. *European Neuropsychopharmacology* 7(2): 147–155.

Levine, J., A. Aviram, A. Holan, et al. 1997. Inositol treatment of autism. *Journal of Neural Transmission* 104(2–3): 307–310.

Levine, J., Y. Barak, M. Gonzalves, et al. 1995. Double-blind, controlled trial of inositol treatment of depression. *American Journal of Psychiatry* 152(5): 792–794.

Levine, J., I. Goldberger, A. Rapaport, et al. 1994. CSF inositol in schizophrenia and high-dose inositol treatment of schizophrenia. *European Neuropsychopharmacology* 4(4): 487–490.

Levine, J., A. Mishori, M. Susnosky, et al. 1999. Combination of inositol and serotonin reuptake inhibitors in the treatment of depression. *Biological Psychiatry* 45(3): 270–273.

Nemets, B., B. Talesnick, R. H. Belmaker, et al. 2002. Myo-inositol has no beneficial effect on premenstrual dysphoric disorder. *World Journal of Biological Psychiatry* 3(3): 147–149.

Nemets, B., A. Mishory, J. Levine, et al. 1999. Inositol addition does not improve depression in SSRI treatment failures. *Journal of Neural Transmission* 106(7–8): 795–798.

Nierenberg, A. A., M. J. Ostacher, J. R. Calabrese, et al. 2006. Treatment-resistant bipolar depression: a STEP-BD equipoise randomized effectiveness trial of antidepressant augmentation with lamotrigine, inositol, or risperidone. *American Journal of Psychiatry* 163(2): 210–216.

Palatnik, A., K. Frolov, M. Fux, et al. 2001. Double-blind, controlled, crossover trial of inositol versus fluvoxamine for the treatment of panic disorder. *Journal of Clinical Psychopharmacology* 21(3): 335–339.

Seedat, S., and D. J. Stein. 1999. Inositol augmentation of serotonin reuptake inhibitors in treatment-refractory obsessive-compulsive disorder: an open trial. *International Clinical Psychopharmacology* 14(6): 353–356.

Kava Kava

Attele, A. S., J. T. Xie, C. S. Yuan. 2000. Treatment of insomnia: an alternative approach. *Alternative Medicine Review* 5(3): 249–259.

Basch, E., C. Ulbricht, P. Hammerness, et al. 2002. Kava monograph. *Journal of Herbal Pharmacotherapy* 2(4): 65–91.

Boerner, R. J., and S. Klement. 2004. Attenuation of neuroleptic-induced extrapyramidal side effects by Kava special extract WS 1490. *Wiener Medizinische Wochenschrift* 154(21–22): 508–510.

Boerner, R. J., H. Sommer, W. Berger, et al. 2003. Kava-Kava extract LI 150 is as effective as Opipramol and Buspirone in Generalised Anxiety Disorder—an 8-week randomized, double-blind multi-centre clinical trial in 129 outpatients. *Phytomedicine* 10(Suppl. 4): 38–49.

Brinker, F. 1998. *Herb Contraindications and Drug Interactions* (2nd ed.). Sandy, OR: Eclectic Medical.

Cagnacci, A., S. Arangino, and A. Renzi, et al. 2003. Kava-Kava administration reduces anxiety in perimenopausal women. *Maturitas* 44(2): 103–109.

Connor, K. M., V. Payne, and J. R. Davidson. 2006. Kava in generalized anxiety disorder: Three placebo-controlled trials. *International Clinical Psychopharmacology* 21(5): 249–253.

Cropley, M., Z. Cave, J. Ellis, et al. 2002. Effect of Kava and Valerian on human physiological and psychological responses to mental stress assessed under laboratory conditions. *Phytotherapy Research* 16(1): 23–27.

De Leo, V., A. La Marca, D. Lanzetta, et al. 2000. Assessment of the association of Kava-Kava extract and hormone replacement therapy in the treatment of postmenopause anxiety. *Minerva Ginecologica* 52(6): 263–267.

De Leo, V., A. La Marca, G. Morgante, et al. 2001. Evaluation of combining kava extract with hormone replacement therapy in the treatment of postmenopausal anxiety. *Maturitas* 39(2): 185–188.

Gastpar, M., and H. D. Klimm. 2003. Treatment of anxiety, tension and restlessness states with Kava special extract WS 1490 in general practice: A randomized placebo-controlled double-blind multicenter trial. *Phytomedicine* 10(8): 631–639.

Herberg, K. W. 1993. Effect of Kava-Special Extract WS 1490 combined with ethyl alcohol on safety-relevant performance parameters. *Blutalkohol* 30(2): 96–105.

Lehrl, S. 2004. Clinical efficacy of kava extract WS 1490 in sleep disturbances associated with anxiety disorders. Results of a multicenter, randomized, placebo-controlled, double-blind clinical trial. *Journal of Affective Disorders* 78(2): 101–110.

Pittler, M. H., and E. Ernst. 2003. Kava extract for treating anxiety. *Cochrane Database of Systatic Reviews* Issue 1. Art. No.: CD003383. DOI: 10. 1002/14651858. CD003383.

Scherer, J. 1998. Kava-kava extract in anxiety disorders: an outpatient observational study. *Advances in Therapy* 15(4): 261–269.

Thompson, R., W. Ruch, and R. U. Hasenohrl. 2004. Enhanced cognitive performance and cheerful mood by standardized extracts of Piper methysticum (Kava-kava). *Human Psychopharmacology* 19(4): 243–250.

Volz, H. P., and M. Kieser. 1997. Kava-kava extract WS 1490 versus placebo in anxiety disorders—a randomized placebo-controlled 25-week outpatient trial. *Pharmacopsychiatry* 30: 1–5.

Wheatley, D. 2001. Kava and valerian in the treatment of stress-induced insomnia. *Phytotherapy Research* 15(6): 549–551.

Witte, S., D. Loew, and W. Gaus. 2005. Meta-analysis of the efficacy of the acetonic kava-kava extract WS1490 in patients with non-psychotic anxiety disorders. *Phytotherapy Research* 19(3): 183–188.

Ketogenic Diet for Epilepsy and Other Psychiatric Disorders

Farasat, S., E. H. Kossoff, D. J. Pillas, et al. 2006. The importance of parental expectations of cognitive improvement for their children with epilepsy prior to starting the ketogenic diet. *Epilepsy & Behavior* 2006 8(2): 406–410.

Kang, H. C., Y. J. Kim, D. W. Kim, et al. 2005. Efficacy and safety of the ketogenic diet for intractable childhood epilepsy: Korean multicentric experience. *Epilepsia* 46(2): 272–279.

Ketogenic diet may be effective for drug-resistant epilepsy. 2008. *Expert Review Neurotherapeutics* 8(6): 869–871.

Kim do, Y., and J. M. Rho. 2008. The ketogenic diet and epilepsy. *Current Opinion in Clinical Nutrition and Metabolic Care* 11(2): 113–120.

Kossoff, E. H., L. C. Laux, R. Blackford, et al. 2008. When do seizures usually improve with the ketogenic diet? *Epilepsia* 49(2): 329–333.

Kossoff, E. H., H. Rowley, S. R. Sinha, et al. 2008. A prospective study of the modified Atkins diet for intractable epilepsy in adults. *Epilepsia* 49(2): 316–319.

Kossoff, E. H., Z. Turner, and G. K. Bergey. 2007. Home-guided use of the ketogenic diet in a patient for more than 20 years. *Pediatric Neurology* 36(6): 424–425.

Kossoff, E. H., Z. Turner, R. M. Bluml, et al. 2007. A randomized, crossover comparison of daily carbohydrate limits using the modified Atkins diet. *Epilepsy & Behavior* 10(3): 432–436.

Levy, R., and P. Cooper. 2003. Ketogenic diet for epilepsy. *Cochrane Database of Systatic Reviews* issue 3. Art. No.: CD 001903. DOI 10.1002/1461858. CD001903.

Martinez, C. C., P. L. Pyzik, and E. H. Kossoff. 2007. Discontinuing the ketogenic diet in seizure-free children: recurrence and risk factors. *Epilepsia* 48(1): 187–190.

Neal, E. G., H. Chaffe, R. H. Schwartz, et al. 2008. The ketogenic diet for the treatment of childhood epilepsy: A randomised controlled trial. *Lancet Neurology* 7(6): 500–506.

Sampath, A., E. H. Kossoff, S. L. Furth, et al. 2007. Kidney stones and the ketogenic diet: Risk factors and prevention. *Journal of Child Neurology* 22(4): 375–378.

Wiznitzer, M. 2008. From observations to trials: The ketogenic diet and epilepsy. *Lancet Neurology* 7(6): 471–472.

Autism

Evangeliou, A., I. Vlachonikolis, H. Mihailidou, et al. 2003. Application of a ketogenic diet in children with autistic behavior: pilot study. *Journal of Child Neurology* 18(2): 113–118.

Behavior

Murphy, P., S. S. Likhodii, M. Hatamian, et al. 2005. Effect of the ketogenic diet on the activity level of Wistar rats. *Pediatric Research* 57(3): 353–357.

Pulsifer, M. B., J. M. Gordon, J. Brandt, et al. Effects of ketogenic diet on development and behavior: preliminary report of a prospective study. *Developmental Medicine & Child Neurology* 43(5): 301–306.

Bipolar Disorder

El-Mallakh, R. S., and M. E. Paskitti. 2001. The ketogenic diet may have mood-stabilizing properties. *Medical Hypotheses* 57(6): 724–726.

Yaroslavsky, Y., Z. Stahl, and R. H. Belmaker. 2002. Ketogenic diet in bipolar illness. *Bipolar Disorders* 4(1): 75.

Omega-3 Fatty Acids / Fish Oil and Depression

Conklin, S. M., S. B. Manuck, J. K. Yao, et al. High omega-6 and low omega-3 fatty acids are associated with depressive symptoms and neuroticism. *Psychosomatic Medicine* 69(9): 932–934.

Conklin, S. M., P. J. Gianaros, S. M. Brown, et al. 2007. Long-chain omega-3 fatty acid intake is associated positively with corticolimbic gray matter volume in healthy adults. *Neuroscience Letters* 421(3): 209–212.

Frangou, S., M. Lewis, J. Wollard, et al. 2007. Preliminary in vivo evidence of increased N-acetyl-aspartate following eicosapentaneoic acid treatment in patients with bipolar disorder. *Journal of Psychopharmacology* 21(4): 435–439.

Freeman, M. P., J. R. Hibbeln, K. L. Wisner, et al. 2006. Randomized dose-ranging pilot trial of omega-3 fatty acids for postpartum depression. *Acta Psychiatrica Scandinavica* 113(1): 31–35.

Freeman, M. P., J. R. Hibbeln, K. L. Wisner, et al. 2006. Omega-3 fatty acids: Evidence basis for treatment and future research in psychiatry. *Journal of Clinical Psychiatry* 67(12): 1954–1967.

Grenyer, B. F., T. Crowe, B. Meyer, et al. 2007. Fish oil supplementation in the treatment of major depression: a randomised double-blind placebo-controlled trial. *Progress in Neuropsychopharmacology and Biological Psychiatry* 31(7): 1393–1396.

Hallahan, B., J. R. Hibbeln, J. M. Davis, et al. 2007. Omega-3 fatty acid supplementation in patients with recurrent self-harm. Single-centre double-blind randomised controlled trial. *British Journal of Psychiatry* 190: 118–122.

Hibbeln, J. R. 2002. Seafood consumption, the DHA content of mothers' milk and prevalence rates of postpartum depression: A cross-national, ecological analysis. *Journal of Affective Disorders* 69(1–3): 15–29.

Hirashima, F., A. M. Parow, A. L. Stoll, et al. 2004. Omega-3 fatty acid treatment and T(2) whole brain relaxation times in bipolar disorder. *American Journal of Psychiatry* 161(10): 1922–1924.

Jazayeri, S., M. Tehrani-Doost, S. A. Keshavarz, et al. 2008. Comparison of therapeutic effects of omega-3 fatty acid eicosapentaenoic acid and fluoxetine, separately and in combination, in major depressive disorder. *Australian and New Zealand Journal of Psychiatry* 42(3): 192–198.

Lin, P. Y., and K. P. Su. 2007. A meta-analytic review of double-blind, placebo-controlled trials of antidepressant efficacy of omega-3 fatty acids. *Journal of Clinical Psychiatry* 68(7): 1056–1061.

Locke, C. A., and A. L. Stoll. 2001. Omega-3 fatty acids in major depression. *World Review of Nutrition and Dietetics* 89: 173–185.

Nemets, H., B. Nemets, A. Apter, et al. 2006. Omega-3 treatment of childhood depression: A controlled, double-blind pilot study. *American Journal of Psychiatry* 163(6): 1098–1100.

Rogers, P. J., K. M. Appleton, D. Kessler, et al. 2008. No effect of n-3 long-chain polyunsaturated fatty acid (EPA and DHA) supplementation on depressed mood and cognitive function: A randomized controlled trial. *British Journal of Nutrition* 99(2): 421–431.

Stoll, A. L., K. E. Damico, B. P. Daly, et al. 2001. Methodological considerations in clinical studies of omega 3 fatty acids in major depression and bipolar disorder. *World Review of Nutrition and Dietetics* 88: 58–67.

Stoll, A. L., C. A. Locke, L. B. Marangell, et al. 1999. Omega-3 fatty acids and bipolar disorder: A review. *Prostaglandins, Leukotrienes & Essential Fatty Acids* 60(5–6): 329–337.

Stoll, A. L., W. E. Severus, M. P. Freeman, et al. 1999. Omega 3 fatty acids in bipolar disorder: A preliminary double-blind, placebo-controlled trial. *Archives of General Psychiatry* 56(5): 407–412.

Wozniak, J., J. Biederman, E. Mick, et al. 2007. Omega-3 fatty acid monotherapy for pediatric bipolar disorder: A prospective open-label trial. *European Neuropsychopharmacology* 17(6–7): 440–447.

Valerian

Balderer, G., and A. A. Borbély. 1985. Effect of valerian on human sleep. *Psychopharmacology* 87(4): 406–409.

Coxeter, P. D., P. J. Schluter, H. L. Eastwood, et al. 2003. Valerian does not appear to reduce symptoms for patients with chronic insomnia in general practice using a series of randomised n-of-1 trials. *Complementary Therapies in Medicine* 11(4): 215–222.

Diaper, A., and I. Hindmarch. 2004. A double-blind, placebo-controlled investigation of the effects of two doses of a valerian preparation on the sleep, cognitive and psychomotor function of sleep-disturbed older adults. *Phytotherapy Research* 18(10): 831–836.

Dominguez, R. A., R. L. Bravo-Valverde, B. R. Kaplowitz, et al. 2006. Valerian as a hypnotic for Hispanic patients. *Cultural Diversity and Ethnic Minority Psychology* 6(1): 84–92.

Donath, F., S. Quispe, K. Diefenbach, et al. 2000. Critical evaluation of the effect of valerian extract on sleep structure and sleep quality. *Pharmacopsychiatry* 33(2): 47–53.

Francis, A. J., and R. J. Dempster. 2002. Effect of valerian. Valeriana edulis, on sleep difficulties in children with intellectual deficits: randomised trial. *Phytomedicine* 9(4): 273–279.

Kuhlmann, J., W. Berger, H. Podzuweit, et al. 1999. The influence of valerian treatment on "reaction time, alertness and concentration" in volunteers. *Pharmacopsychiatry* 32(6): 235–241.

Morin, C. M., U. Koetter, C. Bastien, et al. 2005. Valerian-hops combination and diphenhydramine for treating insomnia: A randomized placebo-controlled clinical trial. *Sleep* 28(11): 1465–1471.

Müller, S. F., and S. Klement. 2006. A combination of valerian and lemon balm is effective in the treatment of restlessness and dyssomnia in children. *Phytomedicine* 13(6): 383–387.

Poyares, D. R., C. Guilleminault, M. M. Ohayon, et al. 2002. Can valerian improve the sleep of insomniacs after benzodiazepine withdrawal? *Progress in Neuropsychopharmacology and Biological Psychiatry* 26(3): 539–545.

Vitamin D and Depression

Armstrong, D. J., G. K. Meenagh, I. Bickle, et al. 2007. Vitamin D deficiency is associated with anxiety and depression in fibromyalgia. *Clinical Rheumatology* 26(4): 551–554.

Berk, M., K. M. Sanders, J. A. Pasco, et al. 2007. Vitamin D deficiency may play a role in depression. *Medical Hypotheses* 69(6): 1316–1319.

Gloth, F. M., III, W. Alam, and B. Hollis. 1999. Vitamin D vs. broad spectrum phototherapy in the treatment of seasonal affective disorder. *Journal of Nutrition, Health and Aging* 3(1): 5–7.

Jorde, R., K. Waterloo, F. Saleh, et al. 2006. Neuropsychological function in relation to serum parathyroid hormone and serum 25-hydroxyvitamin D levels. The Tromsø study. *Journal of Neurology* 253(4): 464–470.

Wilkins, C. H., Y. I. Sheline, C. M. Roe, et al. 2006. Vitamin D deficiency is associated with low mood and worse cognitive performance in older adults. *American Journal of Geriatric Psychiatry* 14(12): 1032–1040.

CHAPTER 8

Mayo Clinic Staff, MayoClinic.com, January 12, 2007, http://www.mayoclinic.com/health/alzheimers-disease/DS00161.

Gingko biloba

Burns, N., J. Bryan, and T. Nettelbeck. 2006. Ginkgo biloba: no robust effect on cognitive abilities or mood in healthy young or older adults. *Human Psychopharmacology* 21(1): 27–37.

Carlson, J., J. Farquhar, E. DiNucci, et al. 2007. Safety and efficacy of a ginkgo biloba–containing dietary supplement on cognitive function, quality of life, and platelet function in healthy, cognitively intact older adults. *Journal of the American Dietetic Association* 107(3): 422–432.

Dodge, H., T. Zitzelberger, B. Oken, et al. 2008. A randomized placebo-controlled trial of ginkgo biloba for the prevention of cognitive decline. *Neurology* 70(19): 1809–1817.

Elsabagh, S., D. Hartley, O. Ali, et al. 2005. Differential cognitive effects of ginkgo biloba after acute and chronic treatment in healthy young volunteers. *Psychopharmacology* 179(2): 437–446.

Hartley, D., L. Heinze, S. Elsabagh, et al. 2003. Effects on cognition and mood in postmenopausal women of 1-week treatment with Ginkgo biloba. *Pharmacology Biochemistry and Behavior* 75(3): 711–720.

Kennedy, D., P. Jackson, C. Haskell, et al. 2007. Modulation of cognitive performance following single doses of 120 mg Ginkgo biloba extract administered to healthy young volunteers. *Human Psychopharmacology* 22(8): 559–566.

Kennedy, D., C. Haskell, P. Mauri, et al. 2007. Acute cognitive effect of standardized Ginkgo biloba extract complexed with phosphatidylserine. *Human Psychopharmacology* 22(4): 199–210.

Kennedy, D., A. Scholey, and K. Wesnes. 2000. The dose-dependent cognitive effects of acute administration of Ginkgo biloba to healthy young volunteers. *Psychopharmacology* 151(4): 416–423.

Kennedy, D., A. Scholey, and K. Wesnes. 2001. Differential, dose dependent changes in cognitive performance following acute administration of a Ginkgo biloba / Panax ginseng combination to healthy young volunteers. *Nutritional Neuroscience* 4(5): 399–412.

Le Bars, P. L. 2003. Magnitude of effect and special approach to Ginkgo biloba extract EGb 761 in cognitive disorders. *Pharmacopsychiatry* 36(Suppl. 1): S44–S49.

Le Bars, P. L. 2003. Response patterns of EGb 761 in Alzheimer's disease: influence of neuropsychological profiles. *Pharmacopsychiatry* 36(Suppl. 1): S50–55.

Le Bars, P. L., and J. Kastelan. 2000. Efficacy and safety of a Ginkgo biloba extract. *Public Health Nutrition* 3(4A): 495–499.

Le Bars, P. L., M. M. Katz, N. Berman, et al. 1997. A placebo-controlled, double-blind, randomized trial of an extract of Ginkgo biloba for dementia. North American EGb Study Group. *Journal of the American Medical Association* 278(16): 1327–1332.

Le Bars, P. L., M. Kieser, and K. Z. Itil. 2000. A 26-week analysis of a double-blind, placebo-controlled trial of the ginkgo biloba extract EGb 761 in dementia. *Dementia and Geriatric Cognitive Disorders* 11(4): 230–237.

Le Bars, P. L., F. M. Velasco, J. M. Ferguson, et al. 2002. Influence of the severity of cognitive impairment on the effect of the Ginkgo biloba extract EGb 761 in Alzheimer's disease. *Neuropsychobiology* 45(1): 19–26.

Mazza, M., A. Capuano, P. Bria, et al. 2006. Ginkgo biloba and donepezil: a comparison in the treatment of Alzheimer's dementia in a randomized placebo-controlled double-blind study. *European Journal of Neurology* 13(9): 981–985.

Mix, J., and N. Crews, W. 2000. An examination of the efficacy of Ginkgo biloba extraxt EGb 761 on the neuropsychological functioning of cognitively intact older adults. *Journal of Alternative and Complementary Medicine* 6(3): 219–229.

Mix, J., and W. Crews. 2002. A double-blind, placebo-controlled, randomized trial of Ginkgo biloba extract EGb 761 in a sample of cognitively intact older adults: Neuropsychological findings. *Human Psychopharmacology* 17(6): 267–277.

Moulton, P., L. Boyko, J. Fitzpatrick, et al. 2001. The effects of Ginkgo biloba on memory in healthy male volunteers. *Physiology & Behavior* 73(4): 659–665.

Napryeyenko, O., I. Borzenko, and GINDEM-NP Study Group. 2007. Ginkgo biloba special extract in dementia with neuropsychiatric features. A randomized, placebo-controlled, double-blind clinical trial. *Arzneimittelforschung* 57(1): 4–11.

Nathan, P., S. Tanner, J. Lloyd, et al. 2004. Effects of a combined extract of Ginkgo biloba and Bacopa monniera on cognitive function in healthy humans. *Human Psychopharmacology* 19(2): 91–96.

Novella, S. 2008. Ginkgo biloba and memory. *Neuroscience.*

Persson, J., E. Bringlöv, L. Nilsson, et al. 2004. The memory-enhancing effects of Ginseng and Ginkgo biloba in healthy volunteers. *Psychopharmacology (Berl).* 172(4): 430–434.

Rai, G., C. Shovlin, and K. Wesnes. 1991. A double-blind, placebo controlled study of Ginkgo biloba extract ("tanakan") in elderly outpatients with mild to moderate memory impairment. *Current Medical Research and Opinion* 12(6): 350–355.

Rigney, U., S. Kimber, and I. Hindmarch. 1999. The effects of acute doses of standardized Ginkgo biloba extract on memory and psychomotor performance in volunteers. *Phytotherapy Research* 13(5): 408–415.

Schneider, L., S. Dekosky, M. Farlow, et al. 2005. A randomized, double-blind, placebo-controlled trial of two doses of Ginkgo biloba extract in dementia of the Alzheimer's type. *Current Alzheimer Research* 2(5): 541–551.

Scripnikov, A., A. Khomenko, O. Napryeyenko, et al. 2007. Effects of Ginkgo biloba extract EGb 761 on neuropsychiatric symptoms of dementia: findings from a randomized controlled trial. *Wiener Medizinische Wochenschrift* 157(13–14): 295–300.

Singh, B., H. Song, X. Liu, et al. 2004. Dangshen (Codonopsis pilosula) and Bai guo (Ginkgo biloba) enhance learning and memory. *Alternative Therapies in Health & Medicine* 10(4): 52–56.

Solomon, P., F. Adams, A. Silver, et al. 2002. Ginkgo for memory enhancement: A randomized controlled trial. *Journal of the American Medical Association* 288(7): 835–840.

Stough, C., J. Clarke, J. Lloyd, et al. 2001. Neuropsychological changes after 30-day Ginkgo biloba administration in healthy participants. *International Journal of Neuropsychopharmacology* 4(2): 131–134.

van Dongen, M., E. van Rossum, A. Kessels, et al. 2003. Ginkgo for elderly people with dementia and age-associated memory impairment: A randomized clinical trial. *Journal of Clinical Epidemiology* 56(4): 367–376.

van Dongen, M., E. van Rossum, A. Kessels, et al. 2008. The efficacy of ginkgo for elderly people with dementia and age-associated memory impairment: New results of a randomized clinical trial. *Journal of the American Geriatrics Society* 48(10): 1183–1194.

Wesnes, K., T. Ward, A. McGinty, et al. 2000. The memory enhancing effects of a Ginkgo biloba / Pax ginseng combination in healthy middle-aged volunteers. *Psychopharmacology* 152(4): 353–361.

Woelk, H., K. Arnoldt, M. Kieser, et al. 2007. Ginkgo biloba special extract EGb 761 in generalized anxiety disorder and adjustment disorder with anxious mood: a randomized, double-blind, placebo-controlled trial. *Journal of Psychiatric Research* 41(6): 472–480.

Huperzine A

Aisen, P. 2007. A multi-center, double-blind, placebo-controlled therapeutic trial to determine whether natural huperzine A improves cognitive function. *Clinical Trials.*

English, J. 1999. Huperzine-A: Natural Club Moss Extract Shows Promise for Enhancing Memory and Alertness. *Vitamin Research Newsletter.* http://www.imminst.org/forum/Huperzine-A-The-Irish-Moss-Nootropic-t2266.html.

Sun, Q., S. Xu, J. Pan, et al. 1999. Huperzine-A capsules enhance memory and learning performance in 34 pairs of matched adolescent students. *Zhongguo Yao Li Xue Bao* 20(7): 601–603.

Ved, H., M. Koenig, J. Dave, et al. 1997. Huperzine A, a potential therapeutic agent for dementia, reduces neuronal cell death caused by glutamate. *NeuroReport* 8(4): 963–967.

Xu, S., Z. Cai, Z. Qu, et al. 1999. Huperzine-A in capsules and tablets for treating patients with Alzheimer disease. *Zhongguo Yao Li Xue Bao* 20(6): 486–490.

Xu, S., Z. Gao, Z. Weng, et al. 1995. Efficacy of tablet huperzine-A on memory, cognition, and behavior in Alzheimer's disease. *Zhongguo Yao Li Xue Bao* 16(5): 391–395.

Zhang, R., X. Tang, Y. Han, et al. 1991. Drug evaluation of huperzine A in the treatment of senile memory disorders. *Zhongguo Yao Li Xue Bao* 12(3): 250–252.

Zhang, Z., Y. Tong, X. Wang, et al. 2007. Huperzine A as add-on therapy in patients with treatment-resistant schizophrenia: An open-labeled trial. *Schizophrenia Research* 92(1–3): 273–275.

Zhang, Z., X. Wang, Q. Chen, et al. 2002. Clinical efficacy and safety of huperzine Alpha in treatment of mild to moderate Alzheimer disease, a placebo-controlled, double-blind, randomized trial. *Zhonghua Yi Xue Za Zhi* 82(14): 941–944.

Melatonin

Almeida Montes, L. G., M. P. Ontiveros Uribe, S. J. Cortes, et al. 2003. Treatment of primary insomnia with melatonin: A double-blind, placebo-controlled, crossover study. *Journal of Psychiatry & Neuroscience* 28(3): 191–196.

Andrade, C., B. S. Srihari, K. P. Reddy, et al. 2001. Melatonin in medically ill patients with insomnia: A double-blind, placebo-controlled study. *Journal of Clinical Psychiatry* 62(1): 41–45.

Atkinson, G., P. Buckley, B. Edwards, et al. 2001. Are there hangover-effects on physical performance when melatonin is ingested by athletes before nocturnal sleep? *International Journal of Sports Medicine* 22(3): 232–234.

Baskett, J. J., J. B. Broad, P. C. Wood, et al. 2003. Does melatonin improve sleep in older people? A randomised crossover trial. *Age and Ageing* 32(2): 164–170.

Braam, W., R. Didden, M. Smits, et al. 2008. Melatonin treatment in individuals with intellectual disability and chronic insomnia: A randomized placebo-controlled study. *Journal of Intellectual Disability Research* 52(Pt. 3): 256–264.

Campos, F. L., F. P. Silva-Junior, V. M. de Bruin, et al. 2004. Melatonin improves sleep in asthma: a randomized, double-blind, placebo-controlled study. *American Journal of Respiratory and Critical Care Medicine* 170(9): 947–951.

Cardinali, D. P., E. Gvozdenovich, and M. R. Kaplan. 2002. A double-blind placebo-controlled study on melatonin efficacy to reduce anxiolytic benzodiazepine use in the elderly. *Neuroendocrinology Letters* 23(1): 55–60.

Cardinali, D. P., L. I. Brusco, and C. Liberczuk. 2002. The use of melatonin in Alzheimer's disease. *Neuroendocrinology Letters* 23(Suppl. 1): 20–23.

Carr, R., M. B. Wasdell, D. Hamilton, et al. 2007. Long-term effectiveness outcome of melatonin therapy in children with treatment-resistant circadian rhythm sleep disorders. *Journal of Pineal Research* 43(4): 351–359.

Dalton, E. J., D. Rotondi, R. D. Levitan, et al. 2000. Use of slow-release melatonin in treatment-resistant depression. *Journal of Psychiatry & Neuroscience* 25(1): 48–52.

Dodge, N. N., and G. A. Wilson. 2001. Melatonin for treatment of sleep disorders in children with developmental disabilities. *Journal of Child Neurology* 16(8): 581–584.

Dowling, G. A., R. L. Burr, E. J. Van Someren, et al. 2008. Melatonin and bright-light treatment for rest-activity disruption in institutionalized patients with Alzheimer's disease. *Journal of the American Geriatrics Society* 56(2): 239–246.

Jan, J. E., D. Hamilton, N. Seward, et al. 2000. Clinical trials of controlled-release melatonin in children with sleep-wake cycle disorders. *Journal of Pineal Research* 29(1): 34–39.

Jan, M. M. 2000. Melatonin for the treatment of handicapped children with severe sleep disorders. *Pediatric Neurology* 23(3): 229–232.

Jockovich, M., D. Cosentino, L. Cosentino, et al. 2000. Effect of exogenous melatonin on mood and sleep efficiency in emergency medicine residents working night shifts. *Academic Emergency Medicine* 7(8): 955–958.

Kayumov, L., G. Brown, R. Jindal, et al. 2001. A randomized, double-blind, placebo-controlled crossover study of the effect of exogenous melatonin on delayed sleep phase syndrome. *Psychosomatic Medicine* 63(1): 40–48.

Kunz, D., R. Mahlberg, C. Müller, et al. 2004. Melatonin in patients with reduced REM sleep duration: two randomized controlled trials. *Journal of Clinical Endocrinology & Metabolism* 89(1): 128–134.

Leppamaki, S., T. Partonen, O. Vakkuri, et al. 2003. Effect of controlled-release melatonin on sleep quality, mood, and quality of life in subjects with seasonal or weather-associated changes in mood and behaviour. *European Neuropsychopharmacology* 13(3): 137–145.

Paavonen, E. J., T. Nieminen-Von Wendt, R. Vanhala, et al. 2003. Effectiveness of melatonin in the treatment of sleep disturbances in children with asperger disorder. *Journal of Child and Adolescent Psychopharmacology* 13(1): 83–95.

Pillar, G., E. Shahar, N. Peled, et al. 2000. Melatonin improves sleep-wake patterns in psychomotor retarded children. *Pediatric Neurology* 23(3): 225–228.

Smits, M. G., E. E. Nagtegaal, H. J. van der, et al. 2001. Melatonin for chronic sleep onset insomnia in children: A randomized placebo-controlled trial. *Journal of Child Neurology* 16(2): 86–92.

Suresh Kumar, P. N., C. Andrade, S. G. Bhakta, et al. 2007. Melatonin in schizophrenic outpatients with insomnia: a double-blind, placebo-controlled study. *Journal of Clinical Psychiatry* 68(2): 237–241.

Takeuchi, N., N. Uchimura, Y. Hashizume, et al. 2001. Melatonin therapy for REM sleep behavior disorder. *Psychiatry and Clinical Neurosciences* 55(3): 267–269.

Tjon Pian Gi, C. V., J. P. Broeren, J. S. Starreveld, et al. 2003. Melatonin for treatment of sleeping disorders in children with attention deficit/hyperactivity disorder: A preliminary open label study. *European Journal of Pediatrics* 162(7–8): 554–555.

Van der Heijden, K. B., M. G. Smits, E. J. Van Someren, et al. 2007. Effect of melatonin on sleep, behavior, and cognition in ADHD and chronic sleep-onset insomnia. *Journal of the American Academy of Child & Adolescent Psychiatry* 46(2): 233–241.

Yang, C. M., A. J. Spielman, P. D'Ambrosio, et al. 2001. A single dose of melatonin prevents the phase delay associated with a delayed weekend sleep pattern. *Sleep* 24(3): 272–281.

Zhdanova, I. V., R. J. Wurtman, M. M. Regan, et al. 2001. Melatonin treatment for age-related insomnia. *Journal of Clinical Endocrinology & Metabolism* 86(10): 4727–4730.

Phosphatidylserine

Amaducci, L. 1988. Phosphatidylserine in the treatment of Alzheimer's disease: Results of a multicenter study. *Psychopharmacology Bulletin* 24: 130–134.

Cenacchi, T., T. Bertoldin, C. Farina, et al. 1993. Cognitive decline in the elderly: A double-blind, placebo-controlled multicenter study on efficacy of phosphatidylserine administration. *Aging (Milano)*. 5: 123–133.

Crook, T., W. Petrie, C. Wells, et al. 1992. Effects of phosphatidylserine in Alzheimer's disease. *Psychopharmacology Bulletin* 28: 61–66.

Crook, T. H., J. Tinklenberg, J. Yesavage, et al. 1991. Effects of phosphatidylserine in age-associated memory impairment. *Neurology* 41: 644–649.

Delwaide, P. J., A. M. Gyselynck-Mambourg, A. Hurlet, et al. 1986. Double-blind randomized controlled study of phosphatidylserine in senile demented patients. *Acta Neurologica Scandinavica* 73: 136–140.

Engel, R. R., W. Satzger, W. Gunther, et al. 1992. Double-blind cross-over study of phosphatidylserine vs. placebo in patients with early dementia of the Alzheimer type. *European Neuropsychopharmacology* 2: 149–155.

Funfgeld, E. W., M. Baggen, P. Nedwidek, et al. 1989. Double-blind study with phosphatidylserine (PS) in Parkinsonian patients with senile dementia of Alzheimer's type (SDAT). *Progress in Clinical & Biological Research* 317: 1235–1246.

Gindin, J., M. Novikov, D. Kedar, et al. 1995. The effect of plant phosphatidylserine on age-associated memory impairment and mood in the functioning elderly. Geriatric Institute for Education and Research and Department of Geriatrics, Kaplan Hospital, Rehovot, Israel.

Hellhammer, J., E. Fries, C. Buss, et al. 2004. Effects of soy lecithin phosphatidic acid and phosphatidylserine complex (PAS) on the endocrine and psychological responses to mental stress. *Stress* 7: 119–126.

Jorissen, B. L., F. Brouns, M. P. Van Boxtel, et al. 2001. The influence of soy-derived phosphatidylserine on cognition in age-associated memory impairment. *Nutritional Neuroscience* 4: 121–134.

Jager, R., M. Purpura, K. R. Geiss, et al. 2007. The effect of phosphatidylserine on golf performance. *Journal of the International Society of Sports Nutrition* 4(1): 23.

Kennedy, D. O., C. F. Haskell, P. L. Mauri, et al. 2007. Acute cognitive effects of standardised Ginkgo biloba extract complexed with phosphatidylserine. *Human Psychopharmacology* 22(4): 199–210.

Kidd, P. M. 1999. A review of nutrients and botanicals in the integrative management of cognitive dysfunction. *Alternative Medicine Review* 4(3): 144–161.

Maggioni, M., G. B. Picotti, G. P. Bondiolotti, et al. 1990. Effects of phosphatidylserine therapy in geriatric patients with depressive disorders. *Acta Psychiatrica Scandinavica* 81: 265–270.

Nerozzi, D., F. Aceti, E. Melia, et al. 1987. Phosphatidylserine and memory disorders in the aged [in Italian; English abstract]. *Clinical Therapeutics* 120: 399–404.

Palmieri, G., R. Palmieri, M. R. Inzoli, et al. 1987. Double-blind controlled trial of phosphatidylserine in patients with senile mental deterioration. *Clinical Trials* 24: 73–83.

Villardita, C., S. Grioli, G. Salmeri, et al. 1987. Multicentre clinical trial of brain phosphatidylserine in elderly patients with intellectual deterioration. *Clinical Trials* 24: 84–93.

Vinpocetine

Balestreri, R., L. Fontana, and F. Astengo. 1987. A double-blind placebo controlled evaluation of the safety and efficacy of vinpocetine in the treatment of patients with chronic vascular senile cerebral dysfunction. *Journal of the American Geriatrics Society* 35(5): 425–430.

Bereczki, D., and I. Fekete. 1999. A systematic review of vinpocetine therapy in acute ischaemic stroke. *European Journal of Clinical Pharmacology* 55(5): 349–352.

Ebi, O. 1985. Open-labeled phase III clinical trials with vinpocetine in Japan. *Therapia Hungarica* 33(1): 41–49.

Feigin, V. L., B. M. Doronin, T. F. Popova, et al. 2001. Vinpocetine treatment in acute ischaemic stroke: A pilot single-blind randomized clinical trial. *European Journal of Neurology* 8(1): 81–85.

Grandt, R., W. Braun, H. U. Schulz, et al. 1989. Glibenclamide steady state plasma levels during concomitant vinpocetine administration in type II diabetic patients. *Arzneimittelforschung*. 39(11): 1451–1454.

Gulyas, B., C. Halldin, P. Karlsson, et al. 1999. Cerebral uptake and metabolism of (11C) Vinpocetine in monkeys: PET studies. [in Hungarian]. *Orvusi Hetilap* 140(30): 1687–1691.

Gulyas, B., C. Halldin, J. Sandell, et al. 2002. PET studies on the brain uptake and regional distribution of [11C]vinpocetine in human subjects. *Acta Neurologica Scandinavica* 106(6): 325–332.

Gulyas, B., C. Halldin, J. Sovago, et al. 2002. Drug distribution in man: A positron emission tomography study after oral administration of the labelled neuroprotective drug vinpocetine. *European Journal of Nuclear Medicine and Molecular Imaging* 29(8): 1031–1038.

Hindmarch, I., H. H. Fuchs, and H. Erzigkeit. 1991. Efficacy and tolerance of vinpocetine in ambulant patients suffering from mild to moderate organic psychosyndromes. *International Clinical Psychopharmacology* 6(1): 31–43.

Horvath, S. The use of vinpocetine in chronic disorders caused by cerebral hypoperfusion. *Orvosi Hetilap* 142(8): 383–389.

Lohmann, A., E. Dingler, W. Sommer, et al. 1992. Bioavailability of vinpocetine and interference of the time of application with food intake. *Arzneimittelforschung* 42(7): 914–917.

Szakall, S., I. Boros, L. Balkay, et al. 1998. Cerebral effects of a single dose of intravenous vinpocetine in chronic stroke patients: a PET study. *Journal of Neuroimaging* 8(4): 197–204.

Szatmari, S. Z., and P. J. Whitehouse. 2003. Vinpocetine for cognitive impairment and dementia. *Cochrane.Database.Syst.Rev.* (1): Art. No. CD003119. DOI: 10.1002/14651858. CD 003119.

Tamaki, N., and S. Matsumoto. 1985. Agents to improve cerebrovascular circulation and cerebral metabolism—vinpocetine [in Japanese]. *Nippon Rinsho* 43(2): 376–378.

Tamaki, N., T. Kusunoki, and S. Matsumoto. 1985. The effect of vinpocetine on cerebral blood flow in patients with cerebrovascular disorders. *Therapia Hungarica* 33(1): 13–21.

Vas, A., B. Gulyas, Z. Szabo, et al. 2002. Clinical and non-clinical investigations using positron emission tomography, near infrared spectroscopy and transcranial Doppler methods on the neuroprotective drug vinpocetine: A summary of evidences. *Journal of Neurological Science* 203–204: 259–262.

CHAPTER 9

Aron, A., H. Fisher, D. J., et al. 2005. Reward, motivation, and emotion systems associated with early-stage intense romantic love. *Journal of Neurophysiology* 94(1): 327–337.

Fisher, H., A. Aron, and L. L. Brown. 2005. Romantic love: An fMRI study of a neural mechanism for mate choice. *Journal of Comparative Neurology* 493(1): 58–62.

Fisher, H. E., A. Aron, D. Mashek, et al. 2002. Defining the brain systems of lust, romantic attraction, and attachment. *Archives of Sexual Behavior* 31(5): 413–419.

Volkow, N. D., G. J. Wang, J. S. Fowler, et al. 1999. Association of methylphenidate-induced craving with changes in right striato-orbitofrontal metabolism in cocaine abusers: Implications in addiction. *American Journal of Psychiatry* 156(1): 19–26.

CHAPTER 11

Baxter, L. R., Jr., J. M. Schwartz, K. S. Bergman, et al. 1992. Caudate glucose metabolic rate changes with both drug and behavior therapy for obsessive-compulsive disorder. *Archives of General Psychiatry* 49(9): 681–689.

Brody, A. L., S. Saxena, J. M. Schwartz, et al. 1998. FDG-PET predictors of response to behavioral therapy and pharmacotherapy in obsessive compulsive disorder. *Psychiatry Research* 84(1): 1–6.

CHAPTER 12

George, M. S., T. A. Ketter, P. I. Parekh, et al. 1995. Brain activity during transient sadness and happiness in healthy women. *American Journal of Psychiatry* 152(3): 341–351.

Katie, B., and S. Mitchell. 2002. *Loving What Is.* New York: Harmony.

Lee Duckworth, A., T. A. Steen, and M. E. Seligman. 2005. Positive psychology in clinical practice. *Annual Review of Clinical Psychology* 1: 629–651.

Nelson, N. 2003. *Power of Appreciation: The Key to a Vibrant Life.* New York: Pocket.

Szloboda, P. 2008. Gratitude practices: A key to resiliency, well-being & happiness. *Beginnings* 28(1): 6–7.

CHAPTER 14

Abramson, L. Y., M. E. P. Seligman, and J. D. Teasdale. 1978. Learned helplessness in humans—critique and reformulation. *Journal of Abnormal Psychology* 87: 49–74.

Amat, J., E. Paul, C. Zarza, et al. 2006. Previous experience with behavioral control over stress blocks the behavioral and dorsal raphe nucleus activating effects of later uncontrollable stress: Role of the ventral medial prefrontal cortex. *Journal of Neuroscience* 26: 13264–13272.

Bolognini, M., B. Plancherel, J. Laget, et al. 2003. Adolescent's suicide attempts: Populations at risk, vulnerability, and substance use. *Substance Use & Misuse* 38(11–13): 1651–1669.

Haglund, M. E., P. S. Nestadt, N. S. Cooper, et al. 2007. Psychobiological mechanisms of resilience: Relevance to prevention and treatment of stress-related psychopathology. *Development and Psychopathology* 19(3): 889–920.

Koepp, M. J., R. N. Gunn, A. D. Lawrence, et al. 1998. Evidence for striatal dopamine release during a video game. *Nature* 393(6682): 266–268.

Lyons, D. M., and K. J. Parker. 2007. Stress inoculation–induced indications of resilience in monkeys. *Journal of Traumatic Stress* 20(4): 423–433.

Sauzier, M. 1998. Disclosure of child sexual abuse. For better or for worse. *Psychiatric Clinics of North America* 12(2): 455–469.

Southwick, S. M., M. Vythilingam, and D. S. Charney. 2005. The psychobiology of depression and resilience to stress: Implications for prevention and treatment. *Annual Review of Clinical Psychology* 1: 255–291.

Valliant, G. 1998. *Adaptation to Life.* Cambridge, MA: Harvard University Press.

CHAPTER 15

Klerman, G., M. M. Weissman, B. Rounsaville, et al. 1984. *Interpersonal Psychotherapy of Depression.* New York: Basic Books.

Klerman, G., and M. M. Weissman. 1993. *New Applications in Interpersonal Psychotherapy.* Washington, D.C.: American Psychiatric Press.

Oberman, L. M., V. S. Ramachandran, and J. A. Pineda. 2008. Modulation of mu suppression in children with autism spectrum disorders in response to familiar or unfamiliar stimuli: The mirror neuron hypothesis. *Neuropsychologia* 46(5): 1558–1565.

Ornish, D. 1998. *Love and Survival.* New York: HarperCollins.

Rizzolatti, G., and C. Sinigaglia. 2007. Mirror neurons and motor intentionality. *Functional Neurology* 22(4): 205–210.

Weisman, M., J. Markowitz, and G. Klerman. 2007. *Clinician's Quick Guide to Interpersonal Psychotherapy.* New York: Oxford University Press.

CHAPTER 16

Berns, G. 2006. *Satisfaction: Sensation Seeking, Novelty, and the Science of Finding True Fulfillment.* New York: Henry Holt.

Csikszentmihalyi, M. 1990. *Flow: The Psychology of Optimal Experience.* New York: HarperCollins.

Offer, D., E. Ostrov, K. I. Howard, et al. 1990. Normality and adolescence. *Psychiatric Clinics of North America* 13(3): 377–388.

Rilling, J., D. Gutman, T. Zeh, et al. 2002. A neural basis for social cooperation. *Neuron* 35(2): 395–405.

Rilling, J. K., D. E. Dagenais, D. R. Goldsmith, et al. In press. Social cognitive neural networks during in-group and out-group interactions. *Neuroimage.*

Wood, R. M., J. K. Rilling, and A. G. Sanfey. 2006. Effects of tryptophan depletion on the performance of an iterated Prisoner's Dilemma game in healthy adults. *Neuropsychopharmacology* 31(5): 1075–1084.

CHAPTER 17

Kosfeld, M., M. Heinrichs, P. J. Zak, et al. 2005. Oxytocin increases trust in humans. *Nature* 435(7042): 673–676.

Raine, A., T. Lencz, S. Bihrle, et al. 2000. Reduced prefrontal gray matter volume and reduced autonomic activity in antisocial personality disorder. *Archives of General Psychiatry* 57(2): 119–127.

ACKNOWLEDGMENTS

I am grateful to many people who have been instrumental in making this book a reality, especially all of the patients and professionals who have taught me so much about how the brain relates to having a magnificent mind. I am especially grateful for the loving support of my parents. The staff at Amen Clinics, Inc., have been of help and tremendous support during this process, especially my personal assistant, Catherine Hanlon, along with Dr. Leonti Thompson, Professor David Bennett, Mike Marino, Chris Hanks, Breanne Amen, Jesse Payne, Kaitlyn Amen, Jill Prunella, Kandace Kadow, and Krystle Miller. Dr. Earl Henslin, as always, has been helpful and a joy to have as a friend and mentor. As usual, I am grateful to David and Sandy Brokaw of the Brokaw Company, who gave many helpful suggestions. I also wish to thank my wonderful literary team at Harmony Books, especially my very patient editor, Julia Pastore, and publisher, Shaye Areheart. I am ever grateful to my literary agent Faith Hamlin and the team at Sanford J. Green-burger Associates for their longstanding love and support. Finally, I am grateful to Tana, my wife, my joy, and my best friend, who patiently read every word and gave many thoughtful suggestions. I love all of you.

INDEX

Note: Page numbers in *italics* refer to illustrations.

ABOUT THE AUTHOR

Daniel G. Amen, M.D., is a clinical neuroscientist, psychiatrist, author, and CEO and medical director of Amen Clinics, Inc., in Newport Beach and Fairfield, California; Tacoma, Washington; and Reston, Virginia. He is a Distinguished Fellow of the American Psychiatric Association and Assistant Clinical Professor of Psychiatry and Human Behavior at the University of California–Irvine School of Medicine. Dr. Amen lectures to thousands of mental health professionals and laypeople each year. His clinics have the world's largest database of brain images related to behavior.

Dr. Amen did his psychiatric training at the Walter Reed Army Medical Center in Washington, D.C., and his child psychiatry training in Hawaii. He has won writing and research awards from the American Psychiatric Association, the U.S. Army, and the Baltimore-D.C. Institute for Psychoanalysis. Dr. Amen has been published around the world. He is the author of numerous professional and popular articles, twenty-two books, and a number of audio and video programs. His books have been translated into seventeen languages and include *Change Your Brain, Change Your Life*, a *New York Times* bestseller; *Healing ADD; Healing the Hardware of the Soul, Healing Anxiety and Depression* (with Dr. Lisa Routh); *Preventing Alzheimer's Disease* (with Dr. Rod Shankle); and *Making a Good Brain Great*, which was chosen as one of the best books in 2005 by Amazon.com and which also won the prestigious Earphones Award for the audiobook; and *Sex on the Brain*.

Dr. Amen has appeared on the *Today Show, Good Morning America, The View, The Early Show*, CNN, HBO, and many other national television and radio programs. In 2008 he wrote and produced the popular PBS special *Change Your Brain, Change Your Life.*

ALSO BY DANIEL G. AMEN, M.D.

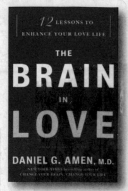

The Brain in Love
12 Lessons to Enhance Your Love Life
978-0-307-58789-3
$14.00 paper (Canada: $17.99)

Change Your Brain, Change Your Life
The Breakthrough Program for Conquering
Anxiety, Depression, Obsessiveness, Anger, and
Impulsiveness
978-0-8129-2998-0
$16.00 paper (Canada: $19.95)

Making a Good Brain Great
The Amen Clinic Program for Achieving and
Sustaining Optimal Mental Performance
978-1-4000-8209-4
$15.00 paper (Canada: $18.95)

Amen Clinics, Inc., Northwest
3315 South 23rd Street
Tacoma, WA
(253) 779-Hope

Amen Clinics, Inc., DC
1875 Campus Commons Drive
Reston, VA 20191
(703) 860-5600

AMENCLINIC.COM

Amenclinic.com is an educational interactive brain website geared toward mental health and medical professionals, educators, students, and the general public. It contains a wealth of information to help you learn about our clinics and the brain. The site contains over three hundred color brain SPECT images, thousands of scientific abstracts on brain SPECT imaging for psychiatry, a brain puzzle, and much, much more.

VIEW OVER THREE HUNDRED ASTONISHING COLOR THREE-DIMENSIONAL BRAIN SPECT IMAGES ON

Aggression
ADD, including the six subtypes
Dementia and cognitive decline
Drug abuse
Premenstrual syndrome
Anxiety disorders
Brain trauma
Depression
Obsessive-compulsive disorder
Stroke
Seizures

AMEN CLINICS, INC.

Amen Clinics, Inc., were established in 1989 by Daniel G. Amen, M.D. They specialize in innovative diagnosis and treatment planning for a wide variety of behavioral, learning, emotional, and cognitive problems for children, teenagers, and adults. The clinics have an international reputation for evaluating brain-behavior problems, such as ADD, depression, anxiety, school failure, brain trauma, obsessive-compulsive disorders, aggressiveness, marital conflict, cognitive decline, and brain toxicity from drugs or alcohol. Brain SPECT imaging is performed in the clinics. Amen Clinics, Inc., have the world's largest database of brain scans for behavioral problems.

The clinics welcome referrals from physicians, psychologists, social workers, marriage and family therapists, drug and alcohol counselors, and individual clients.

Amen Clinics, Inc., Newport Beach
4019 Westerly Place, Suite 100
Newport Beach, CA 92660
(949) 266-3700

Amen Clinics, Inc., Fairfield
350 Chadbourne Road
Fairfield, CA 94585
(707) 429-7181